SOCIAL PROB
WELFARE IDI

AC4.95

SOCIAL PROBLEMS AND WELFARE IDEOLOGY

Edited by
Nick Manning

Gower

Published by
Gower Publishing Company Limited,
Gower House,
Croft Road,
Aldershot,
Hants GU11 3HR,
England

Gower Publishing Company,
Old Post Road,
Brookfield,
Vermont 05036,
U.S.A.

Reprinted 1989, 1993

Library of Congress Cataloging in Publication Data

Social problems and welfare ideology
    Bibliography: p
    1. Social problems—addresses, essays, lectures
    2. Social policy—addresses, essays, lectures
    3. Public welfare—addresses, essays, lectures
    I. Manning, Nick P.
    HN28.562   1985   361.1   85–12496

British Library Cataloguing in Publication Data

Social problems and welfare ideology.
    1. Social problems   2. Great Britain—
    Social conditions—1945–
    I. Manning, Nick
    361.1'0941   HN390

    ISBN 0–566–00938–2
    ISBN 0–566–05067–6 Pbk

Typeset in Great Britain by
Guildford Graphics Limited, Plaistow, Nr. Billingshurst, West Sussex
Printed in Great Britain by Ipswich Book Co. Ltd., Ipswich,
Suffolk

Contents

Preface

This book explores the ways in which, as C. Wright Mills put it, personal troubles become public issues. It arose out of a profound dissatisfaction with both the existing (usually American) literature on social problems, and with the British social administration tradition. The former suffered from a suffocating blandness in which political and economic conflict and argument frequently disappeared beneath a language of social consensus. The latter has suffered from an institutional focus in which problems of welfare planning have overshadowed the analysis of popular concerns, and their collective solution.

We have aimed, therefore, to address the political and economic conflicts which shape the emergence of social problems generally, and in particular areas; and we have tried to set aside some of the conventional limits of social administration, both in terms of the range of social problems examined, and in terms of the theoretical concepts brought to bear in their analysis.

The structure of the book is as follows. The first chapter examines the concept of 'social problem' in three contexts: first, its origin and current definition in the social problems literature; second, the process by which certain personal troubles and social conditions are promoted to social problem status; third, the action of governments through social policy as the major arbiters of what social problems are and how they should be solved. Chapters 2 to 6 then examine in depth a range of social issues to explore the ideas raised in the first chapter. Finally, Chapter 7 draws together the evidence and conclusions of the earlier chapters about different social problems and the social policies pursued towards their solution. This evidence is then linked back to Chapter 1, to reflect upon the adequacy of our initial view of the process of social problem formation, and the relative strengths of different views of state intervention for the solution of social problems through social policy. The crucial importance of ideology is discussed here: first, as the key process through which economic and political conflicts are translated into notions of social problems; second, as the process by which the state can explain its repeated failure to solve social problems through social policy without producing fresh problems; and third, consequently, as the process through which popular and academic perceptions of social issues as social problems become distorted to the advantage of powerful groups in society.

Preface

All the contributors have at some time been members of the Board of Studies in Social Policy and Administration and Social Work at the University of Kent, and this has made possible a greater collaborative effort than is possible in a standard collection. Thus, each of the case studies covers at least the history of state policy in the relevant area, the standard facts and explanations available, and a criticism of the way the problem is conventionally perceived. Nevertheless, each chapter has been written independently and remains the responsibility of the contributor.

This book would not have been possible without the many students, now numbering nearly 1,000, upon whom its prototypes have been inflicted. Thanks are due to them and the other members of the Board of Studies who have found the time to discuss these ideas.

Biographical Notes

John Baldock read Philosophy, Politics and Economics at Oxford University and now lectures in social policy at the University of Kent. He has published articles on youth work and penology, and is the author of a forthcoming book on the rationing of welfare.

David Denney has taught sociology and social work at the University of Kent, and Mid-Kent College of Higher and Further Education. His social work practice includes experience of Probation (Birmingham, and London) and Social Services (West Sussex). He is currently tutor in social administration at Plater College, Oxford.

Peter Ely worked in the Middlesex Probation Service for nine years and for the London Borough of Brent social services department for two years. He has directed Home Office funded research on alternatives to custody for juvenile offenders. He is currently a lecturer in social work at the University of Kent.

Nick Manning teaches social policy at the University of Kent. His publications include *Therapeutic Communities* (with Bob Hinshelwood, 1979), *Socialism, Social Welfare and the Soviet Union* (with Vic George, 1980), and *Sociological Approaches to Health and Medicine* (with Myfanwy Morgan and Mike Calnan, 1985). He is the founding editor (with Bob Hinshelwood) of the *International Library of Group Psychotherapy and Group Process* (therapeutic communities section) (Routledge and Kegan Paul) and the *International Journal of Therapeutic Communities* (Human Sciences Press). He is currently writing up a study of community care in Australia.

Stewart Miller is a lecturer in social administration at the University of Kent. He has researched in the areas of social work organisation and the social administration curriculum, and is at present writing a book on power and social policy. A graduate of Glasgow University, he has also taught at the University of Manchester.

Mike Oliver is currently a senior lecturer in special needs at Avery Hill College, having previously lectured at the University of Kent and worked as a development officer for Kent Social Services. His publications include *Social Work with Disabled People* (1984), and numerous journal articles. He is active in a number of disability organisations, including the Spinal Injuries Association and the British Council of Organisations of Disabled People.

Jan Pahl is a Research Fellow at the University of Kent. She is attached to the Health Services Research Unit and teaches for the Board of Studies in Social Policy and Administration. Her publications include *Managers and their Wives* (1971, with R. E. Pahl), *A Refuge for Battered Women* (1978) and *Private Violence and Public Policy* (1984). She is now completing research on the allocation of money within the family, and is directing a study of the needs of families with mentally handicapped children.

1 Constructing Social Problems
Nick Manning

The study of social problems originated in the nineteenth century in reaction to the enormous social changes brought about by the industrial revolution. In England, America and Europe a variety of observers including politicians, journalists and social scientists struggled to make sense of the new society which capitalism had generated. A range of reactions from the most conservative to the most radical testified to a greatly changed social world, where it seemed that both unlimited opportunity and unlimited degradation could be found.

What were the intellectual tools available for comprehending this situation? Social science itself may be traced back into the eighteenth century and one of the strands emerging from the revolution in Western thought known as the 'enlightenment'. This movement believed passionately in the application of reason to human affairs, which could be therefore improved by the use of the systematic accumulation of empirical evidence, in place of the mystifications of religious belief, traditional authority, and sheer ignorance. It was hoped that the previous treadmill of human existence – epidemic, famine, early death, war and other 'social problems' of the day – could be bettered through rational analysis.

In the event this treadmill was to be broken by nineteenth century industrialisation rather than eighteenth century reason. The reaction of early writers to industrial change was to elaborate theory at the expense of, rather than with the help of, empirical observations. For example, David Hume and Adam Smith's work respectively gave rise to early psychology and political economy. The latter particularly concerned itself with ideals such as free trade and a 'minimum' state, rather than with the social conditions actually developing.

Theoretical elaboration about the general nature of this new society was dominated in the nineteenth century by Herbert Spencer in England, and his disciple William Sumner in the United States. Their sociology was modelled directly on biology, and in particular on Darwin's ideas. In fact their work was the mainstay of the dominant social philosophy of the middle nineteenth century – social Darwinism. This held that, by analogy with Darwin's mechanism of the 'survival of the fittest', it was natural and indeed essential that individualistic competition, a minimal state, and the 'natural selection' of social class should be encouraged.

Although seemingly an analysis of change and development, this was ultimately a conservative theory opposed to change. It argued that industrialising society was a natural development in which the strong (i.e. the wealthy and powerful) rightly dominated the weak (i.e. the poor and powerless). Appalling social conditions were essential to social development and social selection. For example, higher mortality rates amongst the lower social classes merely demonstrated their vulnerability and weakness in the fight for survival. From this point of view social problems did not merit massive state intervention for they were a natural aspect of social development.

Clearly this theory needed no empirical support, since whatever happened was by definition naturally selected. However, in marked contrast to this detached theorising, a second reaction to the new industrial society focused very explicitly on social conditions. The degradation to which the new industrial working class was subjected by the free market economy caused alarm and condemnation:

To whom, then, is this wealth of England wealth? Who is it that it blesses? . . . In the midst of plethoric plenty, the people perish; with gold walls, and full banks, no man feels himself safe or satisfied

(Carlyle, 1843, p. 263)

This duality of fortunes gave rise to Disraeli's famous observation that the rich and the poor were 'Two nations between whom there is no intercourse and no sympathy'. However, public recognition of this situation did not result from social science, but rather from another familiar source – investigative journalism, whereby members of one of Disraeli's nations ventured out to observe and report on the condition of the other. The analogy with the then dramatic geographical exploration of Africa was quite explicit:

But O Cook, O Thomas Cook & Son, pathfinders and trail clearers . . . unhesitatingly and instantly, with ease and celerity, could you send me to Darkest Africa or Innermost Tibet, but to the East End of London, barely a stone's throw distant from Ludgate Circus, you know not the way!

(Jack London (1903) quoted in Keating, 1976)

In other words, there was a 'darkest England' just as there was a 'darkest Africa' (Booth, 1890).

This, as we shall see, is an early attempt to generate a social problem by using the media as a way of influencing the political agenda of the day. Such attempts also drew upon more statistical evidence towards the end of the century. The gathering of such facts by many local statistical societies was part hobby and part business, since accurate and up to date market information was in growing demand. However, these surveys also included information on general social conditions, which it was hoped would be compatible with the still prevailing philosophy of competitive individualism.

Unfortunately, facts about nineteenth century poverty challenged rather than supported prevailing social theories, stimulating both more careful surveys and the beginnings of new theory. Thus when William Booth (of the Salvation Army) said 'The Social Problem has scarcely been studied at all scientifically' (1890), he meant not that there was a shortage of facts, but that as Charles Booth (of the London surveys) said:

The problems of human life must be better stated. The a priori reasoning of Political Economy ... fails from want of reality. At its base are a series of assumptions very imperfectly connected with the observed facts of life. (1887)

However, the powerful revelations of poverty by surveys conducted around the turn of the century seemed to carry sufficient weight, theory or no theory, to suggest the presence of a social problem of significant proportion. For example, Rowntree's evidence in 1901, that about one third of the working population of York were in primary (i.e. physical) poverty, spoke for itself. And this, as we shall see, has become another classic method of demonstrating the existence of a social problem.

During the twentieth century these early developments continue to influence the analysis of social problems. Indeed, the standard approaches can clearly be traced a long way back. For example, the uncovering of 'the facts' has been a central focus of the British study of social policy by social administrators. The theoretical problems involved have however been tackled mostly by sociologists, while journalists and social reformers have continued to lobby politicians in the hope of promoting the status of particular social problems.

What Are Social Problems?
Much of the literature on social problems is American – and there is a great deal of it. In this section we will outline the general approaches contained within that literature as a basis for building up a working definition of social problems.

One way of organising this literature is to outline its historical development, and the changes that can be seen during the twentieth century. An alternative is to lay out and discuss the range of approaches to be found in contemporary work. We shall do both since different approaches have developed sequentially, so that contemporary work is made up of the historical accretion of different social problem 'eras'.

Rubington and Weinberg (1977) have identified the appearance of five different approaches to social problems: social pathology (1905), social disorganisation (1918), value conflict (1935), deviant behaviour and labelling (both 1954).

The first grew out of the 'progressive era' in the United States in the early twentieth century. This was a loose movement of social reformers, academics and liberal politicians who shared a sense that society could be changed for the better. They felt that the individual opportunities opened up by nineteenth century capitalism were being endangered by *the pathology of individuals* such as powerful business and union leaders, political bosses in large cities, and the lack of education amongst immigrants and poor Americans. With little access to power this movement relied on education and persuasion to try to remedy perceived pathologies.

The failure of progressives to remedy their social problems through individual education, led to a more sophisticated sense that social problems were a result of strains and tensions in a rapidly changing society in which institutions experienced *social disorganisation* from time to time. For example, the breakdown of tradition and change in social expectations which European immigrants to America experienced were not remediable at the level of the individual. They were caused by the disorganisation of social and cultural patterns.

Both social pathology and social disorganisation imply an agreement, often implicit, about what the 'good (=organised) society' is. However, America had become a remarkably heterogeneous society of indigenous Indians, English, Scottish and Irish settlers, ex-African slaves, southern and eastern European immigrants, Mexicans and Central Americans. These groups were not well mixed but spread across large cities and vast rural distances. Whose 'good society' was being pathologically undermined, or disorganised? C. Wright Mills (1963) suggested in a classic phrase that there was a particular 'professional ideology of social pathologists'. He reviewed thirty-one text books on social problems, published between 1902 and 1940, and found that they contained many shared assumptions about problems in terms of 'deviation from norms, orientation to rural principles of stability, cultural lag, social change, . . . adaptation and "adjustment".' These he suggested were in fact 'the norms of independent middle class persons verbally living out Protestant ideals in the small towns of America'.

Mills's own work spanned the period which Rubington and Weinberg characterise as the *value-conflict* approach to social problems. This challenged the sociological search for a value-free social science, which the experience of the great depression and World War II had undermined. American society, Mills argued, was to be better understood as riven by conflicts between major groups such as white-collar workers, middle class professionals and the 'power élite' (a dominant alliance of big business, political and military leaders). From this point of view, social problems varied according to which of these groups was defining them. It was not enough therefore to identify some troublesome social conditions as constituting a problem, without also identifying the subjective judgment by a group of people that the condition threatened some values which they cherished. Fuller and Myers (1941) stated therefore that 'Social problems are what people think they are and if conditions are not defined as social problems by the people involved in them, they are not problems to those people, although they may be problems to outsiders or to scientists' (p. 320).

Nevertheless, each of these social problem perspectives did not disappear with the appearance of new formulations. Social pathology and social disorganisation for example were to reappear in the literature on *deviant behaviour* in the 1950s, in the context of functionalist sociological theory. From this point of view, behaviour by individuals which transgressed social norms threatened the supposed unity of a social system in which given social roles were essential functional prerequisites for the complex interdependence of modern society. There were widely accepted rules about the appropriate behaviour in areas such as work, leisure, family and sexual life, property ownership. Transgression of these rules was therefore a problem to be analysed and remedied. Indeed, it was the sociologist's job to spot such transgressions and bring such 'latent' social problems, as Merton and Nisbet (1971) later described them, to light before they could seriously threaten the social system.

Clearly, this line of analysis fell back on the assumption of widely surprisingly, then, in the field of deviant behaviour, a further model appeared in the 1960s building on Mills's criticisms, known as the *labelling perspective*. From this point of view deviant behaviour was not the objective transgression by individuals of shared social norms, but rather it was a process by which one group of people had the power to label another group of people as deviant, whether or not the latter agreed. And whereas earlier Mills had described the professional ideology of social pathologists who had the power to create labels (such as 'criminal'), Becker (1963) now described such people as 'moral entrepreneurs' who occupied a lofty position in the 'hierarchy of credibility': lawyers, doctors, politicians, journalists, and so on. Social problems then were not just 'what people think they are', but rather what powerful and influential people think they are. At the extremities of this approach, for example in Scheff's work on mental illness (1966), there was no deviant behaviour, or at least none that was not shared within all walks of life; there was merely the differential power to label. For example, a middle class crime such as embezzlement attracted a very different label from working class crime such as property theft.

Social Perceptions or Social Conditions?

These sequential, but overlapping, approaches to social problems in fact fall into two very general types which underlie the conventional analysis of social problems. Social pathology, social disorganisation, and deviant behaviour all assume some features of normal society, in which a social problem can be identified by the demonstration of some social condition which is at odds with those normal features. Value-conflict and labelling by contrast suggest that we cannot presume in advance what normal society is, since different groups adhere to different values. Social problems are consequently merely social conditions which some people dislike, but which may not concern others. There is, therefore, no objective measure of whether social conditions constitute a social problem.

Manis (1976) has called this second approach the 'public opinion model' (p. 19). It suggests that a social problem is ultimately defined by what the main groups in society consider to be undesirable social conditions, which they would like to change. Essential to this approach is the focus on what these groups perceive as problematic rather than on the actual conditions that they deplore. For example, the National Front in this model may disapprove of the effects of immigration even if their idea of those effects is highly biased or even downright wrong, for it is what they believe to be the facts which guides their moral condemnation, their explanations, and their political actions. Or, again, the problem of battered wives may be perceived as the consequence of male hegemony in our society, of lack of suitable accommodation as Erin Pizzey (1974) has argued, or of a complex psycho-social interaction including male aggression and female masochism as some psychiatrists, social workers and other professionals argue. Within this model 'public opinion' does not mean an undifferentiated group, but consists of various interests. These can be characterised at one level as big business and government, mediated through the mass media; at another level the interests of journalists in creating news to sell newspapers; or the interests of professionals in sustaining social problems through which they earn their living; or the real if not often articulated interests of the working class, or various exploited or disadvantaged minority groups, as victims of social problems.

Here social problems are emphatically not taken as given by objective social conditions. Rather, this perspective is an interpretive one in which social order itself is taken as problematic in that it is continually being constructed and reconstructed in everyday interaction. Here the research problem is the way people actually create their feeling that a social phenomenon may be a social problem. Important evidence for this is the way social problems emerge and subside in the consciousness of certain groups. For example, only recently has family violence become a social problem, yet it has existed for centuries.

This point of view can be seen clearly in work by Becker and others within the labelling perspective:

Social groups create deviance by making the rules whose infr...
deviance and by applying those rules to particular people and lab...
outsiders. From this point of view deviance is not a quality of the ac...
commits, but rather a consequence of the application by others of ru...
sanctions to an offender. The deviant is one to whom that label has success...
been applied; deviant behaviour is behaviour that people so label.

(Becker, 1963, p. 8)

Here then the focus is directly on the process of perception by others (be they the public, political-intellectual minorities, or the mass media), of social conditions which they decide to label as a social problem. Hence our attention is drawn to the study, for example, of the role of the mass media in shaping perceptions about black immigrants. The principal consideration of social problems in this perspective is the study of the natural history of social problems. For example, we can look at the way Erin Pizzey gained access to the mass media, and changed public and professional perceptions of battered women. We may also come to witness the waning as well as waxing of social problems. Under what conditions will the social problem of immigration or family violence disappear, while the prevalence of these phenomena actually remains unchanged? For example, why did poverty apparently disappear in the 1950s but re-emerge in the 1960s when incomes were higher? And what happened to all those dope fiends of the 1950s who suffered 'insatiable cravings' for marijuana, and faced potential death from their addiction, as our newspapers would have had us believe? Has the marijuana of the 1980s got weaker, or rather has the social problem as then perceived been reconstructed and re-evaluated?

However, there are disadvantages which arise from this approach to social problems:

1   It does not encourage us to search for actual conditions which may become perceived as problems, such as the stimulation of lung cancer by smoking, or the long term effects of polluting the biosphere.

2   It does not encourage any intervention into public debate to offer scientific evidence which may resolve a dispute which can surround or even create a social problem.

3   Similarly, intervention to widen or offer an alternative conception or solution in public debate is discouraged, when social problems are merely defined by public attitudes, which can be volatile and ambiguous (Taylor-Gooby, 1982).

4   Much of the work, for example in the sociology of deviance, is at a small scale level. It tends not to study or question a society in its entirety. Hence, the study of class divisions, or the nature of powerful élites such as the military, big business or politicians is bypassed in favour of the

more dramatic sketches of drug takers, homosexuals or criminals as perceived social problems.

5   Finally, and closely-related, is the fact that definitions of social problems are dictated more often by the interests of the powerful in our society. By taking given social problems for study, this perspective tends to accept perceptions that can be proffered by the powerful, for, as Marx noted many years ago, the dominant ideas or ideologies in a society at any given time tend to be those of the ruling class.

In the face of these difficulties, Manis (1976) asks whether a return to the direct observation of social conditions can be justified. Is it the social conditions themselves or is it the relatively subjective perception of those conditions which determines the problem? For example, is it the number of women or babies that are battered, or the number of immigrants, or the extent of loneliness amongst the elderly, which is the problem; or is it only when sections of the population decide to define those conditions, whatever their level, as undesirable that there is a problem? In other words, can scientific enquiry isolate the objective (underlying) conditions and therefore identify the problem, or do we have to ignore those conditions and look merely to what the public feels about them? Manis suggests that we elevate to a central position the notion that scientific enquiry can determine, through the systematic application of its theories and methods, what social conditions are 'detrimental to human well-being' (p. 25). Social problems are thus identifiable without reference to public opinion, though of course through the publication of scientific facts it is hoped to sway public opinion round to perceiving a social problem as the scientist does, and hence generate sufficient political power to try to implement measures designed to change those social conditions threatening human well-being.

Taking social problems as given in this way emphasises the objective factors assumed to constitute the problem. As we have seen, two principal kinds of definitions can be used:

1   where a social problem is any set of conditions which is troublesome: the actual incidence of family violence, or rape, or other crime; the actual proportion of the population which is elderly; the actual number of homeless;
2   where a social problem is defined as any deviation from some group norm, value or rule in society.

The deviations are seen as objective, that is 'out there in the world', and thus not a product of social definition. Implicit in this approach is the assumption that deviation from the normal is pathological or is a threat to the social order, and hence emphasises a conservative or consensus view of social life. But more recently sociologists of this ilk have explored the positive aspects of conflict through deviance, as a chance to instigate social change and adaptation. However, even these more radical views still presume that the social problem is defined by the conditions themselves out in society. For example, whether one views growing divorce rates as a dangerous threat to the family as a vital institution in our society or as a welcome liberation from a repressive and controlling relationship, the problem is still defined by the objective incidence of divorce.

However, there are also a number of disadvantages we can identify with this approach to social problems:

1 That the location of facts will not tell us what will in fact be selected and defined as problems by groups in society.
2 Further, we cannot therefore explain the waxing and waning of social problems which occurs unrelated to changes in the actual social conditions.
3 We have to presume what the interests of society or 'human well-being' are in advance, and social scientists do not agree on this.
4 In fact social scientists tend to study conditions actually defined by the articulate as inconvenient (such as burglary) rather than those conditions objectively most harmful (such as fraud or embezzlement). In other words, they are influenced by public perceptions in their choice of topics for study, without analysing such influences.
5 This bias in problems studied is not random but rather reflects the interests and concerns of government, business or grant-giving agencies. That is, it concentrates on those who break rules, rather than those who make or enforce them, on individual violence rather than institutional violence, on 'war crimes' rather than the waging of war.

Both these approaches then have failings: Manis relies on science as the judge of social problems, and equates actual conditions, such as the number of people unemployed, with the problem. The public opinion model on the other hand supports, implicitly, establishment definitions of problems, and the public's appetite for the dramatic and unusual.

The Development of Social Problems
We have discussed in the previous sections the historical and contemporary range of perspectives on social problems. We argued that there has been an underlying oscillation between two general types. In this section we will consider a developmental approach which attempts to take a more dynamic view of the way social problems develop, and hence overcome some of the problems associated with earlier formulations.

It is apparent from the previous section that a social problem generally refers to some perceived social condition which offends a group of people (or their 'human well-being') and which is potentially changeable through collective social action. However, we have seen that much of literature has been concerned with identifying social problems, rather than with the way social groups try and change the conditions they dislike. What is the nature of this social action?

Spector and Kitsuse (1977) suggest that we should focus more clearly on the process by which social problems are tackled, rather than whether they exist. This they argue is a more fruitful way of understanding social problems. While this bears some similarity to the 'natural history' definition of the public opinion model, it goes beyond the changing concerns of public opinion to address the issue of how and why different groups try to press their claims for social action, normally in the political arena:

Social problems are the activities of groups making assertions of grievances and claims to organisations, agencies, and institutions about some putative conditions.

(Spector and Kitsuse, 1977, p. 75)

A social problem is not therefore a static condition, but a sequence of events that can vary from problem to problem. Nevertheless, there is a discernable pattern in this sequence with Spector and Kitsuse lay out in terms of four stages.

First, a group asserts that a condition exists, and that it is offensive. Second, an official government or other influential agency responds, typically in a routine or ineffectual way. In British and American politics this is well illustrated by the use of Royal Commissions, or Presidential Commissions (Sheriff, 1983). These are typically made up from the relevant 'political-intellectual minority', in Green's (1975) terminology, which invites the submission of evidence from interested parties, and makes recommendations. The procedure can take a long time, thus either reducing the relevance of the report or allowing the initial issue to cool off. The government of the day (it may well have changed during this time) may or may not respond positively to the recommendations, but is not bound by them, and frequently fails to take much action (Bulmer, 1980, 1983).

The third stage in this sequence involves, in addition to a restatement of the original claim, new claims about the unsatisfactory response of stage two. This may well loop back to a new round of stage two, and indeed group claims can get stuck in this loop and disappear. However, the final stage is the point at which the original group decides that alternatives to stage two must be set up. For example, it may decide to construct its own remedial action such as a self-help service. Alternatively, it might focus on the inadequacy of the political structures to meet its interests, and attempt to alter them more or less drastically to be more satisfactorily responsive.

Perhaps we can explore the strength of this model by comparing the fortunes of the poverty 'lobbies' in Britain and the USA since the 1960s. In both countries in the early 1960s despite nearly two decades of continuous economic growth, it was asserted that the social condition of poverty was widespread and that the government should do something about it. In America, the civil rights movement had called attention to the miserable exclusion of blacks from the fruits of American prosperity. In addition, a singular statement by Michael Harrington in *The Other America* (1963) pointed out that poor whites and other ethnic groups were similarly excluded. In Britain, analysis of the experience of poor people in the Welfare State by Abel-Smith and Townsend in *The Poor and the Poorest* (1965) led to the setting up of the Child Poverty Action Group (CPAG) to press the claims of all poor people, and especially children, for a better standard of living.

These claims were met by a relatively positive response from both governments. In the USA, a 'war on poverty' was declared by President Johnson in 1964 through the Economic Opportunity Act:

... We have never lost sight of our goal – an America in which every citizen shares all the opportunities of his society, in which every man has the chance to advance his welfare to the limits of his capacities ...

The distance that remains is the measure of the great unfinished work of our society.

To finish this work I have called for a national war on poverty.

Our objective – total victory ...

Because it is right, because it is wise, and because for the first time in our history it is possible to conquer poverty, I submit the Economic Opportunity Act of 1964.

> (President Johnson's message to Congress, March 17 1964,
> quoted in James, 1970, p. 65)

The 1964 Act set up the Office of Employment Opportunity to operate two types of anti-poverty programme: delegated programmes to encourage good work habits through re-training and education; and direct programmes involving the poor themselves, volunteers, and 'experts' in community action programmes. However, this 'war' was only allocated about 10 per cent of all expenditures for poor people (i.e. all income maintenance programmes). Nevertheless, the numbers in absolute poverty declined between 1960 and 1970 from just over 20 per cent to just over 10 per cent (Starnes, 1976, p. 40).

Perhaps this contradicts Spector and Kitsuse's model. Could there be a stage three and four when poverty was tackled so effectively? in the event, the answer was 'yes'. A British observer concludes in *America Against Poverty* that:

the improvement in absolute poverty was not directly attributable to federal domestic policy ... most of the improvement had been among the able-bodied poor in, or available for, work. Thus full employment, to which the federal government's main contribution was the Vietnam war, was the most potent poverty killer.

(James, 1970, p. 109)

Consequently, those unable to work, especially the disabled, elderly, single parents and children, gained little from the war on poverty. It had been shaped by political opportunism – 'a terrific slogan in an election year' (Marris & Rein 1974, p. 317), and an assumption that poverty was a cultural disease rather than a product of structural inequalities in American society.

Stage three developed in the early 1970s when welfare rights organisations began to address the problem of those poor who could not work, particularly single black mothers dependent on government aid. For these people it was felt the government response had been quite inadequate. For these people, civil rights meant rather less than welfare rights. However, despite urban rioting in the late 1960s, this claim was unsuccessfully translated into stage four, and the national campaign for welfare rights foundered in the later 1970s for want of political leverage and in the face of the slowing of growth in the American economy.

In Britain, there was a more fragmented government response. Various official reports concurred with the CPAG's diagnosis of urban deprivation. However, these amounted to several small claims in Spector and Kitsuse's terms, to which specific government departments responded. In addition to the Home Office's Community Development Projects (CDP), the departments of the Environment, Education and Science, and Health and Social Security set up urban initiatives. These were generally accorded mere experimental status and aimed at isolated and discrete problems such as poor housing, poor schools and urban crime. As in the American case, financial commitment was limited and even coincided with cuts in general welfare expenditure (Loney, 1983).

It is easier to demonstrate a stage two response in Britain, for at the conference which launched the Home Office's CDP, the Chief Inspector of the Children's Department explicitly acknowledged that he was looking for 'a new method of social control – what one might call an anti-value, gilding the ghetto, or buying time' (CDP Inter-Project Editorial team, 1977, p. 146). Thus the response to stage one claims were unlikely to satisfy those making them, for as Professor Peter Townsend (1976) argued 'bureaucracies have vested interests in defining problems for which they are responsible in forms which show that these problems are of "manageable" proportions'.

The stage three reaction to these government palliatives can be seen in the persistent political lobbying undertaken by the CPAG in the

1970s, for which they claim some success. For example, they were prepared to leak secret cabinet information to embarrass the Labour Government to honour its commitment in principle to the Child Benefit Scheme. Similarly critical comments by the CDP eventually provoked the Home Office into shutting them down. However, once again this activity failed to reach stage four whereby alternative methods could be set up to meet the original claims registered at stage one. The CPAG did not have the political leverage, nor the means, to do anything further about child poverty.

These examples illustrate both the merits and limitations of Spector and Kitsuse's model. In their favour we find a method which usefully combines both the objective social conditions (numbers and kinds of poverty) with the subjective struggle over the significance of those conditions. It shows clearly how a social problem can be established but change in the context of political fortunes. However, it has little to say about how claims are registered, and become legitimate. Nor do we know what constitutes an official agency, nor what determines government reactions, and in particular the circumstances in which claims can be pressed to stage four where alternatives become politically feasible. We will explore these issues in the following sections.

The Mass Media and Social Problems

In this and the next section we will consider two vital omissions in the Spector and Kitsuse model. The first is the role of the mass media as a key link between claim makers and official agencies. The second is the nature of the modern state as the most important agency to which people turn for a solution to their problems.

The mass media are a vital aspect of both the definition and development of social problems through their influence on public opinion. Even Manis's emphasis on scientific enquiry into social conditions that are detrimental to human well-being nevertheless acknowledges that public recognition and support for action are important for the implementation of scientific findings. The other models we have discussed focus quite centrally on public attitudes as the key to social problem definition, and the development of grievance claims within the political system.

While there are various channels for and influences upon public consciousness, such as work, friends and family, there can be little doubt that the mass media have become a central mechanism for the collective consumption of 'social facts', and the collective expression of judgements about social problems. These media, the press, television and radio, are principally involved through the presentation of news, documentaries, entertainment and advertising.

In Britain, broadcasting has been set up on a presumption of neutrality and balance. The government either heavily regulates commercial channels or organises non-commercial channels. By contrast, the press are traditionally entitled to much wider freedom. This is generally held to be because, since the eighteenth century, they have been used as a channel for the expression of public opinion (Burns, 1977), whereas it has been assumed that television and radio are potentially more manipulative of, then expressive of, public opinion.

These two notions of neutrality and freedom of expression have been elaborated into two models of the mass media held by professional journalists, and the commercial media respectively. In the first, it has been argued that journalism, as a profession, is organised with respect to its own set of values and priorities, which are committed to presenting the known facts and informed comment so that the public may come to their own views about issues of the day. Evidence to support this view is drawn from examples of journalists being involved with both criticising and defending the establishment. For example, journalists have been involved not only in exposing, the drug thalidomide, and Nixon's involvement in the Watergate break-in, but also in denouncing terrorism, exposing social security fraud and criticising trade union power. From this point of view, the media are involved in *educating* public opinion as to the facts and arguments about public issues.

In the second model, it is suggested that market forces determine the content of commercial press, radio and television. The buying public have the power to alter that content by consuming media products they like, and ignoring those they do not. Rather than the media educating the public, the public educate the media. Evidence in this case comes from commercial successes and failures. For example, newspapers such as *The Evening Standard* or *The Times*, or programmes such as TV-AM, which have been in difficulty, have had to try to alter their content to attract more public support, or go out of business. In this model, then, the public is the dominant partner in a relationship which *reflects* rather than educates public opinion about important issues.

The twin notions of neutrality and freedom of expression have been criticised, however, on the grounds that neutrality may restrict legitimate opinion to that which reflects the status quo, and freedom of expression requires a highly expensive commercial enterprise available to few people. For example, studies of journalists in action suggest that they have highly routinised ways of handling news. Thus industrial relations reporting implies that businessmen are calm and reasonable (usually interviewed in quiet studios), while union members are irresponsible and selfish (normally interviewed outside studios) (Glasgow University Media Group, 1976). A different bias has been observed in reporting social problems. They tend to be trivialised to a human interest level where individual victims suffer from 'natural' disasters. They rarely tackle structural questions about the shaping of social conditions. Thus, disabled individuals make good items, whereas the causes of poverty do not (Brunsdon and Morley, 1978).

These criticisms have given rise to a third model in which the media are seen to be under the control of an economic/political élite or élites, who use them in a conspiratorial manner to *manipulate* public opinion. Commercial press, television and radio, it is pointed out, are owned by big business, and that ownership is increasingly concentrated in a few hands. For example, a great deal of daily news is produced by wholesalers such as Associated Press or Reuters and sold as a packaged commodity to the press, and other mass media. State owned media, such as the BBC, are not immune from this influence, although they are not private property. For example, in 1926 at a time of acute industrial and political unrest, the director, J. W. C. Reith, wrote in a memorandum to the Prime Minister:

Assuming the BBC is for the people and that the government is for the people, it follows that the BBC must be for the government in this crisis, too.

(Quoted in Burns, 1977, p. 54)

More formally in the Ullswater Committee Report of 1936 on the relationship between the BBC and the government, it was stated that:

It is meritable that the state, in establishing a sole broadcasting authority, should reserve to itself those powers of ultimate control; but we have no reason to suppose that, in practice, divergent views of the lines of public interest have been held by the Corporation and by Government departments . . .

(ibid., P. 55)

More informally it has been suggested that the BBC operates within a middle class Southern English cultural world which reinforces a view of the world harmonious with élite interests.

This third model implies then that public opinion is not in the hands of the public or educative journalists, but in the hands of an élite which tries to exclude opinions contrary to its own interests, or to minimise the significance of adverse social conditions.

In Table 1.1, these three models of the media are directly related to our three models of social problems outlined earlier in this chapter. For example, journalists who regard themselves as public opinion educators regard social problems as residing in social conditions *per se*. The problem of thalidomide was the effect of the drug, and the task of the media was to bring that scientific evidence to public view. On the other hand, the commercial press regard themselves as reflecting public concern about issues, in the fight to maintain their circulation figures. Hence, they attempt to mirror what they feel is of public interest, for example, inflation, union power, or nationalistic interest in the

Table 1.1   Social problems and the media

Social problem is . . .	Mass media effect is to . . .
Scientific knowledge about conditions detrimental to human well being.	Educate public opinion as to the facts.
Public attitude about perceived threats.	Reflect public opinion concerns.
Claim on official agencies about perceived grievances.	Shape perception of grievances and reduce legitimacy of claims (e.g. by 'naturalising' individual misfortunes).

Falklands War. The third model however regards the media as manipulating public opinion away from ideas that may embarrass or challenge the dominant élite. Hence the media are related to public actions, or inactions, in terms of 'legitimate' claims about 'reasonable' grievances to which official agencies are expected to respond.

Just as we have argued the superiority of the Spector and Kitsuse grievance – claims model of social problems, we would similarly support the model of the media as a shaper and legitimiser of such grievance claims. The media's self image as either educative or reflective of public opinion is not satisfactory in the light of patterns of ownership, control and structure within the media.

However, as we said earlier in this section, public opinion is also shaped by people's own experiences of work, family and friends. Also within the media there is a tension between élitist interests and the evidence that journalists collect. How these various influences work out is of importance to social problems. News can 'travel fast' outside the media, particularly in large factories or offices, and some journalists may break with their prescribed routines. We shall deal with these issues in the next section on the state, and again in the final chapter of the book when we pull together our different studies of social problems through the notion of ideology.

The State and Social Problems

The state is the most obvious source of agencies to which grievance claims, with or without media support, are addressed. Similarly, the state is the major purveyor, through its various departments, of solutions to social problems, frequently in the form of social policy. However, the link between any set of claims and any social policy response is tenuous. Other interests and other policy areas are normally involved. For example, new policies to contain the consumption of harmful substances such as tobacco may upset industrial and advertising interests, reduce the volume of indirect taxation, overburden police surveillance, curtail freedom of choice, and so on. Not only do those concerned with these interests attempt to influence politicians and civil servants, but government departments themselves such as those of trade, sport or the Treasury may object to such a new social policy to deal with the problem of tobacco (Calnan, 1982).

To understand the fate of grievance claims, and hence the fate of social problems, we must therefore understand the nature of the modern state. In Britain, as in all industrial societies, the state has grown rapidly with industrialisation whether this is judged in terms of public expenditure, administrative activities, or statutory control. Perhaps the most notable feature is that public expenditure [measured conventionally as a proportion of the gross national product (GNP)] amounts to nearly fifty per cent of GNP, of which half again or about one quarter of GNP is accounted for by social policy activities making up the welfare state. No wonder we turn to the state to solve social problems!

Why has the state become so large? A traditional explanation is that industrial society creates new needs, such as for an educated and skilled workforce and a healthy urban environment, which cannot be effectively provided for through traditional or market mechanisms. In addition, it destroys the ability of ordinary people to deal with needs such as insufficient income or dependent relatives. These are then met by the state. Two different models of the state have been traditionally used to explain this process. The first suggests that the state is a *rational* response to the creation of needs and social problems in a democratic society. Social administration in British universities has been an important element in this model, seeing itself as the systematic identifier of needs and social problems which the welfare state would meet. A second model however suggests that such rationality is bounded by the interests and perceptions of a political *élite*. Thus the history of nineteenth and twentieth century social policy is permeated by accounts of those members of the élite driven by their social consciences to meet needs (Baker, 1979). However such needs are perceived from this point of view through the particular cultural assumptions of the élite – hence the division of clients into categories of deserving and undeserving, and so on.

However, contemporary explanations now focus less on the needs of the public and rather more on two other factors. First it has been argued that the requirements of modern capitalism for cheap but skilled labour, a stable political environment, a buoyant domestic market, and an infrastructure of public utilities seem to have led to government activity more often than human need has done. Second, the Labour movement's ability to threaten political instability, increase the cost of labour, and make needs visible has also stimulated government intervention. Only when pressed by capital or labour does the state seem to respond to reformist requests (Gough, 1979). Again we can identify two models of the state which are used to explain these processes. The first suggests that the modern state is a *corporatist* institution (Middlemass, 1979) in which chief interests in society, such as employers and trade unions, are drawn into a tripartite relationship with the state to hammer out basic agreements about wages, taxes and so forth, completely bypassing the periodic formal electoral process. A more traditional version of this model stressed the activities of pressure groups competing in a *pluralist* political system to get the state to meet their interests. However the assumption that anyone can organise their interests via a pressure group has been found to be false – most effective lobbying is actually carried out by relatively few, large, corporate interests.

A second model is the *Marxist* view that the state is basically concerned to sustain the conditions necessary for capital accumulation (Jessop, 1982). However since this requires the cooperation of workers, who have the power of the vote, the state is forced to concede to working class interests in things such as pensions, health care and housing to retain its legitimacy. This results in a considerable tension between these two pressures, such that, in contrast to the relatively smooth operations of the corporatist state (in Sweden for example), the state is seen as the site of conflicts and struggle.

The mechanisms vary by which these pressures on the state actually appear in terms of concrete policies. What we might call the social relations of government include external demands, the internal politics of policy makers, and the implementation of new policies (Hall, et al., 1975). External demands may appear in terms of economic issues such as changes in exchange or interest rates, political issues such as demands for changes in the abortion law, or social issues such as censorship. However, the weight with which demands can be brought to bear within the relevant part of the state is a crucial determinant of their fate. Much government policy is effectively organised within departments by civil servants with an eye to the interests of their department, and the feasibility of political alignments in the immediate vicinity such as the Commons and the Cabinet. The general political standing of a minister, or the relative strengths of different departments (especially *vis-à-vis* the Treasury) may be crucial. Finally, the ability and commitment of the state to implement policies can be significant. For example, growing numbers of social security claimants are now processed by declining numbers of officials so that the ability to control fraud (apart from the use of special investigators) is declining at a time when government concern is growing.

However, behind these specific mechanisms which connect external demands through to implemented policies is a more general pressure on the state to remain legitimate in the eyes of both the electorate and the business community. In the case of the former, the formal requirements of parliamentary democracy, despite their relatively infrequent operation, do constrain particular governments to meet popular expectations. Indeed, it has been argued that this 'political market' in votes has contributed significantly to the expansion of state activities, as parties vie with each other to attract the voter. The confidence of the business community must similarly be sustained since the modern state's economic affairs are intimately bound up with the health of the private economy, particularly in terms of raising taxes and loans (O'Connor, 1973).

We can now examine the factors in the social relations of the state which are likely to affect social problems in terms of claims about perceived grievances. Clearly some 'personal troubles' become 'public issues' (in C. Wright Mills's (1970) terms), while others do not. Why is this? We can look to see how effectively a potentially public issue can make demands on the state, how it fits with the internal politics of the state, and whether the policies it requires are feasible.

Demands on the state normally appear to be carried by fairly specific pressure groups, such as the Child Poverty Action Group, or the British Medical Association. Such groups have developed an intimate relationship with the mass media, supplying them with free information and stories in return for free publicity. Out of this relationship, particularly the exercise of journalistic routines (about good news values, public concern, etc.), comes an image amongst 'informed' opinion as to how grievances should be perceived, and whether resulting claims are legitimate.

However, this media influence is itself shaped by already prevailing perceptions arising out of people's independent interests and experiences. The media may affect perceptions of grievances and associated claims, but ultimately they cannot create them where there is no general basis for their existence; nor can they make widely felt grievances entirely illegitimate. For this reason a wide basis of support for a public issue in major power blocks, such as the Labour movement or the business community, has been a primary factor in issues successfully 'going public' in the past.

Whether such a public issue is acknowledged as such by the state depends on additional factors. Even though the media and major power blocks support an issue, its fate depends on how well it fits into prevailing political priorities. As we mentioned earlier, departmental politics figure importantly here. An additional element is its fit with prevailing cultural assumptions. For example, to the extent that the issue appears to be a discrete and technical problem which does not challenge assumptions about pre-existing policies, it will generate less opposition. Such cultural assumptions in social policies include in the case of poverty or unemployment, for example, notions of victim culpability and a commitment to the work ethic.

If an issue gets this far it begins to look like a legitimate social problem. However, a final hurdle is whether potential actions to meet the grievances concerned are feasible. Economic cost is a frequent stumbling block. But some policies may also be what Hirsch (1977) termed 'positional goods': they can only be obtained at the logical expense of something else. For example, the more educational qualifications each child obtains, the less each qualification is worth since an important function of qualifications is to grade people, and there is a finite number of positions in any rank order. Of course, sheer physical limits may also exist to some policy options, such as those which require the policing of individual behaviour, for example, under-age drinking and smoking. Finally, as far as social problems rather than policy options are concerned, new social policies have a nasty habit of spawning new social problems in the form of new grievance claims.

Perhaps we can illustrate these processes briefly by looking at two recent social problems, one of which failed to get through this system and one of which succeeded. The first is based on the existence of inequalities in the health of different people, and in their receipt of health care. While information on such inequalities, particularly between different classes, has accumulated since the 1960s, a recent report summarising the data (The Black Report, 1980) showed unequivocally that there were large inequalities which had changed little in the 30 years since the NHS, committed to their reduction, had existed. The report, commissioned by the 1974–1979 Labour Government, concluded that only a substantial increase in expenditure could change this pattern. The report appeared after the 1979 Tory victory, and the new Minister of Health wrote in a curt introduction that there was no possibility of new money being made available, committed as the government was to public expenditure reductions, and very few copies of the report were released initially. However, this particular grievance claim rumbles on, supported by a variety of pressure groups and sections of the media.

A second example is the sustained lobbying of the National Association of Mental Health (MIND) throughout the 1970s for greater recognition of the legal and political rights of compulsorily detained mental patients. This culminated in the passage of the Mental Health (Amendment) Act, 1982, shaped as is often the case by detailed

discussion and horse-trading in the committee
the legislation.

Both of these examples spanned a change of govern.
a new era of financial restraint in British public expendi
plausible, therefore, to suggest that since health equalities
of money, while legal rights will not, the latter will be more h
rise to new social policy. However, there are additional ele.
terms of our earlier discussion. First, the groups supporting the
Report have not come together as a common block to lobby
government. In addition, some of the chief medical groups such as t
Royal Colleges and the British Medical Association have not been
brought into such a coalition. By contrast, MIND is recognised as the
main mental health pressure group, and it enlisted support from those
concerned with civil liberties, social work and so on. Second, the focus of
the two issues was very different. MIND's concerns, while impinging on
some interests (such as the clinical autonomy of psychiatrists), were
quite specific and threatened interests could be accommodated or
persuaded at particular points. By contrast, the Black Report's
recommendations were spread across the whole range not just of NHS
work, but health aspects of the housing environment, food policy,
income maintenance, and so on. Its focus in terms of government action
was therefore as wide as MIND's was narrow.

A third point, and probably the most important, was the difference in
cultural assumptions and values in the two issues. Some authors (e.g.
George and Wilding, 1972a, 1976) have suggested that some social
problems are moral issues which do not involve maximum conflicts of
interest (e.g. the disabled). Other problems are more directly a product
of differences of interest between particular groups such as men and
women (e.g. family violence) or capital and labour (e.g. unemployment).
This position however cannot account for the fate of 'moral' social
problems in terms other than the general drift of social values and the
energy of social reformers. We will suggest in the next section, rather,
that 'moral' social problems *are* part of significant conflicts, which have
become disguised. For example, the fate of mad or epileptic people
discussed in Chapter 4 is closely bound up with medical ambitions,
labour market demands and so on.

Returning to our examples, we can see that the issue of mental
patients' rights looks like a 'moral' social problem. In addition it had the
advantage of addressing specific individual cases, for whom a technical/
legal solution was being proposed. These cultural attributes fit neatly
into government processes which work best, in their own terms, on
technical problems related to individuals, about whom there is no major
conflict. If, on the other hand, MIND had tackled the issues of
understaffed and under-financed hospital and community services for

unemployment on discharge, the
and drug therapy) to effect cures,
urban environment and family life,
the experience of the Black Report.
opted the issue of community care as its
22   *Socia*/On the basis of the above discussion, we
the me...essful on this issue than it has been in the
failu
an that the modern state is the chief site for social
have also described the processing of these claims
mic and political interests, and cultural assumptions.
cial problems are more likely to have their claims met if
...oral, discrete and technical. The response may then
...te the traditional view of social policy as the rational response
needs as demonstrated by reference to social conditions as
facts. Otherwise a social problem may need to wait for support
from a major power block such as the Labour movement before
achieving any satisfactory government response.

In the final section of this chapter we look at the origins of different
interests and cultural assumptions which affect the fate of social
problems, since the social conflict model implied in this section often
takes conflict as given rather than explained.

Ideology and Social Problems

We have seen that the promotion of social conditions as social problems
typically occurs through perceived grievances being organised into
claims which various groups bring to the state. The legitimacy of those
claims is heavily influenced by mass media interpretations of public
opinion, and the priorities and interests of government departments in
terms of existing policies, perceived voter preferences, and major power
blocks such as the Labour movement and the business community.
While Spector and Kitsuse rightly observe that claims-makers may
attempt their own solutions (for example, the organisation of self help
services), state action is the dominant influence on the fate of such
claims.

How is it that the state and the media can exercise such influence over
the acceptability of some problems and not others, and to whom are
they acceptable? We have already seen how American text books were
rooted in the views of rural and small town America (Mills, 1963), and
that the modern state responds to technical and discrete problems.
These preferred perceptions of social problems can be examined
through the concept of ideology.

To tackle this issue we have to look at the nature of thought itself, not
so much in the sphere of science (although that is by no means immune

from social analysis) as in the sphere of 'ruling ideas', as Marx called them. We are interested, in other words, in the common intellectual currency of an historical period which makes up the totality of perceptions and ideas shared by the members of a society about their view of the world. These include such areas as human nature and the society of which we are all a part.

A fundamental aspect of this question of how we think, or rather of how ideas are generated and sustained in the public arena (in politics and areas of collective action especially), is the concept of ideology. Most of us have a general notion of what this means: the biased perceptions of some political faction perhaps. In fact it has a fair history. Mannheim in *Ideology and Utopia* (1960) dates its modern conception from the Renaissance, from Machiavelli who recorded a common observation of his time: that the thought of the palace is one thing, while that of the public square is another. In other words, politicians and public viewed events from different perspectives, essentially according to their particular interests.

From this point on there was the growing realisation that the world we perceive is to a considerable extent shaped for us by the *way* we perceive it – that our consciousness of the world is a human construction rather than a merely mechanical reflection of external reality. Furthermore, this human construction of the world as perceived is different in different historical periods and different social groups, and ultimately is to be located in social classes. This, the Marxist view, provided the most systematic explanation of the way in which our perceptions are affected by the historical period and social position in which we are located. Marx argued that our perceptions of the world were constrained by our class interests – that for example the capitalist could perceive inequality and poverty as inevitable because they enabled him to accumulate wealth. And this insight has been an extremely powerful weapon with which socialist thinkers have attacked the conceptions and ideas favoured by the ascendant class of the industrial revolution – the bourgeoisie. These ideas, it can be claimed, are a product of the class interests of capitalists who through their domination of government, education policy, the mass media and so on, foist their ideas on everybody else.

But of course such a powerful insight could not remain one-sided for long, and opponents of Marxism soon learnt that they could also use this criticism. Socialist ideas can also be attacked for being a particular perception which corresponds to the class interests of socialists – often conceived as the political goal of the downfall of capitalism. Once unlocked, this door can no longer be closed and all ideas are now suspect, with the result that much of current political debate appears to be a somewhat false contest of images or perceptions. Thus Mannheim quotes Max Weber:

The materialist conception of history is not to be compared to a taxi that one can enter or alight from at will, for once they enter it, even the revolutionaries themselves are not free to leave it.

(Mannheim, 1960, p. 67)

This, then, is the brief history of the concept of ideology. How is it used today, and what light does it throw on social problems? Mannheim distinguishes two different types of ideology:

1   The particular conception of ideology means that we are doubtful about the validity of someone's ideas. We suspect that he may be more or less consciously disguising the real nature of a situation which if it were revealed, might be to his disadvantage. Thus we can discredit ideas by showing that they spring from undisclosed personal interests or class bias. This is the thrust of Mills's argument about American social problems text books.

2   The total conception of ideology is a much more sophisticated concept than the particular. It is here that we find our central explanation of views on social problems. This total conception suggests that a total viewpoint or intellectual world is rooted in collective life; that not just a particular deception is in someone's interests, but that there is a correspondence between his social situation and the total perception of the world that he and his colleagues profess. For example, the government's definition of a social problem is bound up with its job of maintaining an ordered equilibrium in society – of maintaining the status quo, of maintaining law and order. Thus the ultimate conception is of a society into which deviant or difficult groups must be fitted – they must be adjusted. For example, the poor in this view must be educated and motivated to 'join in'. Thus, the full or general form of the theory is only reached when not just an adversary's point of view but all points of view, including our own, are subjected to ideological analysis. As Horton (1966) points out, 'one of the tasks of the sociologist is to recognise his own perspective and to locate this in time and social structure'. Not only can we cast doubt on previous conceptions of social problems, but our own position must be similarly doubted. For example, in stressing the essentially conservative nature of previous definitions of social problems we may be creating merely another ideological distortion.

Given this idea of ideology, then, how can we apply it to the views of social problems we have described? Modern conceptions of social problems such as poverty are a rich source of ideological masks. The very knowledge that ideological bias is a factor to be reckoned with in both others' and our own conceptions has resulted in a much more subtle articulation of interests. Ryan (1971) sets out to expose the way 'the new ideology is very different from the open prejudice and reactionary tactics of the old days'. He notes that there has been a series of American ideologies to rationalise injustice. In the past, slavery was justified as good for society and uplifting for slaves, and social Darwinism justified the survival of the fittest, i.e. the survival of the priviledged and powerful at the expense of the weak. Today he sees the dominant ideology as 'blaming the victim'. The miseducated child is blamed for his inability to read and write: he is culturally deprived. The lack of social and economic mobility of blacks is blamed on the unstable black family structure. Or in Sir Keith Joseph's terms, the poor transmit their poverty to their children (Rutter and Madge, 1976). Ryan points out the subtlety that skilled exponents such as Keith Joseph display in a disarmingly genuine concern for the victims so blamed. He really wants to help, yet his perception of the problem leads him inevitably to want to change the victim, not society. This is an example of Mannheim's total ideology – it is a general and honest misconception.

Clarke (1975) suggests that we can map the range of ideologies used about social problems along two dimensions of whether the social condition affects individuals or large collectivities of people, and whether those involved are responsible for their condition or not. (Table 1.2). The degree of responsibility or size determines the extent to which a social problem is seen as morally or politically threatening. In recent times, he argues, social problems ideologies have tended towards the bottom right hand corner of Table 1.2, emphasising the individual and natural rather than the collective and social, for three reasons: that

Table 1.2   Social problems ideologies

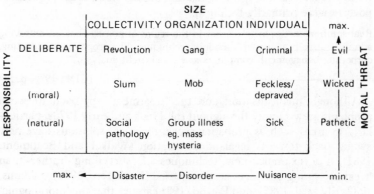

	SIZE				
	COLLECTIVITY	ORGANIZATION	INDIVIDUAL	max.	
DELIBERATE	Revolution	Gang	Criminal	Evil	
(moral)	Slum	Mob	Feckless/depraved	Wicked	
(natural)	Social pathology	Group illness eg. mass hysteria	Sick	Pathetic	

RESPONSIBILITY (left axis)   MORAL THREAT (right axis)

max. ◄— Disaster —— Disorder —— Nuisance —► min.

POLITICAL THREAT

(Adapted from Clerke, 1975, p.411)

reform rather than repression suits consensus politics; that a group's own view of the situation can be conveniently discounted; and that the emergence of professional experts, particularly doctors, can independently legitimise the official view.

This tendency has been discussed more specifically by Haines (1979) as a process whereby social problems are made to appear apolitical, despite the processes of political claims-making that we have described. Haines suggests that while all social problems are actually political, especially in terms of the power to define the terms of the problem, the objective of a claims-making group is ultimately to narrow and close the political debate in favour of its own definition of the situation i.e. to depoliticise it. Indeed, we might suggest that a group enters the political arena with the ultimate aim of leaving it, having vanquished all other versions of the events with which it is concerned. This observation neatly explains the reality behind George and Wilding's (1972a, 1976) distinction between moral and conflictual problems: they have merely perceived the apparent depoliticisation of some problems without understanding that that process is the end result of the political 'enclosure' of a previously conflictual problem. A more historical view would reveal that all 'moral' social problems at some stage were more overtly political.

Depoliticisation entails the transition from a normative to a cognitive universe. Once one definition has come to be predominant, then amelioration and administrative issues are matters of rational planning. The classic paradigm for this process is the medicalisation of social problems such as madness, alcoholism, or delinquency, which we shall examine in more detail in Chapter 4. However, other areas are also prone to depoliticisation. In the report on the British 'war on poverty' we introduced earlier, it was noted that official views of the problem of poverty were primarily technical:

> Real solutions are seen to lie, not in the realm of politics, but in improving administrative practice with modern techniques, like programme budgeting, corporate management, computers and cost benefit analysis.

> (CDP, 1977, p. 54)

Although medicalisation and the 'treatment' approach to social problems grew rapidly throughout the 1960s and early 1970s, particularly in areas such as probation work, technical solutions have now swung back towards legal administration (Walker and Beaumont, 1981). For example, new techniques of 'surveilling' rather than 'treating' young offenders are being tried (Drakeford, 1982; Williams, 1982; Ely et al, 1985), and Parton (1981) argues that the 'moral panic' over child abuse in the late 1970s in the context of the rise of 'new right' concerns about the family has, 'provided the battleground where certain representatives of "soft liberalism" could be more readily harnessed to the traditional virtues and the increased emphasis on "law and order".' (p. 409)

Despite these changing currents in social problem ideologies, social problems have not been solved, but if anything seem to be getting worse. Indeed, it is this pervasive sense of malaise that has given the 'new right' its widespread support culminating in the dominance of Thatcherism in British politics. The consensus which supported the British Welfare State in its first 30 years has broken down. This is not only a result of official disenchantment, but also because of the experience of its social service clients of increasing control over their lives (London Edinburgh Weekend Return Group, 1979). This has traditionally been analysed as a kind of pendulum swing in social values pulled between welfarism and capitalism as ideals (George and Wilding, 1976). However, such an analysis fails to explain why these value swings occur, and how they are related to deeper changes in the modern Welfare State and in particular its economic fortunes (Lee and Raban, 1983).

Such a traditional analysis can be characterised as idealist:

Idealism defends and elaborates theoretically the feeling (which dominates commonsensical explanations) that one has explained an event when one has traced it to an agent.

(Mepham and Ruben, 1979, pp. 47–8)

Thus the explanation of social problems tends to stop short at the perceptions of the key actors involved, and in particular their changing ideologies. Consequently, social problems tend to be understood as separate and discrete issues, each with their own particular constellation of grievances upon which specific claims are based.

In this way, Haines's acute observation about the ways in which some problems become depoliticised into technical issues is in fact an analysis of the struggle between competing ideas:

We need to turn our attention to how certain issues . . . can come to take on an apolitical and technical appearance and can come to be the 'property' of socially-defined 'experts' . . . as *intersubjective constructs* (emphasis in the original).

(Haines, 1979, p. 123)

Although this conflict approach to social problems is an advance over earlier consensus or functionalist views, it remains based on the same theoretical terrain in which separate ideas determine the course of social problems.

An alternative approach is to examine the material basis for social problems, which shapes both the problems and the ideas that key actors have about them. For such a materialism:

consciousness, agency and all aspects of social existence which give rise to ideology and appear to idealism as the foundation of social life, are actually produced by the interaction of needs . . . with the external world.

(Mepham and Ruben, 1979, p. 54)

From this point of view social problems and ideas about them are related to the development and satisfaction of needs in the external world as a whole, rather than to an independent struggle over 'intersubjective constructs'.

How can materialism help us with social problems? Idealist explanations are not only theoretically suspect, they lead to repeated failure as bases for social policies (e.g. poverty policy). We must ask therefore why such explanations persist, and how such social policy failures are tolerated, both by the public and the state. Materialism has here an answer couched in terms of a theory of ideology, which we develop in detail in the final chapter in the light of the case studies.

2 Violence Against Women
Jan Pahl

An Old Bailey judge said yesterday that he had 'considerable sympathy' for a 35 year old man who admitted having sexual intercourse with a seven year old girl. 'It strikes me as being one of the kinds of accident that could almost have happened to anyone', said Judge Brian Gibbens, QC.

The Guardian, 17 December 1983, p. 26

Question: Which is the odd one out? Egg, mat, wife, sex?
Answer: Sex. Because you can beat an egg, a mat and a wife, but you can't beat sex.

Graffiti at Bekesbourne railway station, Summer 1981

In this chapter we shall be concerned with two forms of violence against women: rape and wife abuse. Both clearly come into the category of social problems; both are detrimental to human well-being and both are overtly deplored. Yet at the same time, as the quotations at the head of this chapter indicate, both command a degree of casual acceptance and even, in some quarters, covert approval. This chapter aims to explore some of the ambiguities and complexities inherent in the study of violence against women and to show how a better knowledge of the phenomena we call 'social problems' can lead to a deeper understanding of broader social structures.

The study of violence against women also raises questions about the level of analysis. Whether we are concerned with perception, explanation or action, the question of level is important. Should our attention be focused on the violent event and the two individuals involved in it, or should we be concerned with the social and economic structures within which that event took place? Should rape and wife abuse be treated as separate phenomena, or are they more appropriately seen as two forms of violence against women, part of a broader pattern of gender-based aggression, built into the social and political fabric of a male-ordered world? And is male violence against women universal or is it specific to particular historical configurations and particular modes of production? We shall return to these questions in the conclusion to this chapter, after we have examined the evidence about rape and wife abuse.

Rape: State Policy in Historical Context

Let us begin by considering the legal definition of rape. The most important piece of legislation as far as rape is concerned is the 1976 Sexual Offences (Amendment) Act, which brought together a number of scattered statutory provisions on sexual offences. This Act lays down that a man commits rape if

(a)   he has unlawful sexual intercourse with a woman without her consent, and

(b)   if at that time he knows that she does not consent to the intercourse or is reckless as to whether or not she consents to it.

There are thus, according to the law, two essential aspects to rape, which are, firstly, a man having sexual intercourse with a woman when she does not consent to it, and secondly, his knowing that she does not consent, or not caring as to whether she consents or not.

There are various circumstances in which, though a man has intercourse with a woman against her will, the act still does not, according to the law, constitute a rape. For example, if a man honestly believes that a woman does consent, even though it might seem that his belief is unreasonable, then that is a defence to rape and he may be acquitted. This ruling was relevant in the Morgan case, in which an aircraftman brought three younger members of the RAF to his home, where his wife was asleep in bed. He assured them that they could have intercourse with her, and that, though she was likely to struggle a bit, this would not mean that she was reluctant, but that she was enjoying it. The three aircraftmen went ahead, Mrs. Morgan did struggle, but was overcome, and it was not till it was all over that she was able to put in a complaint of rape. The aircraftmen were eventually convicted, but only after the case had been to the Court of Appeal and the House of Lords; there was a great deal of controversy over the extent to which a woman had to prove that she did not consent to the rape, and this aspect of the crime has always been a controversial one (Toner, 1977, p. 101).

A second circumstance in which a man can have intercourse with a woman without her consent, but in which the act will not constitute rape, is if they are married. A wife cannot in law be raped by her husband, although the majority of battered women, and some women in so-called normal marriages would describe their sexual relationship with their husband at times as rape. However, as the law stands, a wife cannot be raped by her husband, except when a separation order has been granted, or when an injunction is in force; even when the wife has put in a petition for divorce, so long as the petition has not been heard by the court her husband cannot do anything to her which would legally be called rape. This aspect of the law relating to rape demonstrates a key historical tradition in this area of law, that is, the belief that a woman is always the property of some man, first of her father and then of her husband. From this point of view, a husband cannot rape his wife because it is impossible for him to steal his own property. The fact that his wife does not consent, and that he knows she does not consent, seems to be over-ridden by the older legal tradition that upon marriage a woman becomes the property of her husband. According to this tradition, the wrong that was done in rape was the unlawful use of another man's property, and so the punishment for rape, until the Middle Ages, was the payment of compensation by the rapist to the father or husband of the woman who had been raped. More detailed information about the legal aspects of rape is presented in the London Rape Crisis Centre, *Sexual Violence; the Reality for Women,* 1984.

Legal responses to rape, both now and in the past, have been described as reflecting a powerful myth. A myth, as the term is used by social scientists, has been defined as 'the whole world picture held by a social group and the value system anchored in that picture' (Gould and Kolb 1964). Thus any understanding of rape must take account of the value system within which the phenomenon has traditionally been located and the ideological foundations which underpin the myth of rape.

There are three main strands to this myth. The first strand of thinking is that which sees women as private property. This idea is part of the Western European tradition that individuals have the right to own property and that inequality in the ownership of property reflects 'natural' inequalities between human beings. During most of historical time the specific form that this inequality took was to make women the objects, rather than the owners, of property rights: women were among the forms of private property owned and controlled by individual men. This inequality in property rights was considered to be justified by differences between males and females. Those attributed with such rights were held to be stronger, more able, rational and so on; those denied such rights were held to be weaker, less able, emotional rather than rational, and generally in need of care and protection. Thus, under Anglo-Saxon law, the higher the economic or social position of the husband or father of the raped woman, the higher the fine extracted from the man who raped her. And, as we shall see, the punishment of the rapist has never lost its connections with the economic status of the victim – the higher her socio-economic status, the greater the likelihood that she will be considered credible, and that the case will come to court. It is still true that a wife cannot be raped by her husband: 'This is because, in the eyes of the law, he is her proper owner and may use her sexuality as he thinks fit. If he were to force the same act upon another man's wife, then he would be guilty of rape.' (Clark and Lewis, 1977, p. 161)

The second strand in the traditional myth about rape is the idea that women are not able to be autonomously in control of their own sexuality. From this idea flow all the assumptions about women who 'ask for it': a woman has only herself to blame, it is suggested, if she walks by herself in a lonely place, waits for a bus in the evening, hitch-hikes alone, wears attractive clothes, responds to being chatted up – or will not respond to being chatted up. As Wilson says:

In what other crime is the *victim* accused of having encouraged the crime? Is one 'encouraging' muggers by carrying a handbag with money in it? Is one 'encouraging' burglars by owning valuable proeprty?

(Wilson, 1983, p. 69)

This is a classic example of 'blaming the victim' (Ryan 1971). It is sometimes suggested that if women want to avoid rape they should take care not to go out without a male companion, that they should not go out alone at night, that they should not wait for the bus but take a taxi home, and so on. Proposals for a curfew are sometimes put forward: this is usually presumed to be a curfew on women, though it might seem more logically imposed on men since it is they who commit the rapes. The fact that a curfew on men is so unacceptable a solution to the problem of rape, while a curfew on women can be put forward in all seriousness, is a measure of the extent to which it has always been accepted that women cannot be in control of their own sexuality but need to be 'protected'. As we shall see, a woman is as likely to be raped by someone she knows as by a stranger.

A third strand in the traditional myth about rape is the idea of male control of sexuality. Clark and Lewis discuss this idea, and the title of their book, *'Rape: the price of coercive sexuality'* sums up their argument. They suggest that:

The socialisation of both men and women takes coercive sexuality as the normal standard of sexual behaviour. Men are expected to have to apply a certain amount of pressure to have women submit ('agree') to sexual intercourse . . . men are expected to be sexually dominant and to initiate sexual activity; women are expected to be somewhat passive and to agree to sex with reluctance. Understandably, those men who most strongly identify masculinity with sexual dominance and aggression are not likely to see any difference between what they call seduction and women call rape.

(Clark and Lewis, 1977, p. 141)

Looked at from this point of view, the legal definition of rape is very narrow. Many women would argue that the concept of rape might well be enlarged to include all those sexually abusive acts, from sexual harassment to near rape, which reflect male assumptions about the availability of any woman who is not clearly under the 'protection' or ownership of another man. Similarly, the fact that marital rape is not legally rape is a reflection of the idea that upon marriage a woman gives a general consent to whatever form of sexual relations her husband desires.

Though the law deems it not to be rape, recent research shows that rape within marriage is a fairly common occurrence, at least from the viewpoint of the women concerned. In an American study, each of 137 battered women was matched with another woman from the same neighbourhood in an attempt to investigate the links between rape and battering. (It was assumed that the 'matched' women would be non-battered, but the interviews revealed that 29 per cent of them had been physically assaulted by their husbands. As we shall see, this is almost exactly the proportion of battered wives that would be expected to occur in a randomly-selected sample.) The results showed that marital rape is a problem experienced by up to 10 per cent of all married women. In their analysis of the causes of rape within marriage, the researcher concluded:

> Our data suggest further that many of the stereotypes about marital rape and its causes are not valid. There is little evidence that women provoke the rapes by refusing reasonable sexual requests or by being unfaithful. Instead, the husbands who raped their wives appear to like violent sex ... these men appeared to devalue women and to feel that their wives were obligated to serve them sexually in whatever ways they desired.
>
> (Frieze, 1983, p. 553)

Thus rape within marriage, too, seems to be related to male dominance over women and to male control of sexuality.

Conventional Wisdom: The Facts and their Interpretations

In Chapter 1 of this book a distinction was made between two approaches to social problems: one approach suggests that a social problem can be objectively measured, while the alternative approach sees social problems as essentially subjective and as reflecting 'public opinion' of one sort or another (p. 6). It was also argued that this distinction is not so clear as it at first appears to be. Supposedly objective measures may represent particular ideas about measurement which themselves reflect particular value stances. Alternatively, subjective approaches can still be translated into quantitative terms in a way that offers an illusion of objectivity. The example of rape offers an opportunity of exploring these ambiguities.

Let us first consider the question of how many rapes take place. It is important to remember that there are many different stages at which a crime may be enumerated, many different points between the moment when the crime is committed and the point when the criminal is punished, at which the crime itself may be counted. When statistics relating to crime are being discussed, it is important to make clear at what point the statistics were compiled. Thus, for example, it is possible to count the number of rapes experienced by victims, the number of rapes which were subsequently reported to the police, the number recorded by the police as having occurred, the number for which an offender was arrested, or the number of rapes which led to the conviction of a rapist. One of the most striking things about rape is the very great 'shrinkage' which occurs between the first of these stages and the last, between the number of rapes recorded in victim studies as compared with the number of rapes which are eventually punished.

There is considerable dispute about the proportion of women who are likely to experience rape. Most estimates are drawn from studies carried out in the United States. Johnson applied demographic techniques to statistics on rape and concluded that 'nationally, a conservative estimate is that, under current conditions, 20–30 per cent of girls now twelve years old will suffer a violent sexual attack during the remainder of their lives' (Johnson, 1980, p. 145). A large survey carried out in San Francisco in which women were interviewed about their experiences of sexual assault estimated that there was at least a 26 per cent probability that a woman in the city would become a victim of completed rape at some time in her life and a 46 per cent probability that she would be a victim of rape or attempted rape (Russell and Howell, 1983, p. 695).

What proportion of all the rapes that occur are reported to the police? Answers to this question vary wildly, from 4 per cent to 40 per cent (London Rape Crisis Centre, 1982). The London Rape Crisis Centre reported that 25 per cent of all the women who contact the Centre also contact the police. The British Crime Survey estimated that 28 per cent of all sexual offences were reported to the police. However, this is likely to be an underestimate, since children were omitted from the survey and many women were interviewed in the presence of other people: it is likely that some women were interviewed in the presence of the person who raped or assaulted them (Hough and Mayhew, 1983). There are discrepancies, too, between the number of rapes reported to the police and the number recorded by them as having occurred. Again, it is hard to obtain accurate figures, but Toner was able to obtain figures for two police forces which showed that in 1975, 34 per cent of reported rapes were recorded in Cambridgeshire, while 76 per cent of reported rapes were recorded in Northamptonshire (Toner, 1977).

There is shrinkage, too, after the rape has been entered in police records. The study by Clark and Lewis analysed 116 rapes which were recorded as having taken place in Toronto in 1970. The results showed that, of this total, 42 rapes were defined as 'founded' by the police, and these resulted in 32 arrests, of which 17 ended in the conviction of the offender. Clark and Lewis were particularly interested in the 74 'unfounded' rapes. They concluded that whether a recorded rape was defined as 'founded' or not depended on many other factors in addition to the crime itself. Thus the police were more likely to accept the rape as 'founded' if the victim was aged between 20 and 30, if she was married, if she was single and living with her parents, if she was employed as a professional or was a student, if she was completely sober when the rape took place, and if she behaved in an emotional way after it had taken place. That is to say, she was more likely to be believed if she had demonstrated that she had the characteristics of a 'good' woman. On the other hand, the police were more likely to define the rape as 'unfounded' if the victim was aged under 20 or over 30, if she was separated or divorced or if she was cohabiting, if she was a housewife, if she was unemployed or on welfare, if she had been drinking before the rape took place, and if she behaved calmly after it had happened.

What sort of a crime is rape? When and where does it happen? What sorts of men become rapists? It is important to remember that in attempting to answer these questions we are largely reliant on police records; we know relatively little about the rapes which are not recorded or not reported, even though these comprise the majority of all rapes. Certainly there is no lack of popular, traditional notions about what the answers to these questions might be. One such popular notion is that rape is the act of an unbalanced personality in the grip of an uncontrollable sexual urge, and that the act typically takes place between strangers and in a public place. Other popular notions focus on the victim, suggesting, for example, that 'nice' girls don't get raped, so that any woman claiming that she has been raped is somewhat suspect and may indeed be making a false allegation; if it turns out that a rape did take place, such women, it is alleged, may have invited or even enjoyed the experience. Let us consider the truth of these popular traditional notions, drawing on a number of recent studies from both Britain and North America for our evidence.

First, there is little evidence that the majority of rapists have particular types of personality or that they are in any way unbalanced. It seems that the majority of rapists are young, working class men, or at least that most of the rapes which are recorded by the police are committed by this group (Amir, 1971; Clark and Lewis, 1977).

Secondly, the fact that the majority of rapes are planned casts doubt on the idea that rape is the consequence of a sudden and irresistible urge. In a study of 646 police reports of rape in Philadelphia, Amir found that 71 per cent of all rapes had been planned and that an additional 11 per cent had been partially planned; the Rape Crisis Centre found that 64 per cent of rapes had been wholly planned and 24 per cent partially planned; thus in these two studies over 80 per cent of all rapes had been premeditated (Amir, 1971; London Rape Crisis Centre, 1978).

Thirdly, it is incorrect to see the typical rapist as a strange man who jumps from a dark alley to assault a woman whom he does not know. In about half of all rapes, victim and attacker are known to each other: in about 25 per cent of cases they are acquaintances, while in about 25 per cent they are friends. These proportions have been found in a number of different studies (Amir, 1971; Clark and Lewis, 1977; Walmsley and White, 1979; London Rape Crisis Centre, 1982). Nor is it true to say that the characteristic rape takes place in a public place, though rapes that do take place between strangers in public places are more likely both to be reported to the police and to be publicised in the media. In all the three studies referred to above, more than half of the rapes took place at the home of the victim or of her assailant and a further proportion took place in cars.

Fourthly, traditional notions about the victim are often mistaken. As we have seen, it is not true to say that nice girls do not get raped: any woman can be raped but some are more likely to be believed than others. Considering that the proportion of rapes which actually end in court is so small and the ordeal which victims have to undergo in order to appear, it is unlikely that many false allegations actually get into court. The idea that women might invite or even enjoy rape also seems fallacious, given that so many rapes involve more than one assailant and the infliction of physical violence on the victims. Amir found that in 43 per cent of the cases he investigated the woman had two or more attackers and that in 85 per cent of the cases some form of physical violence was used by the attacker or attackers, in order to achieve their aim (Amir, 1971). In a British study, 38 per cent of 321 men convicted of rape had taken part in multiple rapes (Walmsley and White, 1979).

While the majority of rape victims are single and are aged between 15 and 24, there is no evidence to suggest that they are endowed with any peculiar physical or psychological characteristics which make them targets for the crime. Rape victims come from every social class and every educational level and rape can happen to a woman at any age from early childhood to extreme old age. The important differences are between women whose claim that they were raped is believed and those whose claim is not taken seriously.

Clark and Lewis suggest that there are some women who 'cannot' be raped, in the sense that any claim they may make is likely to be discounted. Rape is essentially a socially defined crime, so whether a rape has taken place or not can depend as much on how the situation is defined as on the objective facts. Clark and Lewis conclude 'Men who assault the women that society does not care to protect can usually avoid the penalties of the law' (Clark and Lewis, 1977, p. 94).

Given the reluctance of women to report rapes and the reluctance of the police to take their reports seriously, one might have expected that a majority of the cases reaching court would be serious enough to warrant a conviction. In fact, only a minority of recorded rapes led to conviction. The number of rapes recorded by the police in Britain increased from 784 in 1971 to 1,243 in 1978, but the percentage of those resulting in a conviction decreased from 34 to 26 per cent over the same period (Hay, Soothill and Walby, 1980). Writing of the position in the United States, Connell and Wilson concluded 'of all violent crimes the conviction rate for rape is the lowest' (Connell and Wilson, 1974, p. 125). There is a sense in which rape is perceived both as a very serious crime and as an essentially unserious crime: in order to understand this apparent contradiction we need to look at the problem in broader, structural terms.

Unconventional Wisdom: Another Look at the Problem
Let us first reconsider the traditional myth about rape as outlined in the early part of this chapter. The idea of women as private property, lacking autonomous control of their own sexuality but available to men and controlled by male definitions of sexuality, leads on to the notion of power as an essential element in rape. In his study of several hundred rapists, Groth identified rape as first and foremost an aggressive act. He distinguished three types of rape. These were the anger rape, in which sexuality becomes a hostile act, the power rape, in which sexuality becomes an expression of conquest, and the sadistic rape, in which anger and power become eroticised. Anger rapes made up 40 per cent of all cases, power rapes 55 per cent and sadistic rapes 5 per cent (Groth, 1979).

Once we accept the centrality of power in the problem of rape, it becomes important to look at the structural determinants of power, since powerfulness, whilst it may be mediated through individuals, is ultimately located in social and economic structures. This is an example of the general point, made in Chapter 1, that any individuals' viewpoint is ultimately rooted in collective life: as Manning suggests, 'there is a correspondence between his (sic) social situation and the total perception of the world that he and his colleagues profess' (p. 24). The argument of this chapter is that traditional fallacies about rape continue to flourish because it is in the interest of powerful groups that they should do so. The key question then is: whose interests are served by the continuation of traditional notions about rape? What are the underlying, true causes of rape which have been obscured by long-standing ideological masks?

Feminist scholars have documented the ways in which rape is a consequence of fundamental differences in power between men and women. However, within the feminist analysis there are differences in emphasis. On the one hand rape has been perceived as a consequence of male dominance over women: this might be defined as an élitist analysis, with men as the élite. This approach is exemplified by Brownmiller who sees rape as:

man's basic weapon of force against women, the principal agent of his will and his fear . . . From prehistoric times to the present, I believe, rape has played a critical function. It is nothing more or less than a conscious process of intimidation by which *all* men keep *all* women in a state of fear.

(Brownmiller, 1975, p. 14)

Brownmiller argues, not that all men are rapists, but that all benefit from an interpretation which presents the problem of rape as the problem of women:

a possible deep-down reason why even the best of our concerned, well-meaning men run to stereotypic warnings when they seek to grapple with the problem of rape deterrence is that they *prefer* to see rape as a woman's problem, rather than as a societal problem resulting from a distorted masculine philosophy of aggression.

(Brownmiller, 1975, p. 400)

Thus Brownmiller, like Clark and Lewis, sees rape as the price of coercive sexuality, as one consequence of a pattern of sexual relationships in which men are powerful both physically and ideologically, so that male definitions of the situation prevail over any interpretation a woman may put forward.

On the other hand, socialist feminists have argued against Brownmiller and have suggested that rape has its roots in an exploitative mode of production such as capitalism, which produces socio-economic inequalities which spawn increased violence. This materialist approach is exemplified by Schwendinger and Schwendinger (1983). They criticise Brownmiller's argument, pointing to three objections to her hypothesis that rape is a universal instrument of male power and dominance. First, since rape is censured in most societies, they argue that it would be unrealistic to see it as a universal form of social control. Secondly, they point to the fact that certain modes of production foster non-exploitative relations between the sexes and that in these societies rape is rare or unknown. Thirdly, Brownmiller's assumption of the universality of male supremacy is questioned in the light of anthropological evidence about societies where sexual equality predominates and the division of labour between the sexes is reciprocal. Thus, both approaches see rape as a product of male dominance. But while radical feminists such as Brownmiller see male dominance as a universal condition, socialist feminists such as Schwendinger and Schwendinger see it as one consequence of exploitative modes of production such as capitalism.

When we consider responses to the problem of rape we return to the question of the appropriate level of analysis and to the relationship between explanation and action. Solutions which focus on individuals tend to reflect explanations which see causes as located in individuals, while broader solutions reflect explanations couched in terms of social and economic structures. Thus, 'solutions' which focus on women, seeing them as needing to be protected from the consequences of their own sexuality, are inappropriate when rape is in reality carried out by men. As one of the women interviewed by Toner said:

If you wear a short skirt, people say you've asked for it. If you walk down the street at night, you've asked for it. If you walk down the street in the middle of the afternoon you can still get raped. Even if you lock yourself in a flat, some burglar might come and rape you. If you are a woman, you ask for it. There is no protection.

(Toner, 1977, p. 73)

Questioning the traditional stereotypes and myths about rape has given rise to a different set of responses which dispute male dominance and assert women's right to control over their own lives.

At the individual level, the feminist analysis of rape proposes types of action which are aimed at making women better able to protect themselves. Such actions may take many forms, from self defence classes to Reclaim the Night marches. These marches, torchlit processions which pass at night through city centres, aim to demonstrate women's right to be in the streets whenever they choose to be there; one of the slogans chanted on these occasions insists on women's right to wear what clothes they choose without being accused of being provocative:

Whatever we wear and wherever we go
'Yes' means yes and 'No' means no.

Research investigating the best ways for women to defend themselves has suggested that women who fight back, who scream or who run away, are more likely to avoid rape than women who, when threatened with rape, try to talk their way out of the situation or submit passively (Bart, 1981).

Rape Crisis Centres are one response which combines both individual and structural approaches to action against rape. At the level of the individual these centres offer free and confidential counselling and support for women and girls who have been raped or sexually abused. There are now Rape Crisis Centres in many towns in Britain and all maintain a telephone advice service and provide detailed legal and medical information. At a broader level, Rape Crisis Centres work to educate public attitudes, to bring about changes in the law and in the way the law is administered, to expose the fallacies which lie behind the myths about rape, and to validate the reality of women's own experience of abuse (London Rape Crisis Centre, 1984).

Broader, structural explanations of rape imply responses which are similarly broad. Thus Brownmiller advocates changes around the concept of 'consent' as a way of giving women greater power and men less. She argues that the principle of self-determination for women must be established without question as a way of diminishing the power of the male élite (Brownmiller, 1975, p. 382). If consent were to be recognised as a central element and incorporated into legal definitions of rape, she argues, rape within marriage would legally be rape and rape victims would not be asked to prove that they resisted. Brownmiller suggests that an overhaul of present laws and a fresh approach to sexual assault legislation must go hand in hand with a fresh approach to enforcing the law. She sees it as vital that women should achieve parity with men at every level of the legal and law enforcement professions, pointing to the fact that when policewomen, instead of men, were put in charge of interviewing rape complainants, the proportion of 'false' charges of rape dropped from 15 per cent to 2 per cent, exactly the rate for false reports of other violent crimes. Brownmiller concludes that 'the nation's entire lawful power structure must be stripped of male dominance and control if women are to cease being a colonised protectorate of men' (Brownmiller, 1975, p. 388)

Explanations of rape which see it as a consequence of exploitative modes of production lead on to proposals for action which focus, not just on reducing male dominance and male violence, but also on altering the underlying material order. Schwendinger and Schwendinger, for example, see priorities in terms of reducing poverty and unemployment, changing those conditions which seem to generate high levels of interpersonal violence, enhancing the power and status of women in the workplace, reducing female dependency at home and combatting sexual stereotyping whenever it occurs. Pointing to the fact that the majority of rapes are committed by working class men and that the majority of victims are working class women, they conclude by advocating political struggle by working class and anti-war movements:

It is time to recognise that rape is distributed in our social structure in predictable ways and that sexual assault as well as other violent crime is influenced by political, economic and ideological conditions.

(Schwendinger and Schwendinger, 1983, p. 221)

In the first half of this chapter we have looked at legal definitions of rape and at the historical context which gave rise to those definitions; we have exposed conventional wisdom to the light of findings from recent research; and we have explored some less conventional and more radical approaches to the problem of rape. In the second half of the chapter we shall be looking in the same way at wife abuse, before returning to the more general issue of violence against women.

Wife Abuse: State Policy in Historical Context

There is no reason to believe that wife abuse is any more common today than in the past, or any more common in Western Europe and North America than in other parts of the world. What is new is the definition of this condition as a social problem and the development of policy responses to it. From being what C. Wright Mills described as a 'personal trouble of milieu', wife abuse has become a 'public issue of social structure' (C. Wright Mills, 1970, p. 14). Has it been seen in this way in the past? Why has it become seen as a problem now? As what sort of a problem is it perceived?

In most societies, wife battering is not defined as a social problem. This does not necessarily mean that it does not occur, but rather that it is defined as a private trouble, or as an acceptable form of behaviour. Thus, for example, it may be claimed that wives are not beaten in the Soviet Union; but the existence of the Russian proverb 'a woman is like meat, the more you beat her the tenderer she becomes', suggests that this claim is not valid. There is a certain amount of documentation by anthropologists of societies in which wife beating occurs, but in general wife beating tends to be mentioned in passing, or implied by descriptions of the sanctions imposed on men who 'ill-treat' their wives or on women who 'disobey' their husbands. Schlegel drew together the anthropological evidence on 45 societies and showed that three-quarters of them permitted husbands to be aggressive towards their wives (Schlegel, 1972).

There is substantial evidence to suggest that wife beating has always existed in Britain and that it has been socially and legally sanctioned until very recently (Dobash and Dobash, 1980). However, the condition has only been perceived as a social problem at two periods in British history. The first of these was in the late nineteenth century and the second from 1971 onwards: the first parliamentary enquiry into wife abuse was held in 1875 and the second in 1975 (Select Committee Report, 1975).

Until the late nineteenth century, British law gave to husbands the right to beat their wives for what was called 'lawful correction', and it was only excessive beating that was frowned upon. The law reflected and upheld a hierarchical and patriarchal family structure. This tradition was summarised by Blackstone in the late eighteenth centry as follows:

the husband also might give his wife moderate correction. For, as he is to answer for her misbehaviour, the law thought it reasonable to entrust him with this power of restraining her, by domestic chastisement in the same moderation that a man is allowed to correct his servant or children.

(Blackstone, 1765)

A precedent was set by Judge Buller in 1782 when he declared that legally a husband could beat his wife as long as he did not use a stick thicker than his thumb. Until the late nineteenth century a married woman had no separate legal status and upon marriage she became the chattel of her husband; her children, her property, her earnings and her body belonged to him, and from many sources we can see that the husband's right to chastise his wife was widely accepted: this right was not finally removed until 1891 (R v. Jackson). Charles Dickens reflects both the contemporary awareness of wife beating, for example, in the savage attack which Bill Sykes makes on Nancy in Oliver Twist, and the nineteenth century's casual acceptance of it: Sam Weller, in Pickwick Papers, talks about what he calls 'the amiable weakness of wife beating'.

In the second half of the nineteenth century, wife beating became for the first time perceived as a social problem. This was partly because of the concern about law and order, since it was thought that a man who assaulted his wife might easily transfer his aggression to other people, and partly because of the work of feminists campaigning for the emancipation of women. Mill's *The Subjection of Women* (1869). and Cobbe's *Wife Torture in England* (1878), were both influential in the campaign to provide more protection for wives, and in 1878 the Matrimonial Causes Act for the first time granted a wife the right to live separately from her husband, to retain custody of her younger children, and to receive maintenance from him, but only in those cases where the husband had been convicted of an aggravated assault on her. The insistence that the husband should actually have been convicted of assault meant that this Act was less effective than it might have been, since a woman living with a violent and brutal man was likely to hesitate before taking court action if she had no choice but to live with him while the action was going through the court. However, this Act did pave the way to the ending of the legal right of the husband to beat his wife, at least in England, even if it did not lead to the end of wife battering (May, 1978).

For the first seventy years of this century, however, wife beating was not perceived as a problem: in Merton's terms it became a latent, as opposed to a manifest, social problem (Merton, 1971). It is not clear why, after all the concern and agitation of the last quarter of the nineteenth century, the problem should have disappeared from sight: certainly it was not because the condition had ceased to exist. The reason may have been the relatively low status of women during that period, the low rates of female employment, and the high degree of regard for the privacy of the home and the sanctity of marriage. Another reason may have been, as Rubington and Weinberg suggest, that conditions are only defined as social problems when it is agreed that action is needed to alter the situation: when there is no solution there is no problem (Rubington and Weinberg, 1977, p. 4). Thus it was not until the first women's refuges began to be set up that wife abuse began to be recognised: both the refuges and the identification of wife abuse as a social problem, were very much products of the women's liberation movement.

One important measure of the seriousness of wife abuse is the dramatic proliferation of refuges in Britain over the past few years. From the setting up of the first refuge for battered women in Chiswick in 1971, the number has grown so that by 1981 there were about 200 refuges scattered across the country. The majority of these refuges are affiliated to the Women's Aid Federations of England, Scotland, Wales and Northern Ireland. They provide safe accommodation for women and their children, advice of whatever sort the woman requires and support for as long as she needs it. The fact that most refuges are usually extremely overcrowded suggests that the women who go to them represent the desperate tip of a very large iceberg. The Women's Aid Federation calculate that in any one year about 12,000 women and 21,000 children will use refuge accommodation, and that at any one time about 1,000 women and 1,700 children will be living in refuges (Women's Aid Federation, 1980). State assistance to refuges, however, has been meagre (Binney, Harkell and Nixon, 1981).

Another form of state response has been to fund research on this topic. My own research was funded by the Department of Health and Social Security and was one of a number of studies of wife battering funded by the Department in the late 1970s (see Borkowski, Murch and Walker, 1983; Delamont and Ellis, 1979; Frankenberg, Johnson, Dawson and Faragher, 1980; Leonard and McLeod, 1980; Pahl, 1978 and 1985). The decision to set aside money for research was a product of public concern following the setting up of the first women's refuges, the growth of the Women's Aid movement, and the publication of Pizzey's sensational book, *Scream Quietly or the Neighbours will Hear* (1974). We are now, therefore, presented with an opportunity to examine, for this particular social problem, the process outlined in the Introduction to this book and originally described by Spector and Kitsuse (1977). The process involves, first, the claim by a group that a harmful condition exists, secondly, the response of a government agency, thirdly, the re-statement of the original claim with the assertion that the response of the agency had been ineffective or inappropriate, and fourthly, the development of new political initiatives on the part of the original group.

The final section of this chapter will present a brief analysis of this process as it took place around the problem of wife abuse in Britain.

Two recent pieces of legislation have aimed at making it easier for abused women to escape from the violence. The first of these was the Domestic Violence and Matrimonial Proceedings Act 1976. This Act made it easier for a woman to get an injunction restraining her husband from using violence against her and her children, and allowed for a power of arrest to be attached to the injunction so that a husband can be arrested if he is found to be in breach of the injunction (Parker, 1985). The second significant piece of legislation was the Housing (Homeless Persons) Act 1977. This laid on local authority housing departments the duty to provide accommodation for women with children who have had to leave home because of violence or threats of violence (Binney, Harkell and Nixon, 1981). These two Acts should in theory have provided substantial help to battered women.

Conventional Wisdom: The Facts and their Interpretation

What is meant by the term 'wife abuse'? It is important to recognise that this form of violence includes both physical and mental assault. The evidence from research is that the violence experienced by wives is both prolonged and severe. In my own study 62 per cent of the women had been subjected to violence for three or more years, and the injuries which they had suffered ranged from cuts and bruises, through broken bones and damaged eyesight, to a ruptured spleen, stab wounds and a fractured skull (Pahl, 1985). The findings of this small study are confirmed by the results of a much larger project undertaken at the same time in all the refuges of England and Wales, by Binney, Harkell and Nixon. This larger study found that 73 per cent of women in refuges had put up with violence for three or more years. Thirty per cent of the women had suffered life threatening attacks or had been hospitalised for serious injuries such as fractured bones. The rest of the sample had experienced assaults which included being kicked, being pushed into fires or through glass, being thrown against walls or down stairs, being punched and having their hair pulled out. Sixty-eight per cent said that mental cruelty was one of the reasons why they left home (Binney, Harkell and Nixon, 1981). One definition of the problem is that 'a battered wife is a wife or cohabitee who has suffered persistent or serious physical assault at the hands of her partner' (Marsden, 1978). However, to this definition must be added the comment of many women, that 'the mental battering was worse than the physical battering'.

There is some dispute about whether we should use the words 'battered women' or 'battered wives'. The former term is a reminder that women can be battered by their cohabitees and ex-husbands as well as by their spouses. The latter term is a reminder that, whatever the legal status of the couple, the violence takes place in a marriage-like situation. That is to say, the couple have children in common, they share a home or have shared a home, and the woman is likely to be financially dependent on the man.

What proportion of all violence takes the form of wife abuse? There are considerable difficulties in answering this question since so much violence, both inside and outside of the home, goes unrecorded. The best sources of evidence are police records, but even these pose problems, especially in the case of crimes such as wife assault and rape, where the victims are often reluctant to report the crime because of feelings of guilt, shame and loyalty. However, there does seem to be agreement between a number of different sources which suggest that assault of wives by their husbands is by far the most common form of family violence. Important evidence comes from the study by Dobash and Dobash (1980), who analysed the police records of Edinburgh and Glasgow. Their analysis showed that the most common form of violence is that which takes place between unrelated males, which makes up 37 per cent of all recorded violent incidents. The second most common form of violence is wife assault, making up 25 per cent of all recorded violent crime. By comparison, other forms of violence between family members, such as assault on husbands, on children, elderly parents and siblings, are relatively insignificant. When one thinks of the attention which is directed towards street violence, concern with assault on wives seems long overdue, representing as it does one quarter of all violent crime (see also McClintock, 1963; Chester and Streather, 1972).

We must remember, however, the differential rates of both the reporting and the recording of crimes of violence. It is unlikely that assault on a policeman will go unrecorded, and so we can consider the recorded total of these offences as a reasonably accurate reflection of the occurrence of assaults. On the other hand, assaults on wives are very much less likely to end up as entries in police records and so the recorded totals must be seen as under-estimates of the true extent of these problems. After careful and detailed interviews with large numbers of abused wives, the Dobashes concluded that only about 2 per cent of all such assaults are ever reported to the police (Dobash and Dobash 1980, p. 164).

A further question concerns the extent of violence in family life and within marriage. What proportion of all marriages are violent? A difficulty here is that so little is known about the extent of violence in ordinary families. Most of our knowledge about wife abuse comes from the accounts of wives who have gone to refuges, or from studies of divorcing couples. In both instances it seems likely that a greater proportion of middle class, as opposed to working class, violence goes unreported (Borkowski, Murch and Walker, 1983).

The only large study to have investigated violence in the general population was carried out in the United States by Straus, Gelles and Steinmetz. The first paragraph reads:

> Drive down any street in America. More than one household in six has been the scene of a spouse striking his or her partner last year. Three American households in five (which have children living at home) have reverberated with the sound of parents hitting their children. When there is more than one child in the home, three in five are the scenes of violence between siblings. Overall, every other house in America is the scene of family violence at least once a year.

> (Straus, Gelles and Steinmetz, 1980, P. 1)

This study showed that, while in any one year violence occurs in 16 per cent of American marriages, if the entire marriage period is considered, violence has occurred in 28 per cent of American marriages. Though wives are violent as well as husbands, the damage inflicted by husbands is more dangerous, causes more harm, and is more frequently inflicted.

In Britain, Hanmer and Saunders' study of community violence to women showed that 59 per cent of the women interviewed had experienced violent or threatening attacks during the previous year, 21 per cent of these at home (Hanmer and Saunders, 1984). What about violence within marriage? Drawing together such evidence as there is, Marsden suggested that serious violence takes place in up to 5 per cent of British marriages and less serious violence in about another 15 per cent (Marsden, 1978). These percentages are, however, extremely tentative and perhaps the most realistic answer to our question was given by the Select Committee Report:

> Despite our efforts, we are unable to give any estimates of what the likely numbers are; several witnesses talked to us in terms of the tip of an iceberg and this seems to us to be correct. Most witnesses agreed, and this is almost certainly correct, that all strata of society are involved, although the better off are perhaps less likely to seek outside help.

> (Select Committee, 1975)

Thus it is as difficult to achieve an accurate, quantitative estimate of the extent of wife abuse as it is to estimate the number of rapes which take place. This is no accident. The fact that it is so difficult to measure these two conditions objectively is an essential element in the maintenance of the structures which support and maintain violence against women.

There are now a large number of studies of wife abuse which between them put forward a variety of explanations (see especially Marsden, 1978; Freeman, 1979; Dobash and Dobash, 1980; Breines and Gordon, 1983). In general it can be said that causal analyses of the problem are divided between the individual and the social-structural approach.

The first approach locates the problem within the individuals concerned and seeks to explain the violence in terms of deviant or pathological personalities. The work of Faulk, for example, which was concerned with men who had been convicted of wife abuse, showed that a majority of them could be classified as being mentally ill in one way or another (Faulk, 1974). However, other studies have not so far confirmed this finding, which was, of course, carried out with an unusual group in that all the men had actually been convicted of assault. Several researchers have found a link between violence and excessive consumption of alcohol. In my own study, 52 per cent of the women said that their husbands often drank to excess, and this is similar to the proportions recorded by Gelles (1974) and Gayford (1975). However, it has been suggested that drunkenness should be seen, not as a 'cause' of violence, but as a condition which co-exists with it. Thus men who wish to carry out a violent act may become intoxicated in order to have the courage to perform the act. After violence has occurred, both the man and his wife may excuse his behaviour on the grounds that since he had been drunk he could not be held responsible for what had happened.

Violent personalities are also seen as being a consequence of childhood experiences. The study carried out by Straus, Gelles and Steinmetz showed that people who grew up in violent homes were more likely to use violence than those who had not. Thus one in ten of husbands who grew up in violent families were wife beaters in the sense of serious assault, and this is over three times the rate for husbands who did not grow up in such homes. However, the researchers point out that it would be a mistake to put too great a burden on what is learned in the family. To see this one needs only to look at the violence rates for children of non-violent parents. These rates show that a considerable amount of violence is perpetrated by people whose parents were not violent to them and not violent to each other. The family may be a training ground for violence, but for a fuller explanation we have to look to the wider society (Straus, Gelles and Steinmetz, 1980).

As in the case of rape, responses to wife abuse reflect different explanations. Those who see the problem in terms of individuals tend to propose remedies which are effective at the level of the individual. These remedies may take the form of counselling, group work, psychotherapy, treatment with drugs such as anti-depressants or tranquilizers, or in-patient treatment in a psychiatric hospital. Some violent husbands do receive treatment of this sort. However, all too often it is the wife rather than the husband who goes for help and who is offered these 'solutions' to 'her' problem. Since she is the one who finds the situation intolerable, it is she who is offered the valium or the hospital treatment. This can have the effect of confirming the notion that the problem of wife abuse is in some way the wife's own fault, or at least her responsibility, and it can confound the problems which she is already facing (Stark, Flitcraft and Frazier, 1979).

At a broader level there are analyses which locate the continuance of wife abuse in what Holman called the 'deficient agency explanation' (Holman, 1978). At this level of analysis appropriate responses are seen in terms of changes in the law, better practice on the part of general practitioners, social workers, health visitors, and members of the police force, and, above all, more refuges (Pahl, 1979b; 1982a; 1982b). At present Women's Aid refuges are the primary agency for helping battered women in Britain. A number of studies have documented the value of refuges in offering women practical help, a roof over their heads and protection from further assault, while fostering mutual support among the women in a way that does seem to enhance confidence and self-esteem (Dobash and Dobash, 1980; Women's Aid Federation, 1980; Binney, Harkell and Nixon, 1981; Clifton, 1984; Pahl, 1978 and 1979a). Yet the total number of refuges still does not come near to the recommendation of the Select Committee on Violence in Marriage that there should be one refuge place per 10,000 of the population. Not only are there not enough refuges, but most of those that exist are desperately under-funded. This bears harshly on the women and children who stay there, in terms of over-crowding and poor facilities, and it places a severe burden on those who are trying to set up or run a refuge. Most refuges are run by voluntary groups who employ paid workers if they can afford to do so; few have any long term financial security. Work in refuges is stressful and demanding and those who work there are paid modestly, if at all, so it is hardly surprising that there are not nearly enough refuges and that those which exist teeter permanently on the brink of closure.

In theory, the Housing (Homeless Persons) Act and the Domestic Violence and Matrimonial Proceedings Act should have provided real solutions to the problems of abused women. In practice, however, they can be used together in a way that leaves women defenceless. For example, before offering a battered woman accommodation, a housing department can insist that a woman obtain an injunction as 'proof' that she has been battered; having obtained the injunction, she is told to return home since she will now be safe there. However, the reluctance of the police to get involved in what they define as private and family matters means that she is often by no means safe at home. So she may once again find herself homeless and forced to return to the housing department. This example illustrates the way in which a focus on 'deficient agencies' can conveniently ignore the structural foundations of a problem: it is impossible to provide long term solutions to the problem of wife abuse without taking account of such ideological constructs as 'the privacy of the home' and the 'sanctity of family life'. As Weir said:

The challenge of Women's Aid is not just that it demands better and more liberal and more flexible state provision, nor is it that it provides alternative structures in which women can live their lives . . . The challenge of Women's Aid is that it demands a fundamental change in the way in which women are defined.

(Weir, 1977, p. 119)

Unconventional Wisdom: Another Look at the Problem

This broader approach locates the problem in a social-structural context and focuses, not narrowly upon the individual, but upon the whole social and economic situation within which the violence takes place. Here explanation is in terms of social context rather than in terms of personality, and here new light can be thrown upon the behaviour of individuals. For example, this approach would look beyond the link between drunkenness and battering, to consider the way in which some cultures see both phenomena as symptoms of masculinity and male dominance. Social-structural explanations would, similarly, look beyond the fact that a drunken man committed an assault, to recognise that if he assaults a policeman he is likely to be prosecuted, while if he assaults his wife it is likely to be labelled a 'domestic dispute' for which police intervention is kept to a minimum. And this approach would see the fact that some women return again and again to their violent husbands, not as the result of some sort of sado-masochism, but as a consequence of the inadequate help given to battered women and the hardships experienced by women who are trying to bring up children by themselves.

Psychological and sociological explanations can be interwoven. Thus Walker, whilst putting forward a theory that battered women suffer from 'learned helplessness', sees this as a product of the weak position of married women, socialised into economic and psychological dependency and trapped in marriage both by their own low self-esteem and by the lack of any alternatives for themselves and their children (Walker, 1979). Stark, Flitcraft and Frazier document the ways in which the helping professions, and especially the medical services, by treating cuts and bruises but ignoring women's accounts of how their injuries were caused, exacerbate the problems of abused wives. Their study shows a health system taking women who had been hit and, over time, turning them into 'battered women' (Stark, Flitcraft and Frazier, 1979).

Evason's study focused on the differences among a group of divorced women, some of whom had been battered by their husbands and some of whom had not. There were no differences between the two groups in terms of education and social class, nor in terms of how long the partners had known each other before marrying, or their ages at marriage. Significant differences appeared between the two groups, however, when attention was focused on the nature of these marriages and on the spouses' expectations and assumptions. The great majority of all the wives would have liked a democratic model of marriage with decisions made jointly; however, husbands were seen by their wives as much more likely to favour the traditional, male-dominant model of marriage, in which a husband is 'master in his home'. Violent husbands were particularly likely to favour the traditional model, 66 per cent of them favouring male dominance, compared with 34 per cent of the non-violent husbands. There were further differences between the two groups of women in the ways in which the couples had organised their money. Evason ends by identifying the financial dependence of married women as an important part of the pattern of structured constraints which keeps women within violent marriages (Evason, 1982; see also Homer, M., Leonard, A. and Taylor, P. 1984; Pahl, 1983).

Any explanation of wife assault needs to be located in the broader social context, and in particular in the context of the structural and ideological forces which shape the relationships between men and women both within marriage and in the wider society. Straus summed up the conclusions of the recent large-scale survey of violence in American families by saying, 'the causes of wife-beating are to be found in the very structure of American society and its family system' (Straus, 1978, p. 41). A very careful and detailed British study of wife beating was carried out by Dobash and Dobash in Scotland. In that study the assaults which the women had endured were investigated, not as isolated incidents, but as part of the whole relationship between the couple, as it had developed from courtship to marriage to child bearing and child rearing. The Dobashes concluded:

We propose that the correct interpretation of violence between husbands and wives conceptualises such violence as the extension of the domination and control of husbands over wives. This control is historically and socially constructed. The beginning of an adequate analysis of violence between husbands and wives is the consideration of the history of the family, of the status of women therein, and of violence directed against them. This analysis will substantiate our claim that violence in the family should be understood primarily as coercive control.

(Dobash and Dobash, 1980, p. 15)

Clearly it is important, not simply to describe the violence inflicted by one individual on another, but to extend the analysis to take into account the social and economic context within which the violence takes place.

Finally, to what extent is it possible to see the problem of wife abuse in terms of the 'stages' set out by Spector and Kitsuse (1977)? As we have seen, the problem of wife abuse, which had, of course, always been known to the women who experienced it, only acquired the status of a recognised 'social problem' at two periods in British history. It was in the early 1970s that groups of women began to publicise the existence of the problem, first by setting up local refuges, and then by the formation of the National Women's Aid Federation to which local groups were affiliated. From its beginning in 1975 The National Women's Aid Federation had five aims:

1 To provide temporary refuge, on request, for women and their children who have suffered mental or physical harassment.
2 To encourage the women to determine their own futures and to help them to achieve them, whether this involves returning home or starting a new life elsewhere.
3 To recognise and care for the emotional and educational needs of the children involved.
4 To offer support and advice and help to any woman who asks for it, whether or not she is a resident, and also to offer support and after care to any woman and child who has left the refuge.
5 To educate and inform the public, the media, the police, the courts, social services and other authorities with respect to the battering of women, mindful of the fact that this is a result of the general position of women in our society.

The fifth of these aims, linking wife abuse to the position of women in society, meant that the Federation was denied charitable status since, revealingly, the Charity Commissioners decided that the fifth aim was evidence that the organisation was political rather than charitable in its intentions. Thus in the first 'stage' of the problem, wherein a group asserts that the condition exists, wife abuse was clearly defined in terms of the structural position of women. Women's Aid, in many of its early statements of the problem, conceptualised violence against wives as a consequence of gender inequality and of the dependence and power-lessness of women within marriage.

In the second 'stage' of a social problem an official government or other influential agency responds. What form did this take in the case of battered women? The 1970s saw many different responses. At local levels groups of women struggled to get funding for refuges, in the face of apathy and, sometimes, antipathy (Binney, Harkell and Nixon, 1981). The Housing (Homeless Persons) Act and the Domestic Violence and Matrimonial Proceedings Act were passed, but evidence soon accumu-lated that, though they had alleviated the problem for some women, there were many gaps in the way these Acts were being implemented (Migdall, 1980; Freeman, 1980; Wasoff, 1982; Faragher, 1985; Parker,

1985). The Department of Health and Social Security, the Scottish Home and Health Department and the Department of the Environment funded a number of research projects. The Select Committee on Violence in Marriage was set up and duly produced its report and recommendations (1975).

The Select Committee Report, well intentioned though it was, tends to support Spector and Kitsuse's suggestion that agency response will typically be routine or ineffectual. Thus, though the report strongly recommended the setting up of large numbers of refuges, no money was made available for this at the national level. Six years after the report appeared, one of the research projects concluded 'This study highlights the vital importance of finding a secure, long term source of funding for women's refuges. This should be the first priority for all those concerned with this problem' (Pahl, 1981, p. v). The Select Committee Report, in its section titled 'Causation', set out an analysis of the causes of wife abuse which was very different from that put forward by Women's Aid:

> We have no evidence that the husband alone is responsible for his violence. The behaviour of the wife is relevant. So, too, is the family's environment, their housing and employment conditions, their physical and mental health, their sexual relationship and many other factors.
>
> (Select Committee Report, 1975, p. VIII)

Prevention of violence was presented as a three-point plan under the headings 'Education', 'Alcohol' and 'Vulnerable Children': in this section the concern with the welfare of children was paramount and there seemed little or no concern about the welfare of battered women themselves: the concern about women was over how they would perform their roles as wives and mothers:

> For what is involved is not the plight of a particular category of unhappy women, but the future of families, involving men, women and – most important of all – their children.
>
> (Select Committee Report, 1975, p. XXV)

At the third 'stage' of a social problem the original group of activists criticises the 'official' response and seeks to redefine the problem in its original terms. This 'stage' was not long in coming. In 1981, the Department of Health and Social Security (DHSS) funded a three day seminar on 'Violence in the Family' held at the University of Kent. The paper presented to the seminar by the Research Group of the Women's Aid Federation (England) was strongly critical of the way the DHSS had funded research on this topic:

> An effective research strategy must be based on the premise that the cause of battering of women is a result of the position of women in society. Men and

women have differential power in the family and society generally and no understanding of male violence to women in the home can proceed without a recognition of this basic fact that informs all social structures and processes. Restricting research strategy to two areas; to the setting up and role of women's refuges and to the attitudes and responses of helping agencies to the problems of battered women reduces the problem of male violence to women in the home to that of the personal or interpersonal. These restrictions are inherently reactionary as they ignore larger social processes, interconnections between social phenomena and even inhibit understanding of the subjective experience of women themselves, assuming this has been sought. We do not regard research in these areas as unnecessary, but that this must go hand-in-hand with studies of the incidence of male violence on women and girls, the ways in which social institutions and organisations promote or challenge male violence to women, and the history of violence to women. To eradicate longstanding, entrenched social behaviour involves much more than a study of the immediate behaviour itself.

> (Women's Aid Federation Research Group, 1981, p. 11)
> (See also Hanmer and Leonard, 1984.)

Conclusion

Rape and wife abuse have been treated separately in this chapter largely because in the past they have seemed to exist separately, covered by different areas of legislation, researched and written about by different people. Yet they have much in common and are now beginning to be seen as part of the more general issue of violence against women. (Hanmer and Saunders, 1984; London Rape Crisis Centre, 1984; Wilson, 1983.) If we return to the questions with which this chapter began it is clear that rape and wife abuse should not be isolated as separate phenomena, but are more correctly seen as rather different manifestations of one problem.

In attempting to understand and explain social problems the level of analysis is of central importance. Focusing on one particular violent event and on the individuals concerned tends to lead to the conclusion that the event can be explained by looking at the individuals: it can appear that the 'cause' of the violence must be the man's personality or the woman's behaviour. But if we examine large numbers of rapes and incidents of wife abuse, and if we see them not as isolated incidents but as examples of violence against women, then common patterns begin to emerge which reflect fundamental social forces.

Two of these social forces are power and ideology. By and large interpersonal violence is inflicted on the weaker and more dependent members of society by the stronger and more powerful. So parents beat up their children, men beat up women, dominant men in prisons assault the weaker and more defenceless prisoners (Brownmiller, 1975). Male violence against women has traditionally been sanctioned and legitimated by ideology. The complexities of the nature of ideology are discussed in the final chapter of this book. At this stage it is only possible to point briefly to some of the ideological foundations of the phenomenon of violence against women. These foundations are deep-seated and they include notions about the 'naturalness' of gender inequality, and of male dominance and female dependence. While violence against women varies in its intensity from one society to another, the existence of these ideologies in pre-capitalist as well as capitalist societies suggests that male violence against women is not specific to particular historical conjunctures or particular modes of production.

It is no accident that bringing the ideologies which suggest gender inequality into the open has been accompanied by the identification of male violence against women as a social problem. Invisibility is a crucial mechanism in sustaining the strength of ideologies which support inequality. As we have seen, the relative invisibility of rape and wife abuse through much of history has had the effect of minimising those problems: it has also served to maintain an analysis which approached violence through individuals. Many people who are genuinely sympathetic with the rape victim or the battered wife are yet resistant to more general explanations which link male violence to gender inequality. Focusing on individuals detracts from the larger view. At one level rape and wife abuse can provoke the sorts of crass comments exemplified by the quotations at the start of this chapter; at another level, analysis of these problems leads us to reconsider fundamental and valued aspects of our social world. The debate, however, does not stop here. All who have written this book, and those who will read it, are themselves a part of the process by which social problems are defined and re-defined. The issues of rape and wife abuse raise the broader question of violence against women, which in its turn raises fundamental issues about the nature of relationships between men and women.

3 Race and Crisis Management*
David Denney

In this chapter we will examine the genesis of social policies in Britain since the 1950s dealing with the question of race. Despite forms of legislation to curb discrimination and offset racist practices since 1965, Britain's black population, those of Afro Caribbean and Asian descent, continue to occupy an invidious position in the labour market, and in the fields of education, social services, and housing. We will see when these substantive issues are examined that over generalisations can be dangerous. These policies will be examined in relation to economic, political and ideological changes. It will be seen that two major strands can be discerned in the development of policy in this area, one emphasising the aspect of social control, the other predominantly transmitting an ideology of consent. The state has intervened in various ways to maintain social cohesion, in an attempt to ameliorate racial conflict. Social control policies, the harder aspects of race relations policy are perhaps exemplified in the various pieces of legislation designed to curb immigration (1962, 1965, 1968, 1971, 1981). The softer more consensually oriented interventions can be seen in the anti discrimination legislation (1965, 1968 and 1976).

There have also been many examples of crisis management, most recently seen in the various statements following the disturbances in Southall, Brixton and St. Pauls in 1981.

The notion of racism contextualises all these policy initiatives, and it is perhaps important to attempt to clarify this concept at the outset. There are perhaps as many 'definitions' of racism as there are sociologists attempting to make sense of the phenomenon. For our purposes however, Kowalczewski's conception seems most apposite. Here it is argued that racism:

Does not simply refer to overt explicit racist attitudes, or the use of deliberate emotive or inflamatory language, but to what Hall describes as inferential racism, a more insidious, pervasive and subtle form which is based upon taken for granted commonsense assumptions, and which does not rest on conscious intentions. It is an explicit sub conscious process in which well intentioned assertions can rest on unintentional racism, through the use of mistakenly held stereotypes or patronising attitudes and assertions which hinder expectations

* In the writing of this chapter I have been greatly assisted by discussions with Bruce Carrington, University of Newcastle-upon-Tyne.

and create misunderstandings. *Inferential racism when located in policies and established practices* goes beyond simple acts of discrimination (my emphasis).

(Kowalczewski, 1982, p. 145)

Any analysis of international labour migration, whether from the Caribbean or Indian subcontinent to Britain during the period following the second world war, or from countries on the southern periphery of Europe, such as Greece, Morocco, Algeria, Turkey, Southern Italy, to the industrialised metropolises of Switzerland, France and Germany, must give equal consideration to the 'push' 'pull' factors influencing such movements. 'Push' factors included abject poverty and massive unemployment, whilst black people were 'pulled' by the hope of a better standard of living, and improved standards of employment. The underdevelopment of some countries as many writers have argued, is in part a legacy of British imperialism (Castles and Kosack, 1973; Sivanandan, 1982).

Whereas by and large levels of immigration from the Caribbean and Indian subcontinent were determined by market forces there was some direct recruitment by British employers in this part of the world. London Transport, and the British Hotels and Restaurants Association actively recruited in Barbados.

A History of Responses to the Black and Asian Presence
It is possible to discern a number of shifts in British race relations policy during the past three decades. In the 1950s and early 1960s with labour shortages in various sectors of the economy, there was a tendency for governments to underplay the social implications of immigration policy.

The 1948 Nationality Act ensured the right of colonial passport holders as well as those holding passports issued by independent Commonwealth countries to enter the United Kingdom freely, to settle and find work and to enjoy 'full political and social rights' (Radical Statistics Group, 1980). Thus was reflected the American melting pot ideology being manifested in the early social policy in this area. It was thought by politicians at this time that any white hostility would pass as the newcomers were absorbed into a flexible and tolerant white society. This essentially assimilationist ideology did place the onus on the 'dark strangers' to adapt to an English and more 'civilised' way of life.

Katznelson (1973) has shown that the 'political élite' in Britain resisted various pressures on both sides of Parliament to place race on the political agenda. In 1962 Harold Macmillan reluctantly gave in to attempts by MPs to impose immigration restrictions. Efforts made by Sorenson and Fenner Brockway to introduce anti discrimination legislation were thwarted on some nine occasions. However, the phase of 'pre-political consensus' of silence was shattered in 1958 by the disturbances in Notting Hill Gate, and Nottingham. Prior to 1958 there had been sporadic outbursts of violence against Asian and West Indian people. White youths expressing neo-fascist sentiments were a major element in the Notting Hill Gate riots, indeed the parallels between this situation and the role played by neo-fascist white youths, such as the skinheads in the Southall riots of 1981, should be noted. The Nottingham riots took place between the 23rd and 30th August and involved racial brawls in public houses. Referring to these incidents, Rex and Tomlinson say of the period:

During the 50s the first West Indian and then Asian settlement began to be evident in the major cities of England. There was increasing hostility to the settlers from white neighbours. The British working class had accepted the notion of common citizenship so long as it was purely theoretical, but when it seemed that the black men from the colonies were to be treated as their equals or rather their own position of superiority vis-à-vis blacks was not recognised they became seriously concerned.

(Rex and Tomlinson, 1979, p. 48)

In some circles the disturbances were merely dismissed as little more than pub brawls, until in September of the same year in the Notting Hill Gate area of London, white youths, teddy boys by and large, attacked black people and their property in the area. Severe sentences were passed by Lord Justice Salmon against a number of these youths. Referring to this incident and the collapse of a 'pre-political' consensus Katznelson argues that

Largely as a result of the violent racial clashes that erupted in London and Nottingham in 1958, the issue of race emerged from the periphery to the centre of political debate.

(Katznelson, 1973, p.129).

Although highly localised these disturbances were to trigger a period of fundamental debate within the House of Commons and were to herald the breakdown of consensus between the two major parties. The debates which followed focused largely on the issue of immigration control.

The 1962 Commonwealth Immigration Act aimed to restrict the automatic right of Commonwealth citizens entry to Britain. With the introduction of this Act intending immigrants had to obtain a Ministry of Employment voucher; these vouchers fell into three categories. Category A vouchers were issued to employers and intending immigrants by the High Commission of their own country, who had a specific job to take up in Britain. Category B vouchers were issued to Commonwealth citizens who possessed a recognised skill or qualification which was required in Britain. Category C vouchers were available to all other applicants regardless of skill with priority being given to those who had served in the armed forces in the second world war. Thereafter category C vouchers were issued on a first come first served basis (Radical Statistics Group, 1980).

Two observations need to be made about the 1962 legislation. Firstly, it was a clear acknowledgement of the need to regulate the inflow of immigrants to the need for labour. Secondly, it must be acknowledged that the intervention was premised on racist assumptions, since the Act assumed that by thinning out the black presence racial conflict would be lessened. In general terms we concur with Hall (Hall et al., 1978b), and numerous other authors who argue that post 1945 patterns of immigration to Britain are inextricably related to the demand for labour in the metropolitan economy. Thus as Hall argues:

In the early fifties when British Industry was expanding and undermanned labour was sucked in from the surplus labour of the Caribbean and Asian sub continent there is a correlation in this period as indeed throughout the whole cycle between numbers of immigrant workers and employment vacancies. In periods of recession and especially in the present phase the numbers of immigrants has fallen, fewer are coming in, and a high proportion of those already are shunted into unemployment. In short the supply of black labour in employment has risen and fallen in direct relation to the needs of British capital.

(Hall et al., 1978b, p.343)

During the 1960s policy initiatives in the field of race relations were directed towards the goal of assimilation. The prevailing view among policy makers was that racial harmony depended upon the elimination of cultural barriers between minority and majority populations. Both parties after the period of fundamental debate between 1958 and 1965 came to accept the need for a policy of immigrant control and integration to be pursued concommitantly. Cashmore and Troyna argue that integration, unlike assimilation aimed to produce a situation in which groups of different cultural backgrounds could contribute to society on an equal footing without losing their essential distinctiveness as individuals. Thus people retain their identity whilst being accepted as equals. The onus to change and adapt shifted from the newcomer towards a situation in which both white and black would work together towards the creation of mutual acceptance (Cashmore and Troyna, 1983).

Why was the belief in assimilation so pervasive in British politics at this time? Why did policy makers come to reject it? It seems that policy makers subscribed to assimilation for a number of reasons. Previous reference was made to the fact that in the early post war period of immigration there was a belief in the essential tolerance of the British people. There was a prevalent belief that the only difference between the newcomers and the indigenous population was one of colour. Immigrants from the Caribbean were seen to share a common culture, common language, and common religious beliefs. With the arrival of people from the Indian subcontinent and Pakistan, a moral panic was triggered as those groups were seen to be markedly different in most respects from the indigenous population.

In consequence, during the late 1960s, and early 1970s the government began to pursue a pluralistic policy in race relations. Such a policy is premised upon an assumption that society comprises a diverse range of interest groups, with differential access to power and resources, and that power is diffused throughout a society and not concentrated solely in the hands of one group. In the case of racial and ethnic minorities, discriminatory practices impinge on many aspects of their daily lives and in consequence they fail to gain access to sources of power. There is a clear distinction between ethnicity and race, although the terms are frequently used interchangably. Cashmore and Troyna describe an ethnic group as a collection of people subjectively perceiving themselves as distinct in some way. A racial group is a 'label' placed on a collection of people by others who feel themselves to be superior. The essence of this position was encapsulated in a speech made by Roy Jenkins in 1966 when he defined integration, 'Not as a flattening process of assimilation, but as equal opportunity accompanied by cultural diversity in an atmosphere of mutual tolerance'.

Jenkins idealistic vision was not to be realised, for in the years which followed, Enoch Powell's polemics against immigration were to fuel the growth of racism and intensify racial divisions. The 1962 Act, as we have already seen, marked the end of the *laissez-faire* period in policy making. As Cashmore and Troyna contend the Conservative Government of the day had accepted the racist definition of the situation and turned the attention of the media towards the 'numbers game'. Thus the social problem was conceptualised in terms of how to best restrict the numbers of people entering the country. Despite Jenkins' noble intentions there was a convergence at the political level in this respect, as exemplified by the Labour Party's White Paper on Commonwealth Immigration in 1965. In this singularly contradictory document there appears to be an underlying belief that the secret of good race relations is to keep the numbers of Commonwealth immigrants down to a minimum. The annual issue of Category A and B vouchers was cut substantially, and there was a general tightening of eligibility for entry. Moore has argued that by introducing his White Paper, Harold Wilson was responding to considerable pressures from numerous quarters to restrict immigration. The 1965 White Paper, as Moore goes on to argue, shifted the basis of the argument, clearly conceptualising black immigration in terms of a social problem (Moore, 1975). To an extent the White Paper discredited the Race Relations Act of the same year.

The aim of this latter Act was to curb the excesses of intolerance amongst the white population whilst concomitantly maintaining racial harmony and social cohesion. The Act made racial discrimination illegal in places of public resort for example, hotels, restaurants, and sought to end discriminatory practices in leases. The investigation of discriminatory practices was carried out by the Race Relations Board, a body which was severely circumscribed in its activities and as a result was 'ineffective and toothless' (Lester and Bindman, 1972). The individual, for instance, had no resort to the courts, with complaints having to be made in writing to the Race Relations Board who had no authority to summon witnesses. The number of complaints made to the board was small, and it became clear that many complaints fell outside the scope of the Act.

In 1967 events outside the UK were to have a pronounced effect upon race relations in this country. The Kenyan Government's commitment to Africanisation was to result in the arrival of UK passport holders to Britain. It was at this juncture that Mr Enoch Powell began to mount his vociferous campaign against immigration. In one of his inflammatory speeches he articulated populist fears of a 'black takeover'. As Martin Barker comments the 'ordinary Englishman' had told Powell, with some degree of sadness that by the year 2000 there would be 5–7 million black people in Britain, thus giving the black man a 'whip hand' (Barker, 1981.).

Powell employed the racial category as later he was to use Ireland, the EEC, and the House of Lords, as a vehicle through which to articulate a definition of Englishness (Hall et al., 1978b).

Some Conservative politicians following the Powellite line predicted the arrival of some 250,000 Kenyan Asians, whereas the real figure was in the region of 66,000 (Hiro, 1971). Conservative politicians on the right of the party argued for a control on the number of Kenyan Asians entering the country. The Labour Government of the day went further, effectively removing the right of entry by the 1968 Commonwealth Immigrants Act. This measure which clearly reflected the spirit of the 1965 White Paper withdrew the right of settlement from those 'outside' who did not have a strong connection with the UK. In order to be closely connected an individual must have been born in the UK or descended from a parent or grandparent born in the UK. Registration in the UK as a citizen by naturalisation also constituted a closer connection. In addition another voucher scheme was created which enabled holders who were UK passport holders and close dependents to enter and settle in Britain.

The 'close connection' was a device designed to ensure that white settlers in East Africa retained their right of entry to Britain by virtue of the fact that they held UK passports, whilst black settlers holding the same passport did not (Radical Statistics Group, 1980). Complaints were subsequently made to the European Commission of Human Rights, who found the 1968 Act to be discriminatory.

In 1971 an apparent shift occurred in the pattern of state intervention which altered the course of immigrant policy. The 1971 Immigration Act replaced the 1962 and 1968 Commonwealth Immigration Acts creating the 'patrial' status which without doubt worked to the disadvantage of the black person. Some writers have likened this new category as a move towards the contract system or gastarbeiter approach that operated in Germany. Gastarbeiter refers to the system operating in West Germany whereby immigrant labour notably from Turkey is imported on a system of temporary permits. Labourers can be expelled when conditions in the labour market change. Put simply, all white British together with millions of white emigrant Commonwealth settlers are patrials, whilst most black Commonwealth citizens are not patrials. Patrials can enter Britain without being subject to control, whilst non patrials need permission and a work permit to enter the UK. They are initially admitted for one year and permission can be renewed each year for three more years to stay in the UK at the discretion of the Home Secretary. Migration from the EEC is virtually unrestricted. Sivanandan has argued that by 1971 British immigration policy had consciously functioned to reduce the status of potential immigrants from the Commonwealth to contract labour. Commonwealth immigrants were by this time given the same status as workers from any other country with the exception of the EEC and Ireland. This Act effectively sanctioned state discriminatory practices (Sivanandan, 1976).

This trend blossomed until in 1979 with the election of Margaret Thatcher, race appeared as an issue in an undisguised form. During the seventies there was a distinct ideological shift in this area, until by the end of the seventies we see the dawning of what Barker has referred to as 'The New Racism'. Drawing on Powell's notion of essential 'Englishness', Thatcher during the election campaign often made reference to the threat imposed by 'outsiders'. There is a certain naturalness about the desire to be a bonded exclusive community, a nation aware of its distinctiveness from other nations (Barker, 1981). Thatcher asserted that:

The British character has done so much for democracy, for law and order and so much throughout the world that, if there was any fear that it might be swamped, people are going to be hostile to those coming in.

(*Daily Mail*, 31 January 1978, quoted in Cashmore and Troyna, 1983)

Thus like Powell in 1968 no derogatory comment was made directly about 'immigrants' she was merely reflecting the essential feeling of her fellow Englishmen and women. This stands in stark contrast to the conceptualisation of the eternally beneficient Englishman, willing to accept a Commonwealth brother or sister. Whatever happened to the quintessentially accepting Englishness of the post war period of economic expansion?

The British Nationality Act 1981 introduced by Margaret Thatcher's Government was ostensibly designed to clarify the concept of British citizenship. In fact it resulted in British citizenship not being automatically gained by birth and residence in Britain. Thus if neither parent was born in the UK or was not lawfully settled here, then the child would be unable to obtain citizenship unless she or he could prove that they had not been absent from the country for more than ninety days in any one of the first ten years of life.

Thus the trend that began in 1962 was brought to fruition in the 1981 Act, with Britain operating what can only be called a racist form of social policy towards black people. As Cashmore and Troyna argue the main concern of the Act was to 'control and preserve' (Cashmore and Troyna, 1983).

State Intervention

At the outset it was argued that the intervention made by the state in this area constitutes a highly complex intermingling of coercive and consensual measures. The benign liberalism was reflected in a tokenistic manner through the sixties to the mid seventies, and it was only with the advent of Thatcherism that consensually orientated policy and the pluralism in which it is contextualised begins to pale into insignificance. Reference has already been made to the attempts of Brockway and Sorenson to persuade Parliament to legislate on the subject between 1952 and 1964. The first crucial piece of legislation, as we have seen, was discredited in 1965, by the White Paper of the same year.

In 1968, a new Race Relations Act aimed at dealing with all forms of discrimination was put upon the statute books. The Race Relations Board was reconstituted and given the duty to investigate complaints of racial discrimination particularly in the areas of housing, employment, and education. Its duties were to promote harmonious race relations and to advise the Home Secretary on matters relating to race. It became the Community Relations Council, and was also given the task of co-ordinating a number of independent local Community Relations Councils. Although it was given this brief, the task had severe limits placed upon it.

The Act was an important one in that it made crude, overt forms of racial discrimination less common (Radical Statistics Group, 1980). Other evidence suggests that the Act was ineffective in achieving any real reduction in racist practices. Research carried out by the PEP indicated that although there was a marginal reduction in discrimination with regard to those black people with advanced qualifications in employment, and a marked reduction in relation to the obtaining of mortgage facilities, there still remained a high level of discrimination in all manual job recruitment.

The 1976 Race Relations Act made it an offence to publish or distribute written material, or use in any public place language which is threatening, abusive or insulting, to black and brown people, or is likely to encourage racial hatred against a racial group. The 1976 Act no longer required the complainant to prove that the accused intended to encourage racist sentiments. Incitement to racial hatred thus became an offence, which on the surface appeared to be a promising development, but in practice progress in this field has been depressingly slow. The body which came to be invested with the power to conduct formal investigations into allegations of discrimination was the Commission for Racial Equality. The number of investigations undertaken by the Commission was low. There is also little doubt that the CRE have worked closely with the police mostly at the level of training. There has also been co-operation in attempts to set up machinery at local level in order to prevent troubles before they arise. Since hatred of the police is so deeply ingrained in some inner city areas one must ask what credence the CRE can have if such contacts are maintained. On the other hand if both organisations are to carry out their statutory function some contact would appear to be inevitable. What is clear however is that a vast proportion of the work of the CRE is ameliorative and aimed at creating a consensus, fundamentally containing what is seen as the problem of an increasingly politically conscious black population.

Urban deprivation

There have been a number of initiatives in this area, the first being the Local Government Act 1966 Section 11. Under this provision the authorities with new immigrant populations, could claim grant aid from central government to employ staff required to meet the demands of the population. By new immigrant population is meant a population settling within the last 10 years exceeding 2 per cent of the population.

This measure has been subjected to considerable debate at both central and local government level. The Labour Home Secretary Merlyn Rees said in connection with the Act:

I recognise that with the increasing number whose families are of overseas origin but who were born here and who therefore cannot be described as immigrants these provisions are ill suited to our present times. We are now faced not so much with problems of newness, although these still exist, as with special problems of racial advantage arising particularly from colour and different cultural background.

> (Foreword to the document 'Proposals for Replacing
> the 1966 Local Government Act Section 11).

At the time of writing, Section 11 of the 1966 Local Government Act has not been replaced.

The Home Office has also been responsible for the Urban Programme (1968) which coincided with a speech made by Harold Wilson on race and immigration. In this speech Wilson stated that expenditure in the inner cities must be made on the basis of need. The intention was to arrest the decline of the inner city areas, although only £25 million were made available over a four year period. It should also be added that local government had had to find 25 per cent of the cost of each project. There followed a great competition amongst local authorities for funds resulting in the Home Office using wide discretionary powers.

Ben-Tovim and Gabriel (1982) argue that the programme can only be seen against a background of a continuing debate about Commonwealth immigration and race relations, and was devised to defuse a potentially explosive situation. The programme was instigated in 1968 at a time of disquiet in the wake of inflammatory speeches made by Enoch Powell, and a reforming of the far right of the Tory Party. The urban programme was formulated hurriedly in an attempt to keep the 'lid' on the situation. In consequence little attention was paid to what constituted social need, the programme being launched with such haste that little thought appears to have been given to objectives or strategy.

Another initiative of the late sixties was the Community Development Projects which were initiated by the central government in 1969. These were described by the government as neighbourhood based experiments aimed at finding ways of meeting the needs of people living in areas of social deprivation. Twelve such projects were set up, each being monitored by a local polytechnic or university, an attempt being made here to combine social action with academic research. Problems arose since the projects were set up on the assumption that poverty and deprivation emanated from individual and group characteristics. When some of the reports suggested that structural factors and institution-alised racist practices were relevant the government lost interest and scrapped the idea.

Conventional Wisdom About The 'Race Problem'

Racial inequality in the inner city
Despite nearly two decades of anti discrimination legislation and various state interventions, racial inequality remains an enduring

feature of British inner city life. The arithmetic of race relations has been extensively documented, and a dismal picture of poverty and discrimination in the areas of education, employment, housing and social services emerges with regularity (Smith, 1977).

Although it is possible to make the general assertion that the situation of blacks has barely altered since the initial phase of immigration, closer inspection reveals a highly complicated situation. During the sixties and most of the seventies there was a conventional wisdom in the sociology of education that the British school system actually made the West Indian child appear to be 'subnormal', in a disproportionate number of cases (Coard, 1971). The debate in education centred around issues of ethnocentricity in the curriculum, teachers' racist attitudes towards West Indian children and the criteria used to measure ability, which in many cases was culturally biased in favour of the white child. The evidence for underachievement seemed irrefutable. Wide gaps in reading abilities were found between West Indian and other children (Little, 1978). Other work suggested that Asian children performed well relative to the performance of West Indian children (Taylor, 1974).

What remains in doubt is the extent to which West Indian children are disadvantaged as a result of their social class position or their racial origin. As Tomlinson has shown, in her review of research on racial and ethnic differences in educational performance undertaken between the early 1960s and 1980, explanations of the phenomenon of West Indian underachievement have ranged from social disadvantage and socio-economic class differences through to family difference and organisation, cultural factors, childminding, school and teacher expectations stereotyping, female dominance, self esteem, identity problems, and racial hostility (Tomlinson, 1980). Although the Rampton report found that West Indian children suffered race specific disadvantages critics have suggested, if the Committee had taken account of the social origins of the pupils in the six inner city LEAs surveyed, and controlled for class variables, then the differences between black and white working class pupils would have been either less pronounced or even perhaps non existent (Reeves and Chevannes, 1981).

Recent empirical evidence based on studies of the transition from school to work in the inner city areas, has shown that the attainment levels of black and white working class school leavers are similar. As Ken Roberts et al. have remarked their research indicated that schools were not failing their black pupils to any greater extent than their white peers (Roberts, et al., 1983).

Many researchers have found that young blacks face higher levels of unemployment than young whites. Between 1974 and 1977 whereas the total level of unemployment increased by 120 per cent, minority unemployment increased by 35 per cent (Brake, 1980). More recent research indicates that in the eighties, if anything, the position has worsened particularly amongst West Indian youths (Smith, 1981, Jenkins, 1982). Generally black workers earn less than whites, yet on an average work longer hours. They also do more shift work, have fewer opportunities for promotion and upgrading, and tend to take jobs of a menial and repetitive nature (Radical Statistics Group, 1980).

Roberts and his colleagues found that young blacks faced higher levels of unemployment than young whites, but this was not because of their inferior qualifications. They attributed the marginality of this group in the labour market to two essential factors. Firstly, they acknowledge the existence of racial discrimination, of a direct and indirect nature. Secondly, it seems that young blacks have higher job aspirations than their white contemporaries, and will often reject low status jobs which they term as 'shit work' (Roberts et al., 1983).

Other writers emphasise that the disadvantage of young blacks in the employment sphere 'is at most only partially related to their under-achievement in school.' (Jenkins and Troyna, 1983).

As with employment, the position of racial minorities in the field of housing has shown no substantial improvement since the period of initial migration. Although there has been considerable growth in home ownership, the black population is mainly concentrated in decaying inner city areas. Because blacks and Asians were also prepared to occupy inferior forms of accommodation certain inner city area became 'ghettoised', with black people being forced into low quality leased property, so the white population began to move out of the inner city areas into more respectable and better quality housing (Radical Statistics Group, 1980).

It seems from the research available on housing that Asians are more likely to borrow money to buy their own homes, their use of council housing being lower than the national average. An important develop- ment in the late seventies has been the movement of the black population of Afro Caribbean origin into local authority housing. However as Cross points out:

While it may be desirable that the black population penetrated the local authority tenure to such an extent, by the same token it must, therefore, mean that schemes to improve the other housing stock must have less relevance.

(Cross, 1982)

It would seem therefore that although black people have penetrated local authority housing markets, that success has led to them being unable to gain from other projects like the 'Housing Action Areas' since the latter are intended to improve private property.

Black responses

Against a background of blocked ambition, police harrassment and unemployment, black youth has created a number of subcultural solutions. These solutions are contextualised within the daily experience of racial discrimination and harrassment by the police and the extreme right wing organisations like the National Front, and the more covert although nonetheless offensive racism which permeates white working class consciousness fed by an often overtly racist media (Husband, 1980). Brake has argued that whereas all subcultures develop to resolve collectively experienced problems, racism heightens the consciousness of black youth enabling them to see their own position within a framework of structured subordination. A defensive cohesion therefore exists in the inner city whereby young blacks are able to create an alternative black life style (Brake, 1980).

Some writers have described a process of colonisation occurring in the inner city with the growth of revivalist churches, midday hymn singing and mass baptisms in the local swimming baths, the spilling out of Caribbean fruit and vegetables from the shebeen and the Saturday night blues parties (Hall et al., 1978b). Less exotic images also pervaded the streets of the inner cities in the late sixties. The hustler emerged and is described by Brake as

Men on the street with style, like Firestones 'cool cats' laid back yet doing well. They are those who cannot get work, or will not subject themselves to routine labour for white society.

(Brake, 1980, p.127)

Other solutions include the rapid development of the Rastafarian culture or resistance to white domination. Rastafari has been variously conceptualised, and it is not possible to examine the growing literature in this area (Barrett, 1977, Cashmore E. 1979) Rastafari gives rise to a number of cultural and political practices among Afro Caribbean youth on British society, and is more than simply a religious proclivity which holds the deity of Haille Selassie of Ethiopia and the smoking of ganga (marijuana) as sacred. It embodies a clearly articulated political position constituting an ideology which stands in opposition to racism.

Writers have emphasised that Asian youth is not involved in the same type of alientating process as Afro Caribbean youth. Asian youth draws upon a firmly based historical and religious tradition rather than developing its own culture or resistance as is the case with West Indian youth. Livingstone suggests that Asian youth mix very little with white youth or Afro Caribbeans out of school, which is partly attributable to the fact that Asian parents were not interested in youth organisations fearing the effects that these might have in terms of 'bad company' and different cultural and religious traditions (Livingstone, 1978). Brake argues that racist practices compel Asian youths to seek their own solutions, as was evidenced in the groups formed for self protection following the attacks on Asian youths in Brick Lane in 1977.

Although all these aspects of inner city life are of crucial importance in understanding the complex interplay of social policy and resistance to state intervention they tend to transform the young black into a 'victim'. Cashmore and Troyna, when referring to a number of instances in which the large numbers of black youths have played a far more active role in mobilising forces against the police, argue that the notion of the 'victim' is a fairly unproductive concept. Direct tactics have in the past proved a means whereby things get done (Cashmore and Troyna, 1983)

Consensually orientated policies such as community policing and community social work projects (often initiated by middle class white social workers) fail to take sufficient account of the potential for action amongst black people, and the degree to which the dominant currents underlying such policy initiatives have been penetrated. There is now overwhelming evidence to suggest that inadequate housing and recreational facilities and all the other prevalent difficulties faced by black people in the inner cities have led to a growing frustration and anger. At certain conjunctures this has flared up into violence as evidenced in Bristol, Brixton, Leicester, Notting Hill, Southall and other areas in the riots of 1980. Although race riots are not unprecedented in the inner city the riots which occurred in 1980s took on a new significance in the context of 'crisis management'. From early 1980 to July 1981 a number of official causes and explanations were given. Scarman for instance noted that:

The exuberance of youth requires in Brixton (and in similar inner city areas) imaginative and socially acceptable opportunities for release if it is not to be diverted to criminal ends. It is clear that such opportunities do not at present exist in Brixton to the extent that they ought, particularly given the enforced idleness of many youths through unemployment. The amusement arcades, the unlawful drinking clubs, and, I believe the criminal classes gain as a result. The street corners become the social centres of people, young and old, good and bad with time on their hands and a continuing opportunity which doubtless they use to engage in endless discussion of their grievances.

(HMSO, July 1981).

The Scarman enquiry went on to take cognisance of the economic insecurity, enforced idleness due to unemployment, and the hostility of some young black people to the police.

Many policy initiatives focus upon the group of youths who clearly reject white society and its values, as we see in the above quotation. It should be noted however that other writers have seen the response of black youth to most forms of state intervention as being highly differentiated, ranging from a blatant rejection through a compromising acceptance to a belief in the rewards offered by white society (Pryce, 1979).

Unconventional Wisdom: New Analyses of the 'Race Problem'

In recent years several authors have argued from distinctive theoretical viewpoints in an attempt to identify

1 The major paradigms which have dominated race relations and social policy in Great Britain;
2 The weaknesses of these approaches;
3 Alternative modes of explanation.

Of the attempts that have been made to conceptualise the various analyses of race relations the work of Ben-Tovim and Gabriel (1982) is especially useful. They suggest that three types of approach to the analysis of race relations may be discerned. Firstly, idealist analyses emphasising the importance of cultural determinants, secondly, Marxist analyses dominated by the concept of social class emphasising the importance of economic determinants, and thirdly, holistic analyses, stressing the specificity or relative autonomy of the economic, political, and cultural spheres. Such explanations do not accord a prior causal primacy to any one of these areas, in the determination of race relations.

Within the first category Ben-Tovim and Gabriel argue that research has been dominated by the concept of culture. Racial problems are held to derive from two sources. Firstly, they derive from the cultural differences between groups and what is perceived of as the debilitating effects of minority group culture. Secondly, they derive from discrimination which further contributes to minorities in society. The essence of this position, which emerged in the early 1970s, is described by Bourne and Sivanandan as follows:

In essence what they set out to study was not the relations between races as defined by colour, but the relations between ethnic groups as defined by their culture. British society was not to be viewed as some sort of homogeneous cultural monolith (as their predecessors were wont to do), but as multi cultural, multi ethnic society. The business of the ethnic school was to show how these several ethnicities served to ameliorate and buffer the injustices of society.

(Bourne and Sivanandan, 1980, p.343)

Race relations problems arise from two sources. Firstly, through cultural differences which exist between groups, and what is perceived as the debilitating effects of minority group culture. Secondly, problems arise through the effects of discrimination which place minority groups at a further disadvantage. The police recommendations stemming from this tradition, they argue, tend to reflect the preoccupation with the various forms of cultural relationship. The culturalist viewpoint has led to the interventions such as the expansion of English as a second language, compensatory education programmes, and programmes of dispersal within the spheres of housing and education. In activities such as social work, attempts have been made to create 'ethnically sensitive services', and translating facilities for recipients of social work intervention (Denney, 1983). The previously mentioned Section 11 of the 1966 Local Government Act reflects the identification of 'immigrant' problems in terms of language and custom. Much of the state intervention both coercive and consensual previously discussed appears to define the problem as 'the absorption of culturally strange aliens'. Such an approach we would argue tends to divert attention from the contradictions in social structure which give rise to institutionalised racism. Such policies are not contentious, and are therefore less likely to prompt any reaction from the white majority population. Policies based on such assumptions also give the impression that something is being done, albeit in the safety of a cultural perspective which fails to examine the nature of a social structure which gives rise to racism in the first place. Thus the government are able to argue that they have recognised 'the problem' and are attempting to mitigate policies in an attempt to create a 'solution'.

Such concerns are of paramount importance in the second tradition identified by Ben-Tovim and Gabriel which they refer to as the 'race–class axis'. Here the adopting of superiority and the operationalisation of racist ideologies is necessary to legitimate existing forms of class relationship. Black and Asian people were thus driven to migrate by endemic poverty with migration being encouraged in order to fill a gap in the labour market. On arriving here they found themselves to be in substandard housing taking the jobs rejected by the white working class. Thus migration occurred because of underdevelopment of the colonies and ex-colonies, and because the capitalist economy in a period of expansion needed a reserve army of labour from the third world to meet a labour shortage. We have previously seen that when the post war economic boom began to end in the early sixties, social policy shifted away from the recruitment of black labour towards a policy of gearing the entry more closely to the needs of the economy (Hall et al, 1978b; Sivanandan, 1976). We have also seen how this idea can be related to the 1962 Commonwealth Immigration Act through the introduction of the skills related voucher scheme.

The 1971 Immigration Act with the creation of the patrial and non-patrial distinctions effectively discriminates on the basis of social, economic, and racial criteria. For the Marxists, then it is possible to view the history of immigration control from the 1948 Nationality Act to the present 1981 Nationality Act in terms of an 'organic' crisis of capital. By organic these writers refer to the combined effects of economic, political, ideological and cultural processes. Such an analysis goes beyond more conventional Marxist interpretations of crises in which economic vicissitudes of capitalism are linked to crises in capital accumulation and declining rates of profits. These writers have isolated a number of significant events which have characterised this perceived moral and social disinitegration (Hall et al., 1978b; Solomos, Findlay, Jones, Gilroy, 1982).

During the mid to late sixties there occurred a growth in extra parliamentary organisations particularly amongst the young, the anti-Vietnam movement being a case in point. The development of mass youth subculture like mods and rockers also demonstrated the creation of the 'permissive society'. The 'troubles' in Northern Ireland also presented a threat to part of Britain, as did the power of the trade union militants. In the early seventies the struggles of Edward Heath and conservative policies ended in the final surrender to the miners. This was only to be followed by the break up of the Labour Party who were attempting to reconstitute 'consensus' with the social contract.

The election of Margaret Thatcher in 1979 marked the culmination of this tendency with a rapid concentration of political power in the executive. Race became a central component in a right wing ideology in which all that was good and wholesome seemed to be under threat and on the point of disintegration. This combined with a decline in the role of the political parties led to a position in which the ideology of liberal democracy had been 'severely qualified'. When any major social question is raised the issue of race emerges. Race is thus used to construct explanations designed to create consent (Solomos, Findlay, Jones, Gilroy, 1982).

Alfred Sherman has clearly articulated this position:

The imposition of mass immigration from backward alien cultures is just one symptom of this self destructive urge reflected in the assault on patriotism, the family, both as a conjugal and economic unit, the Christian religion in public life and schools, traditional morality, in matters of sex, honesty, public display, and respect for the law, in short all that is English and wholesome.

(Sherman A, 1979)

Mullard in his description of this position rightly points to the centrality of ideology in the analysis of social policies designed to ameliorate the worst excesses of racism. Thus, such conceptions as multi-cultural education, community development projects, and most forms of urban aid are seen as having a number of primary functions. Multi-cultural education for instance can be seen as emanating from a pluralistic desire to create a fuller understanding of the national and cultural background of 'immigrant children'. It could be argued that those who initiate, design and teach these programmes do so in the hope that ultimately a reduction in ignorance will lead to less racial harrassment and discrimination. Such beliefs it can be argued stem from the liberal notion that education in itself is a 'good' thing and ultimately can work towards the amelioration if not the destruction of social problems.

The Marxist would probably take the view that this notion was naive and idealistic serving to divert attention from the central issues. Racism is seen as an enduring and to some extent functional feature of the British social formation. Racism and not ignorance is being the primary problem. Multi-racial education channels a desire to acquire knowledge of black history into safe channels effectively controlling the development of black consciousness. Similarly social workers adhering to a cultural pluralist perspective argue for the creation of more ethnically sensitive services. All these initiatives transmit a ruling class conception of the race problem, as distinct from the problem of racism. If the composition of these organisations is examined, the Marxist would argue, it can be seen that whites occupy the top and blacks the lower positions, thus reproducing in a racial form the white power structure and the social structure which legitimates capitalist relations (Mullard, 1982).

The problem with both the culturalist and the Marxist view is the tendency towards oversimplification. Thus, in the case of the ethnic school, the problem is reduced to that of competing cultural definitions of reality, whereas the race class axis relies upon a sometimes crude form of economistic polemic to explain the highly complex position of black and Asian people in Britain. Ben-Tovim and Gabriel (1982) point to the fact that both explanations fail to specify the nature of racial discrimination in a wide variety of contexts. They argue that the impact of the latter materialist position has been negligible since amongst other things the nature of Marxist discourse is such that governments cannot respond to this form of analysis, due to both the inherent pessimism which follows from such an analysis and the antithetical stance taken towards the liberal democratic state by those adhering to this position.

Relative autonomy and race relations, a third approach.
Some writers, in an attempt to transcend the often monolithic strictures of the culturalist position and reductionist Marxist economism, analyse state intervention in relation to the notion of relative autonomy. Mullard has argued against over-determined materialist explanations conceptualising racist ideologies in terms of their independence from the requirements of the capitalist mode of production. Thus racism is not being seen as being functional to the interests of capital, neither does it originate with capitalism. Racist sentiment has a quasi independent existence competing with other ideological systems (Mullard, 1982).

Tierney (1982) arguing from a similar position, points out that whilst the black and white worker have a similar position in that they are both exploited within the capitalist mode of production, categories of race cannot be conflated since the structural position of black people has been strongly influenced by racial differences as perceived by white people. If the notion of relative autonomy is accepted in relation to policy on race relations we see how it is that some local authorities have been able to adopt policies which make genuine attempts to combat racism. Thus there is no overall economic rationale behind the legislation designed to control immigration. As Paul Foot comments in connection with the 1962 Immigration Act, no-one knew what the effect would be on the rate of Immigration (Foot, 1965). The piecemeal nature of the legislation lends weight to the view taken by Ben-Tovim and Gabriel (1982) that the policy reflects a clash between 'political' and ideological forces.

Such an approach was taken by Rex and Tomlinson (1979) in their study of Handsworth. These writers argue that capitalist interests have not been at the forefront of the campaign for immigration control. They see the campaign as developing within the Conservative Party, and as being executed by politicians such as Powell who see themselves as speaking for national rather than business interests. There has not been any large diversion of funds from 'business' to bodies like the National Front, as was the case in Germany in the 1930s. Rex and Tomlinson go on to argue that the campaign for immigration control was mounted successfully at the time that Harold Macmillan made his famous 'you never had it so good' speech. As they put it, 'Far from being the case that racism has ebbed and flowed with the trade cycle, the tragic truth is while racism flows it rarely ebbs' (Rex and Tomlinson, 1979, p. 285).

Thus we see that Rex is taking a decisive stance against orthodox reductionist interpretations of racism and the social formation in Marxism. He appears to be positing that racist and nationalist political organisations are neither supported by the dominant economic class nor seem to represent its interests. It follows therefore that racism is not reducible to class and no determinate relationship exists between racism and capitalist reproduction. Secondly, Rex and Tomlinson argue that working class racism in post war Britain first surfaced in affluent times in a period of full employment, rising living standards and low inflation.

Returning to the first point that racism is not orchestrated by dominent economic interests it should be stated that whereas political practices, institutions and ideologies have their own specificity and effectivity (and as such are not reducible to the effects, expressions or representations of economic class relations) they have nevertheless differential effects upon economic classes which may determine some of their own conditions of existence. Notwithstanding this, however, it should be stated that such cause-effect relationships between practices and relations at different 'levels' of the social formation, cannot be deduced theoretically, as for example, in Althusserian structuralism (cf Giddens, 1979). Such relationships must be established substantively, for the effects of racist ideologies and practices are uneven in a social spatial and temporal sense.

Conclusion

It can be seen that state policy in this area forms a bewildering set of contradictions, since on the one hand the state imposes ever more stringent immigration controls whilst introducing measures ostensibly designed to eliminate racism. Thus any ameliorative measures designed to increase access to scarce resources must be seen in the context of measures which exclude black and brown people from entry and settlement in the country on the basis of race (Lea, 1980). How for instance could the Conservative Party in 1962 reconcile immigration control with an almost reverential view of the Commonwealth? How could the notion of equal rights, a central value espoused by both parties (although to a lesser degree by the Thatcher Government), be equated with blatantly unequal treatment of blacks in relation to immigration? The Labour Party's ethos of brotherhood and internationalism seems to be contrary to notions of immigration control and racial exclusiveness. It should be noted that the Labour Party promised to repeal the immigration controls imposed by the Tories in 1962, but when in office toughened them.

It seems that government initiatives to control immigration and forms of institutional racism have been made in response to crises. Policies have thus reflected, as Ben-Tovim and Gabriel argue, a need to react quickly to a developing situation. These policies are also indicative of a society in which, as Engels puts it, there exist indissoluble contradictions. How can we begin to understand these contradictions in relation to our analysis of the problem? Firstly, materialistic conceptions of the state and the notion of relative autonomy are not necessarily discreet conceptual categories. Corrigan and Leonard (1978) argue that the state serves the long term interests of the ruling class. In the short term state activities can be seen on occasions as working against the interests of those owning the means of production. Thus in the case of what we have referred to as consensual state intervention there would not appear to be any direct advantage to the ruling class.

What we see instead is a position in which as Cashmore and Troyna put it, a 'complimentarity' exists between capitalism and racism. It is not possible as we have shown to argue in terms of a crude conspiracy, since complex questions such as this demand complex analyses. Race and racism predates the capitalist colonial expansion of the seventeenth and eighteenth centuries (Van Den Bergh, 1978). Racism does effectively fraction working class interests, particularly in times of high unemployment. Thus Cashmore and Troyna go on to contend that if one is unemployed in an industry in which migrant workers enter prepared to work at lower rates of pay, then a simple wish for self protection will encourage the desire to exclude black people, thus providing an underlying rationality behind racist sentiment.

Such is the crude reasoning which has enabled policies to be based on a commitment to the reduction of numbers. Some writers have argued that some of the legislation provides the basis for some positive actions (Ben-Tovim and Gabriel, 1982). To a large extent this applies to the 1976 Race Relations Act, the problem being the creation of a 'political will' with adequate strategies to deal with specific problems, since every small gain made by black and Asian people is countered by crude racist ideologies and class fractioning.

It is noteworthy that the most successful community projects have been conceived and executed by black people, free of the patronising assumptions of white social workers who often feel that it is their professional duty to select issues on behalf of black people (Ohri, Curno, Manning, 1982).

The bleak reality for the future is that policies designed merely to keep the lid on the situation in the inner cities will no longer be practicable for governments of any persuasion. The 'riots' of 1981 were indicative of the fact that many Asian and black people have penetrated the dominant culturalist and integrationist paradigms which have guided policy initiatives.

4 Madness, Epilepsy and Medicine
Nick Manning and Mike Oliver

In the struggles over definitions of various phenomena as problems of one kind or another, certain groups have a vested interest in ensuring that their own particular definition becomes generally accepted. This chapter will consider some of the factors involved in the definitions of epilepsy and madness as social or alternatively medical problems and the conceptualisation of these phenomena as either deviance or illness. It will be argued that both epilepsy and madness have become medicalised, along with a range of other similar phenomena. Despite objections from individual doctors about trivial or inappropriate cases:

Medicine is now being called upon to deal with problems which were once considered moral rather than medical issues – for example, alcoholism, drug addiction, crime, marital disharmony, behaviour disorders and fertility control – as well as the unwelcome fruits of technological and social change – for example, the toll of morbidity from road accidents, smoking and obesity.

(Jefferys, 1975, p.viii)

The main difference, we suspect, between epilepsy and madness and the other phenomena mentioned in the quote is that there would be general agreement today that both epilepsy and madness really are illnesses and therefore appropriately medicalised, whereas the others may not be. We want to suggest that this in fact is not the case, though in order to do so it is necessary to go beyond explanations which see social meanings and definitions merely as the outcome of competing struggles between various interest groups.

Historical Perceptions
Kittrie (1971) has examined a number of deviant phenomena, such as drug addiction, homosexuality, alcoholism, and mental illness and demonstrated how such phenomena were originally regarded as moral, then legal, and now medical problems. As a result of these perceptions, particular deviants were subjected to moral, legal and then medical modes of social control. Similarly, Conrad and Schneider (1980) conclude their review of the medicalisation of deviance by proposing 'that three major paradigms may be identified that have held reign over deviance designations in various historical periods: deviance as sin; deviance as crime; and deviance as sickness.' (p. 27).

This religious–legal–medical scheme can be applied to an historical analysis of the social meanings associated with madness and epilepsy. Thus, at one time or another, they have been regarded as divine possession, possession by the devil, or possession by spirits, either benign or malevolent. Usually whether perceptions have been purely magical or religious, they have nonetheless centred around notions of good or evil, and have given rise to reward for correct behaviour or punishment for evil-doing. Different attitudes sometimes existed side-by-side: horror and adoration, indifference and admiration.

An important source of this religious view in Europe was the biblical story of Jesus casting out evil spirits from epileptic or similarly troubled people. Although other non-Christian cultures such as the Greeks, Romans and Hindus held similar views, only in Europe were they to become the basis of the systematic persecution of such deviants. Feared as a danger for a weakening Church, these deviants were tackled through the Inquisition, epitomised by the manual for witch-hunters, the *Malleus Maleficarum* (Hammer of Witches), published in 1486.

With the decline in the power of the Church, and the growth in power of the Nation State in Europe, heralded by the Reformation and the break with Rome in England (1534), deviant minorities came to be seen in more secular terms. Rather than a theological or moral concern, they became a problem for state bureaucracies to solve rationally, either through financial support and control as in the Elizabethan Poor Law of 1601, or in new residential establishments such as the Hôpital Général founded in Paris in 1656, which at its height housed as much as 1 per cent of the population of Paris. This 'great confinement' as Foucault (1967) describes it was the beginning of the institutional segregation of mad and epileptic people (often along with the poor, unemployed or elderly) which reached its greatest development in the nineteenth century. Although Enlightenment ideas provided a general alternative to theology, there were as yet no specific scientific or clinical approaches to madness or epilepsy.

The golden age
The secularisation of ideas in the seventeenth and eighteenth centuries thus offered no positive interpretations, and madness and epilepsy came to be seen as something less than human – as animal or brutish conditions suitable for brutish treatment. While medical interpretations for the élite, such as George III's madness, used the humoral model of Hippocrates, the general experience of inmates in, for example, the flourishing private trade in madhouses in the late eighteenth century was equivalent to that of caged animals. And even the humoral model dictated unpleasant bouts of blood-letting or vomiting. Other medical interpretations owed more to the whim of the physician than any

working theory. For example, the influential Benjamin Rush, founder of American psychiatry, who flourished in the late eighteenth century, identified such diseases as 'anarchia' evident soon after the American War of Independence:

> The excess of the passion for liberty, inflamed by the successful issue of the war, produced, in many people, opinions and conduct which could not be removed by reason nor restrained by government . . . these opinions constituted a form of insanity.

> (Szasz, 1971, p. 140)

On the other hand, Rush felt that continued loyalty to the British Crown was also an illness he termed 'revolutiona'.

The real opportunity for the development of psychiatry, however, occurred as a result of what Castel (1976), and following him Ingleby (1983), have termed the 'golden age' of the asylum. This period covered the late eighteenth century to the middle of the nineteenth century, and began with the development of non-medical 'moral treatment'. From this point of view, the experience of madness was to be corrected by providing a calm and ordered life, in which the mad person was treated, insofar as was possible, in a humane and respectful manner. Symbolised by the dramatic removal of the chains of the mad in 1794 by Pinel in the asylums of Bicêtre and Saltpetrière, this approach was developed by Tuke in the Retreat at York into an educational process using kindness and respect to help mad people re-establish self-control of their 'animal natures' through moral force. In *Description of the Retreat* (1813), Tuke argued that a patient's 'desire for esteem' rather than 'the principle of fear' guided the organisation of treatment.

Partly in response to this example, and partly in reaction to the excesses of the private madhouses revealed in Parliamentary Select Committee reports in 1807 and 1815, a strong reform movement developed to press for the construction and regulation of public asylums. The construction of these was made compulsory in the 1845 Lunatics Act; within 3 years nearly three-quarters of English counties had complied, and the rest followed suit within 10 years. While it might be expected that the non-medical system of 'moral treatment' would naturally be adopted in these new asylums, in fact the medical profession soon came to dominate them.

The medical profession had officially become involved with madness as early as the late eighteenth century when official (though ineffective) inspection of private madhouses was set up. In addition, many of these used medical claims in their competition for trade and were often built near infirmaries. However, the development of moral treatment at the turn of the century posed a considerable threat to such medical expansion, and it is remarkable therefore to find that by 1830 existing public asylums (built under the 1744 Vagrancy Act) mostly had medical directors, and that the 1845 Act required the keeping of medical records and encouraged medical dominance within the Lunacy Commission. An Association of Medical Officers of Asylums and Hospitals for the Insane had been founded in 1841, and began to publish the *Asylum Journal* in 1853, promoting the theory that insanity was purely a disease of the brain. This relatively rapid takeover of madness by the medical profession has been the source of some debate (which we shall discuss later in this chapter); but it effectively established the medical treatment of madness, and at the end of this 'golden age' the profession could look forward with hope to the successful treatment of madness in the new asylums (Scull, 1979).

The modern age

Such optimism was to be short lived. The asylum movement drew its inspiration not only from medicine and moral treatment, but also the utopian hopes which inspired socialist and religious communards of the early nineteenth century such as Robert Owen. Yet by 1877 a Lancet Commission set up to investigate asylums recorded that 'everywhere attendants, we are convinced, maltreat, abuse and terrify patients when the backs of the medical officers are turned. Humanity is only to be secured by the watching officials.' (Jones, 1972). The asylums had rapidly become overcrowded during the middle of the century, as a result both of pressure on them to take increasing numbers of admissions, and the failure of the asylum doctors to cure many of their inmates. While at the end of the first quarter of the nineteenth century there were 6 public asylums, of an average size of 116 inmates, this became 24 asylums averaging 300 inmates by 1850, and 60 asylums averaging 650 inmates by 1880 (Scull, 1979, p. 198). Institutions of this size be they workhouses, prisons, public schools or asylums tended to develop features common to what Goffman (1961) called 'the total institution', in which an inmate's entire waking life, work or leisure, was subject to surveillance and regulation such that a person's very self was stripped away. Small wonder, then, that the popular image of the asylum by the late nineteenth century was of something to be feared. Although the asylum movement had developed earlier in the century with a positive idea – literally an asylum or retreat from an increasingly stressful world – in reality the incarceration of lunatics became a sub-branch of the general nineteenth century use of institutional control. Clearly, such a place was not attractive, and in the later decades of the nineteenth century considerable concern developed about the possibility of individuals being erroneously locked away. This gave rise in 1890 to the Lunacy Act which was addressed to the proper process of admission such that mistaken confinement could not occur. Its focus on safeguarding those outside could not be more of a contrast with the 1845 Act's intent of bringing the benefits of the asylum experience to mad people.

During this time in Britain many epileptics also found themselves the responsibility of the Poor Law Guardians and were lumped together with lunatics, the poor, the idle and the sick, in workhouses or asylums. The coming of the industrial revolution and the process of industrialisation had serious implications for the epileptic as Jones and Tillotson (1965, pp. 5–6) spell out:

The drift to the town and the growing complexity of industrial machinery at the time meant the development of a class of industrial rejects for whom it was clear that special provision would have to be made ... The problems of severe epileptics in a city such as Bradford, where the wool trade meant fast-moving machinery and crowded workshops, must have been particularly acute.

The usual result for many social deviants unable to adapt to the requirements of the industrial system was the asylum or the workhouse and it was not until the 1880s that a movement to separate epileptics from the mentally ill began. In the following thirty years eight epileptic colonies were built and segregation was added to the existing policy of isolation.

Despite popular fear of asylums, and a correspondingly legalistic control of them, the period since the mid-nineteenth century has come to be called the modern age since it witnessed the consolidation and eventual triumph of the medical view of madness and epilepsy. Epilepsy is probably the oldest known disorder of the brain and one of the earliest and most famous medical treatises on epilepsy appeared in the book *On the Sacred Disease* written by Hippocrates in 400 BC. Hippocrates correctly attributed epilepsy to abnormal cerebral function, and argued that this was caused by an excess of phlegm, one of the four humours, which prevented air-carrying vessels from reaching the brain. This emphasis on the physiological basis for seizures is, according to Lennox (1960) like one tower of a suspension bridge whose twin, however, is more than two thousand years beyond and whose building is not to begin until the nineteenth century. Then, in keeping with the morality of the time, sexual excess and masturbation were regarded as the commonest causes of fits. Accordingly, epileptics were discouraged, if not prevented, from marrying and if they found themselves in institutions they were rigidly separated from members of the opposite sex. Treatment reached its zenith when, as late as 1880, one Dr Bacon reported to the British Medical Association that he had castrated two male epileptics, with the result that, in one case, there was a great improvement. The foundations of the second tower of Lennox's 'suspension bridge' were laid by Hughlings Jackson who in 1873 wrote:

'Epilepsy is the name for occasional, sudden, excessive, rapid and local discharges of grey matter.' Since then, advances in neurological diagnosis, the electroencephalograph, improved techniques of brain surgery and the development of anti-convulsant drugs have all played their part in the present dominance of the medical framework for the evaluation of epilepsy.

The treatment of madness followed a similar path. The opportunist involvement of doctors in the early asylum movement survived the pessimism of the late nineteenth century by repeating the claim that medicine would in time develop the right answers, as it was doing spectacularly for physical illness. It seemed not unreasonable that the success associated with the germ theory of disease (leading to vaccination, antiseptics, and so on) would spill over into the field of madness, in which the notion of diseased brains rather than troubled minds was gaining strength. By the early twentieth century, medicine had metamorphosed from an art into a science, a process epitomised in the impact of the 1910 Flexner report on medical education in the USA. This report, commissioned by the American Medical Association, concluded that a substantial number of medical schools were of insufficient standard, and within a few years about one third had closed down (Anderson, 1968).

Faith in science, including medical science, resonated with the emergence of social reform around the turn of the century. Fabians (in England) and Progressives (in the USA) built on imperialist concerns about the fitness of working class military recruits, to make a strong case for state intervention in working class life. Nowhere was this argument more relevant than in the health field, where it gave a further boost to the medical profession. Consequently, the final transition from medical control of asylums, to the medical treatment of mental illness, was sealed in the early twentieth centiry. Specifically, the successful identification of syphilis as the cause of general paralysis of the insane in 1894 and its confirmation as an infection in the nerve-cells of the cortex in 1913, and the identification of the neuroses in the early 1920s, enabled the medical profession to dominate the 1924–27 Royal Commission on Lunacy and Mental Disorder. The subsequent Mental Treatment Act of 1930, as its title implies, began to prise the control of asylum admissions away from lawyers in favour of doctors (Treacher and Baruch, 1981).

From the 1930s mental hospitals began to move away from their social welfare function to become more concerned with active therapeutic measures. Over the following 25 years we see the development of various somatic treatments for mental illness: insulin coma, electroconvulsive, drugs, and brain surgery. Drugs in particular have enabled doctors to control the disabling symptoms of both epilepsy and mental illness sufficiently to reduce the need for asylums (now called hospitals); and after the steady growth of asylum numbers up to the 1950s, there has been a dramatic reduction in the last 25 years of about 40 per cent in the total number of inmates, to less than 80,000.

The highpoint of medical dominance was reached in the 1959 Mental Health Act, which gave doctors complete control over admissions. During the 1960s psychiatric expansionism, in alliance with a drug industry keen to expand profits, began to inflate the jurisdiction of medical authority: a variety of deviant behaviours such as addiction, hyperactivity in children, homosexuality, crime and so on were treated with drugs. By the 1970s drug advertisements were implying that any normal stress in the life cycle, particularly for women, could be 'treated' with drugs.

However, this process has not gone uncriticised, nor has it entirely eliminated legal or religious conceptions. Religious leaders occasionally become seriously involved in exorcism, and the public's appetite for demonologically framed films has been prodigious. On both sides of the Atlantic there has also been growing concern about the rights of compulsorily detained patients. In the USA this has led to attempts to establish that patients who are committed have a constitutional right to treatment. Courts have witnessed legal representatives trying to determine whether certain psychiatric practices amount to treatment, or not – much to the professional distaste of doctors whose professional edifice rests on the foundation of 'clinical freedom' (Ahmed and Plog, 1976). In England, where compulsory admissions are far less common, similar concerns have nevertheless been expressed by MIND (the National Association for Mental Health) (Gostin, 1977), and new Acts have been passed in 1982 and 1983 to tighten up admission procedures.

Criticisms of psychiatric expansion have appeared both inside and outside the profession. Non-medical explanations of madness, which we shall discuss later, were proposed from political and sociological viewpoints in the 1960s. Psychiatry was accused of using a scientific ideology to disguise and depoliticise activities which were more accurately to be seen as social control than medical treatment. These intellectual critiques were taken up here and there by particular minorities into what Schur (1980) has termed 'deviancy struggles'. Perhaps the best example has been the successful effort in 1973 by American gays to get homosexuality removed as an official diagnostic category in the American Psychiatric Association manual.

This small current of demedicalisation has yet to be reflected in public opinion about madness. Recent surveys have, rather, confirmed a general public endorsement of the medical view of madness as illness, with an apparent growth in tolerance of psychiatric patients, at least in principle (Rabkin, 1975). However, in practice, particular neighbourhoods may be less than welcoming when faced with the possibility of sharing their street with a mental health hostel; and ex-mental patients frequently end up in inner city ghettos (Dear and Taylor, 1982).

Despite occasional conflicts, there is no doubt that the medical framework is also the dominant mode through which epilepsy is perceived and evaluated in society today. The commonly accepted explanation for this is that epilepsy is a physical illness and was wrongly evaluated in previous times and in other societies. Now, at last, advances in medical science are providing a much more satisfactory basis for the treatment and cure of epilepsy. The last twenty years have seen a decolonisation and an attempt to reduce the isolation of epileptics in both Britain and the USA. However, the life of the epileptic outside the institution is, and has been, surrounded by a number of legal constraints. In this respect, Britain has been more humane than some other countries; for example, marriage between epileptics is not prohibited in this country although in Sweden and in a number of states in the USA it has been, or still is, on the statute-books; Britain has only recently (1971) changed the law with regard to divorce and epilepsy, however, in that having epilepsy is no longer recognised as a reasonable ground for divorce.

Travel presents another restriction; many countries are reluctant to admit epileptics as immigrants and Australia actually has laws banning them. Driving, almost an essential to life in modern Britain, was illegal from epileptics until recently, and even today epileptics are only allowed to drive if they have been seizure-free for at least two years. This change in the law has brought little benefit to many epileptics for they find it impossible to obtain motor insurance at reasonable prices.

State Policy

In the preceding section we have referred in passing to the key pieces of legislation that have marked respectively the ascendancy of secular, legal and medical views of madness. However, it would be too simple to present state policies as merely the official response to changing popular and professional views. While of course these are important, the state is also itself changing dramatically over this period, and developing policies in a wide variety of areas. Responses to perceived social problems take place within constraints set by the general conditions of existence of the state itself. These, we have argued in Chapter 1, include the maintenance of a buoyant economy and the securing of political legitimacy, as well as the meeting of legitimate needs. State policy concerned with epilepsy and madness must be seen then in the context of more general policies.

The existence of the state itself is of course a primary indicator of the secularisation of power consequent upon the decline of the Church from the fifteenth century onwards. Mad and epileptic people over this period were transferred as a problem from Church to state. For the state they became mainly a part of the general category of vagabonds, subject to the restrictions of the Elizabethan Poor Law, in force from 1601 to 1834. In addition, the state had taken an interest in setting up an inspectorate for private madhouses in 1774, but the permissive legislation of 1744 and 1806 which allowed counties to build asylums had remained largely dormant well into the nineteenth century.

The growth of state activity concerned with madness in the nineteenth century was really a part of general state expansion (despite popular impressions that this was an era of the minimal or *laissez faire* state). Of relevance here is the nineteenth century concern, from the 1834 Poor Law Act onwards, to regulate and classify those unable or unwilling to work. While the 1601 Act had recognised that the poor could be divided into the able and non-able bodied, the 1834 concern to control rising Poor Law costs, and the availability of a new stringent universal classification mechanism (the workhouse test) allowed the collapse of all the poor into the single category of pauper. However, it quickly became apparent that many residents of the workhouse (the ill, old, feeble-minded) could never work; and much subsequent social policy, well into the twentieth century, has been occupied with classifying out those for whom the workhouse could never be an incentive to join the labour market. Asylums and epileptic colonies were two such alternatives to the workhouse.

The classifying out of such dependent groups into special institutions encouraged the development of specialists claiming to meet each group's particular needs, as we have already seen clearly in the way the medical profession took over the asylums in the middle of the century. And hence a part of the development of state policy cannot be understood without appreciating the lobbying of such pressure groups on the growing state apparatus. In return for their work in classifying and controlling groups such as the mad and the epileptic, the state granted the medical profession a market monopoly on medical practice in 1858, which considerably strengthened their position as a pressure group.

However, to enter an asylum was still a legal transition authorised by a Justice of the Peace. This is why asylums became so overcrowded in the late nineteenth century – the admission procedure was not yet controlled by the asylums themselves. This legal transition was both a legitimate withdrawal from the labour market, and an enforced disenfranchisement of many legal rights, particularly over the control of property – both changes of great significance to a citizen of the nineteenth century whose personal autonomy was heavily dependent on either wages or wealth. For this reason the state, via the legal system, actually increased its direct control of asylum admissions, most notably in the 1890 Act.

We see then in the nineteenth century that state policy for the mad and epileptic was an intimate part of a general concern to identify those who should earn their living in the labour market. Those who could not do so should be returned to the labour market as soon as possible, and therefore active provision (offered in principle by the medical profession) in the form of the asylum was necessary. However, since this meant an important suspension of rights and obligations, admission remained under the direct legal control of the state.

The law did not just operate in the area of production, but reproduction also in that children with epilepsy as well as other handicaps did not immediately benefit from the state provision of universal education from 1870. In fact, the policy of segregation pursued for adults with epilepsy was also followed for children following from the Elementary Education (Defective and Epileptic Children) Act 1899. Thus the majority of children with epilepsy have been and still are educated in segregated establishments of one kind or another.

In the twentieth century, this legal line of development in state policy gives way to medically determined provision, a process reminiscent of the earlier ousting of 'moral treatment'. Yet as we argue in detail in a subsequent section there is no evidence that medicine becomes especially effective in this area in the twentieth century. The explanation, rather, is to be found once again in more general changes in policy. Baruch and Treacher (1978) have pointed out that in the early twentieth century the general health of the working class was of some concern to the British political élite. Either in its own right or in its consequences for British imperial might, working class fitness was seen as an issue right across the political spectrum. Social reform was therefore in the interests of both Imperialists and Fabians.

To the extent that the medical profession had by this time strengthened its claim to the interpretation of madness as illness, it was able to influence the 1924–27 Royal Commission on Lunacy, and the subsequent Mental Treatment Act of 1930. Here for the first time the state began, albeit cautiously, to hand over the control of admissions, that is the decision about who was or was not mad, to the medical profession.

This happy coincidence of interests in social reform was to reappear after the second world war, and gave rise to the setting up and subsequent all-party acceptance of the Welfare State. The establishment of income security and free health care in the 1940s substantially weakened the logic of confining mad people in asylums, and the sustained economic growth of the 1950s ('You've never had it so good') suggested that social problems could at last be relegated to the social planners rather than the politicians. And in this area, of course, we have seen that the technicians available to the social planners were to be found in the ever ready medical profession. Social reform was now not so much an aid to Fabianism and Imperialism as to economic growth and political stability: Britain had become a contented community with common aims and aspirations.

Not surprisingly then the 1957 Royal Commission and 1959 Mental Health Act suggested that, with help from the Welfare State and new medical treatments, the mentally ill could now be returned to, or retained in, the community, and asylums were to become more flexible in taking voluntary patients. Logically, given the ageing physical structure and forbidding reputation of the old asylums, Enoch Powell announced in 1961 that he was going to substantially empty them by 1975. And although this target was not met, a 40 per cent reduction in the asylum population has been achieved to date, despite higher admission rates, as a result of reduced lengths of stay.

Current state policy is to maintain the mentally ill in the community through the support of the Welfare State, while making medical care available through brief in-patient treatment and out-patient support. However, policy for community care has only been slowly implemented in comparison with estimates of need. Wider concerns, such as shortage of money for public expenditure, have been crucial constraints on state policy; although official views have rationalised that this is in any case appropriate: 'Psychiatry is to join the rest of medicine . . . People go into hospital with mental disorders and they are cured.' (Sir Keith Joseph, 1971, quoted in Jones, 1972, p. 340). We shall examine the basis for this claim in more detail later in this chapter, but it illustrates clearly the complete endorsement of the medical notion of madness in state policy.

By contrast, the policy of segregation under legal definitions of epilepsy was not in fact dispensed with as medical definitions superseded legal ones. Rather segregation was often seen as part of the medical treatment, at least until the development of anti-convulsant drugs from the 1930s onwards. Segregation still forms part of the treatment and some epileptics are still hospitalised for long periods of time. Though the colonies have now disappeared and have been replaced by 'special centres', one cannot help but wonder if all that has changed is the words. With regard to epileptic children, it is to doctors that education authorities turn for legitimisation and ratification in the case of individuals and their designated schools. Although the Warnock report (1978) and the 1981 Education Act may have shifted some power away from doctors to educational administrators and psychologists, as Tomlinson (1982) argues, the rationale remains the same:

This move has enabled each of the professional groups involved, teachers, psychologists, psychiatrists, and doctors, to maintain their sphere of authority and simultaneously offer some relief to beleagured colleagues and institutions in their own or associated professions. The problems have been firmly defined as belonging to individual pupils who could be assessed, diagnosed and referred to an appropriate treatment programme.

(Ford et al., 1982, p. 152)

Consequently, it is medicine which now performs the crucial task in both defining what is, and what is not, epilepsy, as well as having responsibility for its treatment. The state, insofar as it has a policy towards the problem of epilepsy, is content to regard it as a medical problem and consequently leave it to the doctors. As Conrad and Schneider (1980, p. 252) point out:

The medicalization of deviance never has been a formalised social policy; . . . it has emerged from various combinations of turf battles, court decisions, scientific innovations, political expediences, medical entrepreneurship, and other influences. The medicalization of deviance has become in effect a de facto social policy.

Conventional Wisdom

We have repeatedly observed that the medical profession in the past had no useful treatment for madness and epilepsy, yet it acquired the right to define, control and treat them. In this section we will examine conventional views of the nature of madness and epilepsy, the role of the medical profession in dealing with them, and the causes and consequences of state policies in this area.

The nature of madness

Conventional wisdom about the nature of madness can be drawn from two general sources – the medical model, and the social model. The medical view of madness draws on the general framework of scientific medicine, in which the body is conceptualised in terms of systems or organs. In terms of diagnosis and therapy, the body is the analogue of the machine whose individual parts could be examined and treated. The main task of diagnosis is one of approximating the patient's pathology to an established disease category through observation, examination and tests. Treatment consists of raising the level of an organism's natural resistance to specific agents, or restoring an identified or presumed disturbance of the biological system (Morgan, Calnan, Manning, 1985). For epilepsy and madness, then, the classification of mental disorders and the identification of normal functioning developed since the early twentieth century have established the full perspective of modern scientific medicine.

A social view of madness has also appeared in the twentieth century, partly as an addition to the medical model, and partly as a rival to it. In the former case, medicine has increasingly recognised that some diseases are caused by social factors such as working environment and life style, and that good health is socially defined. Thus in 1948 the World Health Organisation constitution suggested that health should be defined as 'a complete state of physical, mental and social well-being, and not merely the absence of illness.' In recent years it has been discovered for example that marriage and other significant life events can affect an individual's susceptibility to illness. Thus, Brown and Harris (1978) were able to explain almost entirely why young women became clinically depressed by looking at their adult relationships, child care responsibilities and employment.

However, a more critical thrust within the social view of madness has also developed which directly challenges medical competence to define and treat in this area. One of the most influential origins of this view is undoubtedly Parsons (1964) who has argued that in the USA societal values centre around notions of health, and therefore deviation is more likely to be considered a problem of illness rather than law, ritual purity or political commitment. This is not to say that alternative or competing evaluations will not exist but that, where a particularly deviant phenomenon has newly arisen or is ambiguously regarded, then the central values of the society concerned will be influential in determining not only how a particularly deviant phenomenon is evaluated, but also how the particular deviants are handled and what methods are deemed appropriate to their treatment and control. Thus, Parson's identification of the American commitment to health values accounts in part for the process of the medicalisation of social problems. Parsons suggests that there is a 'sick role' into which the sick are placed which allows them legitimately to give up certain responsibilities such as work, but only in return for a commitment to co-operate with their treatment and to return to work as soon as possible.

From this point of view madness is deviancy for which the medical profession has been given the right of definition, control and treatment. It does not therefore presume that medicine works in its own terms. Indeed, two writers in particular have, on these grounds, cast doubt on the whole psychiatric enterprise. Scheff (1966) suggests that madness (mental illness) is a label which has been placed on those deviants for whom we have no alternative explanation. That is, they are not criminal, drunk, physically ill, etc., and hence they are placed in a 'residual category' for rule breakers, labelled 'mentally ill'. In addition, he suggests that those who are relatively powerless are likely to be labelled by those who are relatively powerful. Thus psychiatrists are disproportionately white, male and middle class, while the mentally ill are disproportionately black, female and working class. A closely related argument has been developed by Szasz (1972) who suggests that mental illness is a myth generated by the mistaken application of the medical model, designed for physical disorders, to people's 'problems in living'.

Both Scheff and Szasz rely upon making a relatively discontinuous break between physical and social reality. Szasz in particular suggests that psychiatry should confine itself to the world of organic (i.e. brain) disorder, and leave other problems alone. Both writers emphasise the illegitimacy of psychiatric involvement in an area of social uncertainty, in which cultural norms and social power are more appropriately seen as the determinants of events, than the effects of medically defined pathogens.

Bureaucracy and professionalisation: the right to define illness

The right to define certain behavioural deviations as illness, it is often assumed, is tied to the rise of science, and that medicine as the most prominent profession to utilise scientific principles thereby becomes the leading professional beneficiary. Thus, Freidson states (1970, p. 303):

> What is distinct about a complex civilisation like ours, compared to a simple society, is the existence of special classes of men who are engaged on a full-time basis in creating knowledge, formulating laws, morals, and procedures, and applying knowledge and moral principles to concrete cases.

These special classes, usually called professions, become part of the official social order and thereby achieve the right to impose their definitions on the rest of society. This is not to deny that special classes with specialised knowledge did not exist in primitive societies, but that they did not achieve the power to impose their definitions on the rest of society.

One particular study of epilepsy in a primitive culture illustrates the relationship between lay and professional definitions and the implications of such a relationship for the treatment of epileptics (Aall-Jilek, 1965). The Wapogoro regard epilepsy as a disease affecting families and when anyone has an epileptic seizure it is regarded as a catastrophe for the whole family. When a western-trained physician such as Aall-Jilek started to treat some of the epileptics herself, she found it necessary to operate within the context of traditional evaluations and beliefs in order to make her treatment effective. Obviously, she had a different definition of epilepsy, seeing it as an individual neurological mal-function, but she had to administer her drugs by involving the whole family in ensuring that individual epileptics took their tablets. Additionally, in order to help her better understand and treat epilepsy among the Wapogoro, she constructed family trees and family case histories, despite the fact that western medical science would argue that there is very little of a hereditary element in epilepsy and, consequently, that epilepsy does not run in families.

However, the relationship between professional and lay definitions is not simply a function of the development/under-development of the economy, nor the industrial/non-industrial state of the particular society, for even in developed industrial societies, some professions lose the right to define some behaviours as deviant. Thus, the clergy as a profession would no longer claim the right to define epilepsy as demonic possession, though one or two individual clergymen might.

Scott (1970, p. 271), working within the interactionist paradigm, attempts to make some generalised statements about this relationship between lay and professional constructions of the stigmatised meanings associated with various illnesses and handicaps:

Expert conceptions of stigma reflect prevailing cultural values, attitudes and beliefs. In a sense it is inevitable. Experts must use the native tongue in order to communicate their constructed meanings to laymen and the modes of expression that a language affords are grounded in the core values of a culture. Moreover, it is laymen who usually grant legitimacy to experts' claims to special knowledge about stigma; any constructive meanings that are dissonant with lay values, beliefs and attitudes will probably be rejected as nonsensical.

Nonetheless, as organised intervention programmes develop for the stigmatised, so the organisational process becomes more and more bureaucratic and these bureaucratising processes both shape and reflect professional constructions and definitions. These constructed definitions then filter through to the clients of the organisations, the stigmatised themselves, who as Scott forcefully shows then come to accept these definitions, for failure to operate within the conceptions of the professional and his organisation means failure to get the services and benefits that they provide. Thus Scott sees the process of bureaucratisation as the intervening variable between the level of development of the society and the ability of professionals to impose their constructed meanings on the rest of society.

Of all the professions that have obtained the right to define deviations, the medical profession is undoubtedly the most powerful; and the question then becomes, how did they attain this powerful position in modern industrial society? Parry and Parry argue that much sociological theorising about class has concentrated on processes of individual mobility and failed to consider how groups of professional associations can achieve group mobility. They achieve this collective mobility through, what Parry and Parry call, professionalism, which for them (1976, p. 83) is:

A strategy for controlling an occupation in which colleagues, who are in a formal sense equal, set up a system of self-government. It involves restriction of entry to an occupation through the control of education, training and the process of qualification. Another aspect is the exercise of formal and informal management of members' conduct in respects which are defined as relevant to the collective interests of the occupation. Occupational solidarity and closure are used to regulate the supply of services to the market. This serves also to provide a basis for the domination of institutions, organisations and other occupations associated with them. Finally, there is the reinforcement of this situation by the acquisition of State support in order to obtain, if possible, a legal monopoly backed by legal sanctions.

Whether the medical profession has achieved its power as a concommitant of the bureaucratisation process or as a result of upward social mobility, it is usually assumed that various deviations have been brought under the control of the medical profession by the process of medical imperialism. The argument goes something like this: the medical profession occupies a very important and powerful position in the class structure of society, sustained through its almost exclusive control over specialised knowledge related to crucial issues like life and death and its ability to control entry into its own ranks. Thus it is not only able to determine who is and is not ill but, to define which areas of behavioural deviation are appropriate for medical intervention. But not all writers would agree that the medicalisation process stems from either the achievement of political power or the occupational strategy of professional imperialism. Zola (1972, p. 487), in many ways one of the severest critics of modern medicine, argues thus:

Moreover, this is not occurring through the political power physicians hold or can influence, but it is largely an insidious and often undramatic phenomenon accomplished by medicalising much of daily living, by making medicine and the labels 'ill' and 'healthy' relevant to an ever-increasing part of human existence . . . nor is this extension into society the result of any professional imperialism for this leads us to think of the issue in terms of misguided human efforts or motives. If we search for the why of this phenomena, we will see instead that it is rooted in our increasingly complex technological and bureaucratic system – a system which had led us down the path of the reluctant reliance upon experts.

Additionally, the consumers of medical services represent such a vast heterogeneous group of individuals that it is difficult to articulate complaints or challenge dominant definitions of particular behavioural deviations. What is more, many of the customers are only too willing to give up autonomy over particular areas of life, for as Johnson (1972, p. 43) reminds us:

Medical practice intrudes into areas of social taboo relating to personal privacy and bodily functions, as well as areas of culturally defined ritual significance such as birth and death.

The efficacy of treatment

Undoubtedly, the most important factor in the achievement of the right to treat a wide variety of deviations has been the enormous success which scientific medicine appears to have had in treating physical illness. However, this apparent success has been criticised from within the profession as misleading. For example, Cochrane (1972) has argued that a great deal of current medical practice is determined by custom and the preferences of individual consultants rather than by scientific knowledge. He shows that there is great variation in practice from hospital to hospital, not because of medical whim, but because there are too few systematic evaluations of specific practices. He argues therefore that all of medicine should be subjected to RCTs (randomised controlled trials) to determine what works and what does not. This paradox of both a reputation based on science and a lack of scientific evaluation has been explained by McKeown (1979) as a result of the medical misuse of history. McKeown suggests that most of the dramatic reduction of disease and death which has occurred since the mid-nineteenth century (that is since the modern medical profession developed), was caused by environmental factors such as better diet, clean water and drainage, and antiseptics. Most specific treatments for infectious diseases were developed after the bulk of the disease had disappeared. He suggests, therefore, that for medicine to claim the benefit of this improvement in health status, and for it to use this to justify current practices, is specious.

In terms of specific treatments for mental illness and epilepsy, the medical profession has had a struggle to find effective agents. Some, such as insulin coma treatment, have been dramatically exposed, after years of use, as ineffective (Bourne, 1953). Others, such as electro-convulsive therapy and lobotomy, continue to provoke heated debate within the profession (Pippard and Ellam, 1981; Kendell, 1981), about which disorders it should be used with and what the costs in terms of side effects and misuse (e.g. punishment) are. A third, and probably most widespread, therapeutic agent is pharmaceutical. A drug 'revolution' since the late 1950s has greatly changed psychiatry which can now control delusions, moods and convulsions. However, controversy still occurs about whether such drugs actually cure rather than contain mental illness (Scull, 1977), and whether the benefits are worth the sometimes considerable side effects.

The rise in importance of drug therapy in particular has enabled medicine to expand its area of treatment rights. For example, many children who cause behavioural problems in school and would have been the concern of the headmaster, parents, local policeman or the School Board, are now given the label 'hyperkinetic' and subjected to drug therapy as the most appropriate means of treatment (Conrad, 1976; Box, 1981). However, many such deviations or illnesses (including most epilepsy), have no immediately apparent physical causes, and their etiology may well be psychological, economic or social. Hence, it may not be appropriate to treat such behaviours according to the model that has proved so successful in combatting physical illnesses. Unfortunately, when the success rate of medical treatment of mental illness, epilepsy, homosexuality, alcoholism and so on, fails to match the success rate for the treatment of measles, smallpox or tuberculosis, then explanations are usually couched in terms of deficiencies in knowledge, rather than the inappropriateness of the treatment method. And hope is held out, therefore, that in the future, deficiencies in knowledge will be remedied and the medical model will triumph.

It should be stressed, however, that as the process of medicalisation of deviant behaviour proceeds, this is not solely due to the entrepreneurial or imperialistic activities of the medical profession. The substitution of a treatment ethic for a punitive one reflects a shift in social values towards humanitarianism. And in many cases this substitution has benefits for the deviants themselves. Conrad (1976, p. 18) points out:

Hyperactive children are now considered to have an illness rather than to be disruptive, disobedient, over-active, problem children. They are not likely to be the bad boy of the classroom; they are children with a medical disorder. Clearly there are some real humanitarian benefits to be gained by such a medical conceptualisation of deviant behaviour. There is less condemnation of the deviants (they have an illness, it is not their fault) and perhaps less social stigma.

So, too, with epileptics; undoubtedly many epileptics are better off as a result of anti-convulsant drug therapy but as has already been pointed out, this is not without costs in terms of side-effects such treatments often produce.

Social policy
Conventional wisdom about social policies that affect epilpetics and the mentally ill has been touched on in the earlier section on state policy. There we suggested that state policies in this area could only be understood as part of more general policy developments in the nineteenth and twentieth centuries. As such, we concluded, medicalisation was never a conscious policy. In fact recent social policy has been dominated by a general desire to limit public expenditure, whichever party has been in power. This change from the expansionist days of the 1950s and 1960s has been significant timing for the mental health field which, as we have already described, has been in the throes of a considerable redistribution of effort from hospital centred activity, to medical and social care out in the community. Public opinion about mental illness has in general supported such a move, displaying an increasingly humanitarian acceptance of these disorders as illnesses (Crocetti, 1974; Rabkin, 1975). However, a chronic shortage of funds has restricted the development of community care.

The nature of medicalisation has also allowed social policies to be shaped by the internal priorities and preferences of the medical profession itself. These have not favoured psychiatry, which is the least popular choice for medical students (Clare, 1976). Consequently, the National Health Service relies heavily on immigrant medical labour – most of its psychiatrists were born overseas (*Royal Commission on the National Health Service*, 1979). While this may not be of relevance for straightforward physical medicine, the significance of cultural and social factors in psychiatric diagnosis and treatment makes such tasks more difficult for overseas doctors (Littlewood and Lipsedge, 1982).

A further consequence of the lowly status of psychiatry within medicine is that since general health policy is heavily influenced by medical interests, mental health policy has received relatively little emphasis, even within the already constrained public expenditure budgets of recent years. Combined with a steady pressure to reduce the numbers in mental hospitals, these factors have resulted in an accumulation of ex-patients amongst the homeless, in cheap boarding houses, or in alternative institutions such as prisons.

A summary of conventional explanations

We can draw together the kind of arguments we have encountered so far into three types, in preparation for the final section of this chapter which considers more critical approaches. The first has suggested that medicalisation is a consequence of both the rise of science and the progress of humanitarian ideas. Thus medicalisation is seen as largely beneficial and marks the pinnacle in the march of evolutionary progress. While the consequent move from physical punishment to deprivation of freedom to medical treatment appears progressive, it is by no means certain that the three main forms of medical treatment – drug therapy, surgery or hospitalisation – are perceived in exactly that light by many of the recipients.

The second argument has suggested that medicalisation is the consequence of struggles between various groups to impose their own particular set of meanings upon particular social phenomena. At present, the medical profession, as a consequence of the power it has in modern society, is able to impose its own definitions upon a wide variety of such phenomena, though why medical labels stick with regard to some groups and not others is always an empirical question. Thus, for example, Alcoholics Anonymous in the 1930s were forced to struggle to get alcoholism accepted as a disease; while homophile organisations in the 1970s campaigned successfully to have homosexuality rejected from the American Medical Association list of identifiable mental illnesses. In his recent book in this area, Rothman (1980) has thus characterised the outcome as a struggle between conscience and convenience.

The third argument is that medicalisation is consequent upon the rationalisation of social values and social organisation with its concomitant bureaucratisation and professionalisation. Doctors, as one of the best organised and most powerful groups, were thus able to achieve dominant positions within these proliferating bureaucracies and were able to spread their influence through a process sometimes referred to as 'medical imperialism'. A related aspect of medicalisation concerns the Protestant Ethic:

There is a historical link between the damnation metaphor and the contemporary medical model of deviance. The latter, which classifies people as healthy or sick, reflects the same dichotomous assumptions as do Calvinist notions of elect and damned. Furthermore, the Protestant ethic of predestination is at least partly responsible for the belief in man's inability to change, which underlies much of the biophysical determinism of the medical model.

(Conrad and Schneider, 1980, p. 264)

Insofar as the Protestant ethic requires hard work within the discipline of the factory, and the smooth integration of human and machine labour, epileptics and the mentally ill have been at odds with the dominant values and organisation of capitalism.

Many accounts of medicalisation combine parts of all three of these arguments, and hance share their weaknesses, which we set out below. Nevertheless they have opened up the possibility of a critical interpretation which can take account of the negative aspects of medicalisation, which are graphically described by Szasz with regard to epilepsy:

In the initial decades of this century much was learned about epilepsy. As a result physicians gained better control of the epileptic process (which sometimes results in seizures). The desire to control the disease, however, seems to go hand in hand with the desire to control the diseased person. Thus, epileptics were both helped and harmed; they were benefitted insofar as their illness was more accurately diagnosed and better treated; they were injured insofar as they, as persons, were stigmatised and socially segregated . . . It has taken decades of work, much of it still unfinished, to undo some of the oppressive social effects of 'medical progress' in epilepsy, and to restore the epileptic to the social status he enjoyed before his disease became so well understood. Paradoxically then, what is good for epilepsy may not be good for the epileptic.

(Szasz, 1966, p. 3)

Unconventional Wisdom

While we accept that the previous explanations we have discussed contain some validity, they are weak in two respects. Firstly, they are frequently partial, in that they consider selected elements such as specific social policies, or medical practices, detached from general social changes, particularly the development of capitalism since the eighteenth century. Secondly, they rely heavily on social values, ideas, or perceptions as the origin of their explanations, without considering where those ideas come from, or indeed whether ideas are post hoc rationalisations rather than the originators of change.

A revisionist history

We can begin to sketch an alternative explanation by returning to the history of medicalisation. The commonest alternative to a history of progressive reform has been to see the problem of deviant groups like the mad as a problem of social control.

The idea of social control has however varied considerably from one author to another. Ingleby (1983) suggests four variants. The first is identified with the work of Rothman (1971, 1980, 1983). His approach fits neatly with the idea of madness as deviancy, whose control is required as a functional necessity in an increasingly bureaucratic and rational society. As such the social order is seen as threatened by social change in the nineteenth century, and consequently in greater need of social control, of which the labelling of mental illness is merely one aspect. Rothman builds up a systematic explanation which pulls together the various approaches we have already outlined in the previous section on 'conventional wisdom', into a more coherent whole. As such his work is an improvement upon the eclecticism we noted in criticism at the beginning of this section; but in common with functionalism it nevertheless relies upon a rather metaphysical 'need for social control', unrelated to specific interests or activities.

A second variant extends the model of psychiatric opportunism we have already examined in the notion of medical imperialism (Strong, 1979). Partly in reaction to the generalities of functionalism, this approach stresses the interests and activities of the agents of social control. However, these agents discussed for example by Scull (1979) and Conrad (1981) are not operating freely, but only to the extent that their services are useful to a political élite. For example, Conrad suggests that it is not enough that medical control is available based on the notion, however tenuous, that an organic pathology exists; it is in addition essential that the behaviours concerned are defined as deviant by a powerful social group, and that alternative or traditional forms of control are no longer seen as efficient, acceptable or available (pp. 111–14).

A third variant merely extends this argument by suggesting that doctors are not serving an arbitrary social group, but rather that under capitalism they are privileged servants of a ruling capitalist class. As a consequence of the transition from feudalism to capitalism, a number of marginal groups such as people with epilepsy were unable to meet the demands of the new productive system for a fit and efficient workforce.

The effect of this was to loosen the bonds which tied almost everyone to the feudal mode of production and consequently give rise to a section of the population who had no appropriate roles to play or functions to perform. These 'dangerous classes' posed a threat to social stability and hence there was a need to provide appropriate means of control to reduce their potential threat.

This alternative account therefore suggests that the need for social control within capitalism was the crucial factor. The basis for such an explanation has been sketched out by Rusche and Kirckheimer (1939, p. 5) in their discussion of changing methods of punishment:

Every system of production tends to discover punishments which correspond to its productive relationships. It is thus necessary to investigate the origin and fate of penal systems, the use or avoidance of specific punishments, and the intensity of penal practices as they are determined by social forces, above all by economic and fiscal forces.

They go on to argue (p. 6):

It is self-evident that enslavement as a form of punishment is impossible without a slave economy, that prison labour is impossible without manufacture or industry, that money fines for all classes of society are impossible without a money economy.

The initial means of social control under early capitalism was the institution – the workhouse, the prison, the asylum and the epileptic colony. As well as performing the function of segregating the productive from the non-productive, the institution also performed an ideological function in that it stood as a visible reminder to the productive of their fate should they fail to conform to the new work ethic of this capitalist mode of production.

The fourth variant of social control theory takes up and focuses explicitly on this last point about ideology, in that social control is seen as a result of the creation of a particular conception of social order, with its own distinct limits and opportunities. Thus Foucault (1973) suggests that the medical profession literally created the body as a system of organs, rather than discovered some pre-existing truth about the body, by developing a particular way of looking at it – the medical 'gaze'. Similarly, Armstrong (1983) has argued that in the twentieth century this medical gaze was extended outwards via the dispensary and the social survey to create an environmental view of influences in the body in a process he describes as 'political anatomy'. From this perspective, medicine exercises social control through its determination of the social knowledge of illnesses – a closely similar argument to our earlier discussion of the conventional sociology of the professions. Despite the obscurity of much writing in this school, which talks of 'archaeologies' and 'genealogies' of knowledge and power, ultimately it explains processes such as medicalisation by merely describing them as part of the larger development of the modern intellectual age, much as Max Weber did before for the modern social age of the bureaucracy.

Science or ideology?

These different approaches to social control help us to make stronger connections between the process of medicalisation, and more general social developments, both in terms of the demand for control technologies and the rationalisation for them. The latter, we observed earlier, drew heavily on the burgeoning of science in the nineteenth century. Yet to accept science as the gradual revelation of truth, is as naive as to accept history as the gradual achievement of progress. The scientific rationalisation for medical intervention can thus be reconceptualised as ideology, in the same way as medical intervention has been reconceptualised as social control. Although Foucault's ideas about knowledge indicate its potential relativity to time and place, his work as we have stressed is descriptive rather than explanatory. For the latter we must look for different accounts.

In Chapter 1 we suggested that ideology could amount either to deliberate deception or to a particular view of the world shaped by self-interest, social norms and so on. In the world of science, while there are deliberate deceptions from time to time, these are rare. More often scientific ideas have been exposed as based on historically specific or culturally bound perceptions. We can look back with the benefit of hindsight to the Copernican debate over the relative movement of earth and sun (Koestler, 1959), or the more recent debates on the Darwinian theory of evolution. We have already mentioned earlier in the chapter Rush's disease categories of 'anarchia' and 'revolutiona', and only 100 years ago masturbation was blamed for madness.

In this century, controversy is still common in the field of psychiatry over the scientific status of madness. Thus in a recent study, Trombley (1981) has revealed in detail the social and cultural influences on the eminent doctors who diagnosed Virginia Woolf as insane; and we have already discussed the views of Scheff and Szasz that mental illness is a scientific myth. However, the source of medical legitimacy, pure science, has also been criticised. Sociologists examining the activities of scientists have discovered that scientific practice is a highly social activity. The public image of the disinterested pursuit of truth is a myth (Mulkay, 1979). Dominant approaches to scientific questions are maintained through the careful exercise of power in the shape of research grants and jobs. Jealousy and competition over the ownership of knowledge are common, while reputations owe as much to impression management as to good science.

Of course, just as medicalisation can help the mad and the epileptic even while controlling them, so scientific infighting can still reveal truths. However, we have grounds to be sceptical. This point is central to more radical critiques of science which point out that modern scientific bureaucracies are closely influenced by commercial criteria. Psychoactive drugs are invented because they are profitable (Klass, 1975), and their efficacy depends on the criteria for judgement: patients usually feel worse, but symptoms are controlled. Drug treatment works more or less, therefore, depending on your point of view. A similar point is made by Scull (1981) about pre-medical 'moral treatment': it depended upon the patient internalising social control before physical restraints could be dispensed with.

Thus it can be argued that truth cannot be divorced from the circumstances of its production, since science, including medical science, is an organised labour process (*Radical Science Journal*, 1981). We shall develop this point at greater length in the final chapter.

The nature of madness and epilepsy

Does this focus on social control and medical ideology change our understanding of the nature of madness? The discussion in the last few pages reinforces the grounds for our earlier scepticism about madness as illness. However, this notion that madness is a label given by the powerful to the powerless, mediated by a scientific ideology, has itself come under increasing criticism.

The basis of this criticism is that social control theories imply that there is a direct relationship between the deviant and the agent of control. In fact, the process is typically complicated by the involvement of the family or other intimate social group in the process of deviance identification. Bott (1976) and Goffman (1969) have both described how families frequently use hospitals or doctors to 'do something about' their intolerable members. Similarly, one of us (Oliver 1979) has shown from a study of a small number of adolescents with epilepsy that those with supportive families were far less likely to end up in penal or mental institutions than those without. While these findings imply that the family should care for its dependent members, to the detriment of women as the typical carer (Finch and Groves, 1983), the psychiatric profession has been quick to redefine the family rather than the individual as sick. It seems then that while madness may not be illness, it could nevertheless be a real condition which offends other social intimates.

Ingleby (1982) suggests that the social control of moral behaviour is too simple an explanation of psychiatric practice. As we have seen, Scheff and Szasz rely on a radical separation between mental and physical illness. Yet the latter can be as subject to great uncertainty in diagnosis as the former (Sedgwick, 1982). The implication here is that either one rejects the medicalisation of physical illnesses which are at all ambiguous, or one admits that so-called mental illnesses are at least referring to a condition of greater substance than deviant behaviour.

Morgan (1975) develops this point by suggesting that all illness has two components – a culturally defined exemption from moral responsibility for the condition, plus some detectable biological process. However, mental illness and much epilepsy has often contained the first, with little or no evidence of the second. And this is the point at which, for example, Szasz's critique of mythical illnesses is directed. Morgan suggests that the modern world of social change and uncertainty invites where possible a reinterpretation of personal difficulties in terms of the stable and orderly world of things, that is in terms of science. Indeed, he suggests (p. 280) that:

We might expect to find the ideological articulation of these beliefs most evident in relation to those areas of social experience which, mediated by moral and emotional conflicts, paradoxically least conform to the positivistic conception of order represented by the world of inanimate things.

Rather than a specific social control strategy, then, medicalisation is an ideological reinterpretation of uncertainty as certainty via the mediation of science. Ingleby (1982) develops this argument to suggest that, in terms of Morgan's second component of illness, the specific disease-like process in mental illness is the quality of 'unintelligibility'. The failure of someone to keep their place or behave in accordance with what Hilbourne (1973, p. 499) calls 'the normal pattern of social exchange and reciprocity' poses a threat to the micro-social order, the painstakingly constructed social reality. Goffman (1971, p. 450) graphically spells out the consequences of such a failure with regard to mental illness:

The manic gives up everything a person can be, and gives up everything we make out of our jointly guarded dealings. His doing so, and doing so for any of a multitude of reasons, reminds us of what our everything is, and then reminds us that this everything is not very much. A somewhat similar lesson is taught by other categories of trouble makers who do not keep their place.

However, since unintelligibility is highly dependent on cultural context, its detection is liable to dispute and hence liable to the political manipulations which radical critics of psychiatry have documented over the years. And here the possibility of the social control of moral deviance re-enters, but via the control of those rules and conventions by which unintelligibility is judged. Taylor (1979, p. 107) makes this point with regard to epilepsy:

Every fit reinforces the view of witnesses that the epileptic cannot be relied upon to participate fully in society, since he is liable at any time to go out of control. Therefore, unless he can be cured he must be set apart; he must be reformed, or else rejected.

Clearly, the question of what criteria should be used raises the possibility that the incidence and nature of madness can vary, so that even everyday 'normality' may be critically redefined. For example, a theme in the work of R. D. Laing (1965) and D. Cooper (1970) is that individual madness may really be an intelligible response to a maddening society or family; and Taylor and Cohen (1976) provide a general theoretical framework within which it is possible to conceptualise fits as 'momentary slips through the fabric' of everyday life. In a similar fashion, Freud reinterpreted jokes, slips of the tongue and dreams as neurotic (Sayers, 1984), and Marx argued that the apparently independent reality of market commodities was really a fetish – i.e. a projection and alienation of powers actually residing in people.

In the everyday world of medical, and psychiatric practice, however, such critical revisions do not occur. Rather, a professional aura legitimates administrative decisions which originate in the world of commonsense. And it is the relevance or irrelevance of this commonsense to a person's experience which Ingleby (1983, p. 182) suggests determines whether they become mentally ill:

A person's capacity to confront his or her own experiences consciously, without becoming mentally ill, will depend at least in part on the adequacy of the shared world of interpretations that makes up his or her 'ego'. To the extent that this world is dominated by ideology, that is by mystifications and delusions that foster the status quo, it will inevitably be harder for a person to come to terms with his or her own reality. Thus, people experiencing stressful emotions will seek to interpret those emotions in a way consistent with their general view of the world; the ideology that they share, however, may deter them from perceiving the true significance of the emotions – indeed, from perceiving them at all.

Thus, Ingleby suggests, if, for example, worlds of (un)employment or parenthood do not live up to their ideals, and if we believe those ideologies strongly, any failures may be literally incomprehensive to us and lead to depression rather than anger or frustration.

Not surprisingly, this approach to madness predicts considerable social variation in the manifestation of mental illness. And indeed in addition to historical growth, madness varies considerably by class (Schwab and Schwab, 1978), race (Littlewood and Lipsedge, 1982), and gender (Brown and Harris, 1978); although no figures are available which would enable us to make similar assertions about the epidemiology of epilepsy.

Social policy
In the twentieth century we can relate social policy in the mental health field closely to the requirements of capitalist production. While we have criticised the crude version of social control as an explanation of

madness, pressures for control arising from the labour market can be seen clearly. As the conditions of capitalist production changed in the twentieth century so the labour needs of capital shifted from the need for a mass of unskilled workers to a more limited need of skilled ones. As a result of this, the Welfare State arose as a means of ensuring the supply of skill, and in order to 'pacify' the ever-increasing army of the unemployed, the under-employed and the unemployable. Consequently, an infrastructure of state employees has arisen whose job it is to pacify this army and hence we have the 'structural pre-conditions' for a move towards community care. It now becomes cheaper to provide care within the community, especially against the twin pressures of demands to cut public expenditure and the increasing pressure from employees working in institutions for higher wages and a limited working week. In both the 'incarceration' and 'decarceration' movements, medicine has had a crucial role to play, but a materialist account suggests that in acting as an agent of control, this role was determined by the needs of capital. Historically we have seen that it was the institution which preceded doctors, who were eventually imported to facilitate increasing specialisation amongst different kinds of institution. It was not the doctors who decided that institutions were appropriate forms of treatment for their charges. Similarly, Scull (1977) has shown that it was not medical technology (chemotherapy) which produced the decarceration movement, which was well advanced long before advances in this technology, but rather it was this technology which was developed as a consequence of the need to control more and more potential disruptives now living in the community.

There can be little doubt that medicine, or rather the medical profession, has had a crucial role in 'rendering deviants harmless' at the cheapest cost possible. While Scull is sceptical about the effectiveness of what he calls 'the technological fix', there can be little doubt that the prescription and administration of drugs does significantly contribute to the maintenance of potentially disruptive deviants within the community in a socially harmless condition. Anti-epileptic medication, for example, can prevent the majority of fits in approximately 80 per cent of diagnosed epileptics (College of General Practitioners, 1960) and it is solely the prerogative of doctors to prescribe this medication.

This is not to suggest that the medical profession has expropriated almost complete power in the area of social control, but as the title of Zola's (1972) influential paper suggests, they are the 'agents' of social control. This is spelled out more clearly by Navarro (1976, p. 121):

One of the functions of the service bureaucracies – including the medical bureaucracy – is to legitimise and protect the system and its power relations. One aspect of this protection is social control – the channelling of dissatisfaction – . . . But to believe that social control is due to the culture of medicine and the pervasiveness of industrialisation is to ignore the basic question of who regulates and most benefits from that control. An analysis of our societies shows that the service bureaucracies – including the medical ones – although willing accomplices in that control, are not the major benefactors. The ultimate benefactor in any social control intervention in any system is the dominant class in that system.

So medicine benefits capitalism and the capitalist ruling class in that the medical profession acts as an effective and relatively cheap agent of social control. But it does more than that (ibid., p. 208):

it contributes to the legitimation of capitalism. And it is because of the legitimation function that the medical profession is serving the interests of the capitalist system and the capitalist class.

This legitimation is performed through what Szasz (1974) has called 'the ideology of mental health and illness' which extends to almost all aspects of society. Scheff (1975) has further suggested that specific labels such as schizophrenia are also ideological labels in that they provide residual categories in which to place otherwise unexplainable deviant behaviour. So too with epilepsy then – it is currently estimated that there are 300,000 epileptics in this country, but there are many more who have black-outs, momentary losses of consciousness, fits of temper, hysteria and even fits of laughter. Hence the label epilepsy is also ideological in that it provides a label for the residual category of those having fits and it legitimates the social control of those so labelled whether it be by surgery, drug therapy or confinement. It further legitimates these techniques of control in that they often pass for treatment and hence are justified for the good of the deviant concerned. This legitimation has been called 'the therapeutic impact of social reaction' (Young, 1975, p. 65).

Some Concluding Remarks

Undoubtedly, then, the medical profession has acquired a crucial place in the process of defining and treating various deviations as illnesses and as a number of writers have pointed out, this is not without drawbacks. Illich (1975, p. 22) is probably the severest critic of modern medicine and argues that much illness is iatrogenic, that is:

The sum of malpractice, negligence, professional callousness, political mal-distribution, medically decreed disability and all the consequences of medical trial and error.

It has been a theme of this chapter that the medical profession has, indeed, iatrogenically created much illness in modern society, not solely or even largely because of the kinds of incompetencies listed by Illich – but by acquiring the right to define certain deviant behaviours as illness instead of lunacy, immorality, irresponsibility, or just plain evil.

Medicine has thus transformed behaviours from one category to another, thereby labelling them as 'illness', and thus can be accused of conceptual iatrogenesis rather than malpractice or inefficiency.

It is often assumed, too, that to define and treat deviations as illnesses is more humane (Zola 1972, p. 489):

The assumption is (thus) readily made that medical involvement in social problems leads to the removal from religious and legal scrutiny and thus from moral and punitive consequences. In turn, the problems are placed under medical and scientific scrutiny and thus in objective and therapeutic circumstances.

However, this argument ignores a number of important factors. Firstly, punishment is a subjective experience and while medical treatment may be objectively (from the point of view of the doctor) therapeutic, it may still be subjectively painful. Additionally, although treatment may be in the patient's own good, his opinions concerning his treatment are usually ignored on the grounds that he is a layman who lacks the special knowledge and detachment that would qualify him to have his voice heard. Finally, the application of the label 'illness' does not automatically provide absolution from individual responsibility, accountability and moral judgment.

The final dangers that should be mentioned with regard to medicalisation of deviant behaviour are that the ascription of the label 'sick' both individualises and de-politicises the particular form of deviation. For example, recently medicalisation has intruded into a number of new areas, particularly the law and education. Thus, we have seen opened a number of law clinics, set up to grant access to legal advice to a substantial section of the population who are unable to obtain it under the existing system; and a number of remedial reading clinics have also been set up to teach two million illiterates to read. It is not disputed that these clinics have been very successful in helping large numbers of individuals, but by opting for individual solutions and utilising the medical model, albeit implicitly by their own choice of nomenclature, they direct attention away from other issues. The fact that large numbers of people in a formally democratic and egalitarian society are denied access to law and legal process, or that more than a million people can be discharged from a universal education system unable to read or write, are matters of great social and political importance. To send such people to clinics merely locates their problems at the individual rather than at the societal level.

In conclusion, we can note with both Kittrie and Freidson the dangers of the medicalising process if it continues unchecked:

The therapeutic model now offers the only system of social control unlimited in its potential applications, for by its very aims the therapeutic state is required to look beyond the question of past misconduct and into those factors of morals, welfare and health which might produce a present or a future state of dangerousness.

(Kittrie, 1971, p. 362)

A profession and a society which are so concerned with physical and functional wellbeing as to sacrifice civil liberty and moral integrity must inevitably press for a scientific environment similar to that provided for laying hens on progressive chicken farms – hens who produce eggs industriously and have no disease or other cares.

(Freidson, 1970, p. 356)

5 Delinquency and Disillusion
Peter Ely

Constructing the Problem

The amount of crime committed by juveniles, and whether this is increasing or decreasing, has received a good deal of research attention. The official statistics are the most obvious source of data. But they are only an outcome of a series of discretionary decisions taken at different stages of the process of reporting, recording and clearing up crimes.

Data not reliable

'Victimisation' studies, in which a sample of the public is interviewed to ascertain the frequency with which individuals have been the victims of crime, show that many offences, mainly of a minor nature, are not reported to the police if the victim feels that there is little to be gained from doing so.

The police also exercise discretion as to whether they record incidents reported to them as crimes. Practice varies significantly between police forces, but the seriousness of the offence is the main deciding factor, and the attitude of the victim, and the context within which the incident occurred (as part of a domestic dispute, for instance) may also play a part.

Once a juvenile suspect has been identified, the police can still decide to deal with him informally, rather than by an official caution or a court appearance. The seriousness of the offence is again a crucial consideration. For less serious offences, the attitude of the complainant, offender, and parents can influence the decision. First offenders and younger juveniles are less likely to be taken to court. Some studies also show a weaker influence from race and social background. In England and Wales, all co-defendants to the same offence must be processed in identical ways, that is either made subject to 'no further action', or officially cautioned, or taken to court. Those denying their participation in the offence cannot be cautioned, and must be taken to court if the police consider them guilty, and the offence sufficiently serious to support this course of action.

Rather than representing a measurement of a discrete and distinct type of behaviour, therefore, the official statistics represent, especially with regard to less serious offences, only a small fraction of juvenile misbehaviour. But Phillips (1979, p. 15) a serving police officer, considers that juveniles are more likely to be detected than adults. They are more likely to confess when interrogated, and to betray other offenders or be betrayed by them. They are more likely to admit to crimes either known or unknown to the police, and to leave indications of their age group at scenes of crime. Parents, schools, and other agencies sometimes assist the police in detecting them. Therefore a much higher proportion of incidents which have been officially recorded as 'crimes', and have been committed by juveniles, are 'cleared up' by the police, than the proportion which are 'cleared up' which have been committed by adults. Juveniles will therefore be less well represented than adults among the unknown offenders whose crimes are not cleared up. The one exception to this picture is that there is little reason to doubt that juveniles are disproportionately well represented among those committing offences of criminal damage ('vandalism'), with regard to which there is an exceptionally low detection and clear-up rate. The total cost of vandalism may be comparable with that of stolen property.

Estimating the overall trends in juvenile crime is a complex matter. In a review of most of the research, Rutter and Giller (1983, pp. 88–9) conclude that 'it is virtually certain that much of the apparent rise in the numbers of offenders has been illusory'. Recidivists have been responsible for more of the increase than have first offenders, so that acts of delinquency have increased to a greater extent than the number of people committing such acts. Changes in legislation and in police recording practice have accounted for some small part of the apparent increase. There has also been a tendency to 'widen the net' so that individuals who would previously have been dealt with informally, are now officially processed and hence appear in the statistics. There may also have been a tendency for the public to report to the police offences which they would not have reported hitherto.

Nevertheless, as we have discussed, there are sound reasons for assuming that, even when all of these factors have been generously taken into account, a real rise remains. The evidence for a real rise in crime rate is also greater for the 1950s and 1960s time period than it is for the 1970s decade. It seems rather dubious whether there has been any significant increase since the mid-70s and the appearance is of a levelling off, or even slight fall, in the overall crime rate in recent years.

(Rutter and Giller, 1983, p. 89)

It would appear that, contrary to the impression usually given, juvenile crime has not increased more than adult crime. 'The proportionate increase in the number of offences by juveniles has been about the same as for adults'. (Brittan, quoted in Tutt, 1981, p. 253).

Finally, it would be inappropriate to minimise either the seriousness or the extent of the problem. One in five males appear before the courts before they reach the age of twenty, and in certain inner city areas this proportion reaches a third or more. Quite apart from the material and personal losses resulting from the offences themselves, the organisations which process these crimes and offenders absorb very significant resources.

Functional for society?

While in the eyes of the public these costs are dysfunctional to society, sociologists have pointed out that there are functional aspects to crime. Thus Durkheim suggested that crime had an integrative function for society as a whole, sustaining conformity and stability. 'Crime brings together upright consciences and concentrates them' (Durkheim, 1964, p. 81). Marx also indicates benefits to society as a whole, partly in the realm of consciousness:

The criminal produces an impression, partly moral and partly tragic, as the case may be, and in this way renders a 'service' by arousing the moral and aesthetic feelings of the public.

(Marx, 1964, p. 375)

But also, materially, crime extends the division of labour by giving rise to all those professions concerned with the law and its enforcement, and stimulates production in every sphere, from literature, and textbooks on law, to the development of currencies resistant to counterfeiting, of chemical analysis to detect the adulteration of commodoties, devices to defend property against theft, and so on.

Box (1971, p. 28) points out that this functional role actually refers, not to the criminal actions themselves, but to society's reaction to them. He considers that this reaction has three functions: it can clarify social rules, perhaps advancing the power of certain interests in the process: it can help maintain such rules, by providing occasions for celebrating them through trials and punishments of offenders: and, it can also lead to modification of the rules. Box places these processes within a political rather than a moral context: 'instead of viewing society as an organic body in which [deviant] parts are cancerous,' he sees society as 'a precarious entity, emerging out of a constant struggle between competing subjective definitions of reality'. (Box, 1971, p. 31). In this respect he considers that the mass media, in reporting the punishments meted out and the remarks of magistrates and judges when passing sentence, perform the same functions as the public punishments of the past; the degradation of the offender, and the transformation of individuals into deviants.

But Walker and Marsh (1984) empirically tested, on a sample of parents, the proposition that severe sentencing will create greater public disapproval of the criminal behaviour in question. They found that while such disapproval was increased by making acts illegal (criminalisation), the severity of sentences did not seem to have an influence. Exceptionally severe sentences tended to cause a backlash of sympathy for the offender. On the other hand, the opinions of fellow parents did affect levels of disapproval. Since the parents seemed to identify with neither the sentencers nor the accused, they took little interest in media reports.

> ... in real life news media reports of sentences do not seem to make much impression, even when they are strikingly lenient or severe, and ... cannot be expected to give repeated publicity to series of sentences which merely exemplify sentencing policy.
>
> (Walker and Marsh, 1984, p. 41)

Most crime reporting in the popular press, however, does not consist of the moralising and rule-celebrating homilies of judges and magistrates but rather the details of the actual crimes, and frequently unsolved, violent crime, the assailants either unknown, young, or black. How is one to explain why victimisation of the elderly, for example, is featured to an extent which is unwarranted by the reported frequency of such offences, tending to create a general apprehension about this form of crime in the minds of the public? It may be a response to market forces, in that the elderly tend to read newspapers. Or it may reflect the outrage to the social rules involved in such offences: the research finding that those actually most likely to be the victims of violent assaults are male, under 30, single, divorced, or separated, who go out drinking and assault other people, (Hough and Mayhew, 1983, p. 27) seems to involve no such outrage.

Manipulating perceptions

Cohen (1972) however, inferred a more conscious use of selective over-reporting when he coined the phrase 'moral panic' to describe the process which takes place when the media report events in such a way as to amplify the extent of the problem, exaggerate the significance of the outrage to society's rules and values, and emphasise the 'alien' nature of the perpetrators. The perception of a disproportionately serious threat to the social fabric is established in the public consciousness, and this has the effect of a self-fulfilling prophecy as more and more deviant acts are redefined in terms of the new object of the panic. This is Cohen's example, was a Bank Holiday disturbance between groups of teenagers ('Mods and Rockers') at Margate.

Subsequent work has indicated that official encouragement can induce such 'moral panics' through the media. Hall et al. (1978b) have carefully demonstrated how the organisation of newspaper journalism requires special 'crime' reporters to cultivate official 'spokesmen', contacts and sources of news in government ministries, the police force and other agencies, upon whom they are dependent for speedily available information – the 'news'. The official statement or 'line' on any issue or incident tends to be sought first as it is the most readily available, and naturally tends to set the parameters of the ensuing discussion. The government's view of the facts is particularly unlikely to be challenged in the area of crime, as alternative views, from offenders for instance, are rarely accessible. Journalists may hesitate to voice strong criticism of the 'official line' themselves for fear that the 'official sources' on which they are dependent for their daily functioning might begin to see them as hostile, and become less co-operative. Thus the structure of media reporting, rather than conspiracy theory, explains why government has disproportionate access to the media. Hall et al., (1978b) locate the origin of the 'moral panic' over 'mugging' in the police force, but infer that leading members of the Conservative Party have made a conscious decision to make the crime problem function as a party political resource, to establish a perception of reality favourable to Conservative interests, and to utilise 'moral panics' in a sustained way to help the party to attain and retain office.

Research has consistently shown that, with the single exception of housebreaking, the poorer sections of the community run the greatest risk of becoming the victims of crime, and are least likely to be able to minimise its effects by private measures such as insurance. Hall et al. (1978b) therefore consider that the fear of crime is likely to operate as an effective resource for social cohesion and control, influencing the less privileged towards acceptance of 'class domination' and the 'educative and ethical leadership of the state'. Through their access to the media, government draws on the latter's supposed capacity to form public opinion rather than express it. The media offer definitions of the situation which reinforce consensual notions – they offer definitions of what significant events are taking place, and also interpretations of how to understand these events. 'Public opinion is constantly and unremittingly tutored in social authoritarian postures by the method of sponsored moral panics' (Hall et al., 1978b, p. 310).

This sociological speculation on the role of the media goes unchallenged by empirical research, as this area of the problem has not attracted attention or funds until recently '. . . fear of crime . . . seems to be exacerbated by the press', comments the head of the Home Office Research Unit (Croft, 1982, pp. 7–8).

Little information is available about public attitudes to crime and punishment . . . it would be interesting, and perhaps useful, to know about the congruence of public opinion and the criminal law, and especially the width of the gap (if any) between the two . . . There is no reliable guide to the attitudes of various groups in terms of age, socio-economic class, or region. It is claimed that, if the general public turned out to be more tolerant of crime and particularly minor crime, and politicians felt obliged to pay deference to those views, then the moral fabric of society would collapse.

The Unit's forthcoming British Crime Survey, a national victimisation study, will investigate perceptions of crime seriousness and public attitudes towards punishment.

Party political interpretations
Taylor (1981) points out that the crime rate is used as a party political weapon with which to attack collectivist policies:

We are saying that if you have a background, a philosophy, let's say, which on the whole . . . treats private effort and private property with some contempt, and does not place the upholding of the rule of law absolutely as the highest priority, then this created an atmosphere in which you get vandalism, disrespect for the law and the vast increase in the crimes which we have seen. And that worries us very much indeed and worries many millions of people.

(Howell 1979, quoted by Taylor, 1981, p. 43)

Taylor suggests that the Labour Party has been unable to use the crime issue in a comparable way because of its commitment to social democracy and the mixed economy of welfare capitalism. But this does not always seem to have been an obstacle:

The inbalance, in our mixed economy, between the private sector (constantly reinforced and encouraged in the years of Conservative Government) and the far smaller public sector, combined with the exaltation of acquisitiveness already noted and the constant sneers at the nationalised industries, may well excite an immature mind to regard all property, public or private, as legitimate loot'.

(Longford Report, 1964, pp. 5–6)

In an earlier work Taylor, Walton and Young (1973) argued that crime is not an inevitable part of any society but is an outcome of the criminal nature of the capitalist system, which itself involves direct or indirect theft from the working class. Abolition of capitalism would therefore bring about the abolition of crime. Clearly there would be many problems in using this argument at the hustings. They point out that the socialist tradition has regarded the 'lumpenproletariat' of criminals and deviants as politically insignificant individuals who would play no decisive role in the class struggle, and were indeed susceptible to use by reactionary forces. Their way of life represents an individualised adjustment to the capitalist system rather than a rebellion.

Pearson (1983, p. 234) also suggests that the argument that crime is the outcome of poverty, poor housing, unemployment, poor health and poor education, apart from being extremely difficult to substantiate by empirical research (Taylor et al., 1973, pp. 218–9; Tarling, 1983), should also be unattractive to the Labour Party, though it represents an element in liberal thinking which has been well established since the

1850s. The fear of crime is not the best justification for attempting to alleviate conditions which are evils in their own right, and to argue for reforms on this ground devalues the suffering of individuals living in disadvantaged circumstances.

Continuities: the ideological message

Pearson (1983) suggests that the nature of public concern about crime and disorder involving the young shows how the problem is functional for the social structure in a more profound way than at the party political level. Pearson's survey of public comment on street crime, extending back through several centuries, reveals a formidable stability and continuity. The current crime wave is regarded as unprecedented, and contrasted with the state of affairs twenty years earlier, when there was emphasis on traditional discipline and the unswerving distinction between right and wrong which maintained the peaceful nature of the British way of life. Looking in the newspaper files of twenty years previously, he found that the then current crime wave was being contrasted with the 'golden age' twenty years before that, and so on back through the centuries. The present is always represented as succumbing to an unprecedented deluge of crime and immorality.

If we accept these generalisations at face value, then generation by generation crime and disorder increase by leaps and bounds. Parental care plumbs increasing depth, while the shortage of authority in the home is said to be mirrored by the increasing leniency of the law and the interference of sentimentalists . . . a relentless history of decline.

(Pearson, 1983, p. 208)

The over-representation of young people in the criminal statistics is repeatedly rediscovered as a new and shocking feature of the problem: and violence and disorder are repeatedly disowned as an alien intrusion into the 'British way of life'. 'It is wonderfully convenient, of course, that this accusation can now be brought against an actual black presence in British cities' (ibid., p. 226).

The same factors are blamed, again and again: working mothers, from the mill-hands of the 1840s to the parents of today's 'latch-key' children: mass education, from the Ragged Schools to the 'permissive jungle' of modern comprehensives: spectator football, associated with violence, rowdyism and unsporting behaviour from the moment of its inception: popular entertainment, blamed for dragging down public morals from pre-industrial festivals to modern television: and allegations that the common people are living in unparalleled luxury have also persisted for centuries.

This repetitious, immovable, and age-old 'tapestry of complaints and fears' is 'continually held up as something entirely new and unprecedented', as regards both the complaints themselves, and the problems to which they direct our attention. This 'ancient tapestry' would also seem to have substantially determined the direction of the 'objective' investigations of academic research: perhaps Pearson's argument is strengthened by the outcome:

Although there are many social changes associated with the rise in delinquency, considerable doubt remains on which (if any) are responsible for the changes in crime. It seems reasonably clear that an increase in opportunities for crime has played some part, but it is uncertain how much general effect this has had on crime. There are several factors commonly thought to have been associated with the rise of crime in the U.K. for which the empirical evidence suggests that this belief is mistaken. Factors in this category include immigration, unemployment, the increase in the proportion of working mothers, industrialization and urbanization, and environmental lead pollution. There are some factors, such as rising levels of divorce, the effects of television, and more frequent hospital admission, which may have played some minor role (the circumstances associated with divorce perhaps more so,) but none of these seems likely to have had a sufficient impact to make a great deal of difference. There are others, such as weakened family ties and reduced family interaction which might have had some impact if they had occurred but there is doubt on whether they have done so. Clearly, there have been some changes in the roles and expectations of women, but we do not know whether these have had any effect on crime. Finally, there are certain changes in society, such as increased affluence, better living conditions, improved physical health, and a reduced size of the average family, which might have been expected to have had benefits, but where no such benefits are identifiable. The reasons for changes in the crime rate remain largely unknown . . .

(Rutter and Giller, 1983, p. 118)

Pearson concludes that there are underlying continuities both in the nature of the actual crime and hooliganism, and in the ways in which the problem is perceived and understood. These continuities are evident in the conflicts between generations: in the conflict between classes: in the tendency to view the past nostalgically and see the future as posing a threat. Then, there is 'the continuing social reproduction of an underclass which as the traditional location of riotous discontent is repeatedly the object of fearful scrutiny . . .' (Pearson, 1983, p. 213). But more generally, Pearson considers that to the powerful, crime and disorder are storm warnings of social and political threat from the working class, so that:

. . . this preoccupation returns to a cluster of themes bearing upon the production and reproduction of consent and social discipline among the working class – and more particularly upon the rising generation, the bearers of the future.

(Pearson, 1983, p. 230)

The extraordinary public interest in the problem therefore relates to the feeling that a government's policy towards juvenile delinquency embodies an ideological statement of that government's political relationship to the present and future working class. The problem with this formulation is that the majority of the working class do not associate themselves with acts of delinquency. Nevertheless the hypothesis does have considerable explanatory power, and it seems quite reasonable to suggest as Pearson does, that crime and political disorder, the lumpen and the productive proletariat, are associated together from the perspective of many powerful interests; just as they are in the minds of contemporary Marxist criminologists.

The History of State Policy: Progress or Continuities?

Policies towards juvenile delinquents are concerned with the manner in which they are tried, the arrangements for their supervision at home, and the places to which they are committed. Also with the limits of the juvenile justice system, which consist of the age range with which it is concerned, the scope of 'status offence' behaviour such as truancy, absconding from home, or sexual activity which is only of concern when the subject has juvenile status: whether orders can be made on children who have not committed an offence: the basis on which decisions are supposed to be made: and the relationship between the available sentences and the facilities for children deprived of a normal home life through parental incapacity. These are mainly technical matters of specialised interest: political concern centres rather on the ideological message sent out by proposed changes to the system.

Government policy may attempt to adjust the formal ways in which services are provided, to accord with its perception of the relative importance of the various needs they are expected to meet: so that the system sends off a general 'message' which expresses the government's ideological interests. This current 'message' from the juvenile justice system is made compatible with those of policies for other systems for socialising young people, such as education, and the family. Government policy is also partially determined by the group interests and conflicts of the bureaucracies and professions charged with its implementation. The study of social welfare institutions cannot be isolated from the study of such interest groups.

The historical development of social policy towards juvenile delinquency might be presented in linear form – the gradual advance of enlightened and evangelistic reformers, generously imbued in earlier times, with remarkable personal qualities and high social status, or in more modern times, with the wisdom and skills of the social sciences: and a correspondingly gradual retreat of the forces of reaction, infused with wrongheadedness, lack of concern, and a cruel will to punish. This long march of the progressives would reach its apotheosis in the 1960s.

But defeat was (temporarily) snatched from total victory by the failure of successive governments to implement the Children and Young Persons Act 1969.

This incremental model does have a certain validity, in that provisions for juvenile offenders have indeed been developed which are separate and different from those for adults. This is one aspect of the establishment of childhood as a separate stage in life preceding adult status, a concept taking firm shape in the nineteenth century, and now elaborated and institutionalised. Nevertheless, alongside this incremental development, can one again discern 'a formidable stability and continuity', similar to that which Pearson distinguished in public comment on crime and disorder, in the influences brought to bear on policy towards juvenile delinquency? It is remarkable how historians of penal reform are able to show that nearly all of today's issues were discussed, in strikingly similar terms, more than a century ago. This applies both to specific and to larger issues. The Home Secretary was being urged to drastically restrict the committal of first offenders to reformative institutions in 1861. The principle that each offence should attract a more serious sentence than the previous one was also being advocated in that year (Rose, 1961, p. 24). In 1828, an official report pointed out that the sons of rich men might be punished at home for behaviour for which the sons of the poor were sent into custody (Pinchbeck and Hewitt, 1969, p. 441). Proposals that institutions for delinquents should be merged into provisions for orphaned and abandoned children were being made in 1881 (Carlebach, 1970, p. 74).

Differentiation between juvenile and adult systems, a humanitarian enterprise, is concerned to protect juveniles from the contaminating effects of association with adult offenders during remand, trial and sentence: and with rendering offenders less likely to transgress. Pragmatic developments have always been hindered by a number of factors. There is the fear of provoking a public reaction, and possibly of encouraging crime, if the services provided seem to benefit offenders unduly, compared to their peers, because of their offending. This 'least eligibility' principle is sometimes expressed by the judiciary, who feel themselves to represent the public, and whose views the government have to take into account. Additionally the judges' 'constant concern with individual liberty and freedom ... sometimes casts them in opposition to the reformers' (Hall Williams, 1977, p. 109) because of the reformers' preference for simplifying or dispensing with the trial process, and for using sentences which relate less to the gravity of the offence than to the alleged 'needs' of the offender. Reformative sentences tend to be longer than retributive ones in order to give time for reformative influences to be brought to bear: and to be indeterminate, their length determined not by a judge but by agents of the executive.

There is a political constituency for ideas of 'social defence', crime protection measures aimed at incapacitation of the offender which override his rights as an individual: but this interest generally converges with that of reformist practice.

Additionally there are votes to be gathered for the idea that simply punishing offenders more harshly will prevent crime. This constituency, whose interests are repressive, are followers of the 'war theory' of criminal justice (Allen, 1974). They are always an obstacle to service developments, and are sometimes powerful enough to move policy in a less humane direction. In 1863 the paradoxically-named Security from Violence Act, passed in response to the contemporary 'garrotting' panic, restored flogging, a penalty abolished only two years previously. This Act remained on the statute book until judicial corporal punishment was ended in 1948, replaced for juveniles by detention centres. These centres provide a second example of a less humane policy development when in 1980 the government introduced more punitive regimes. Evidence as to whether the general level of crime can be influenced by deterrent measures is inconclusive, though specific behaviours can be if the likelihood of detection is high.

Reform ideology: nothing to do with punishment
The final political obstacle to pragmatic developments has been the nature of the pressure for reform. Juvenile justice has lacked aspects of struggle, expressed need, and pressure from working people in general, of 'concessions wrung from above' which characterise more central areas of policy development. There is, naturally, no need expressed by the recipients for the services imposed on them, and the opinions of the offender have been systematically sought as seldom as those of the victim. To most members of the public, whether an offender desists because he has been deterred, or because he has reformed, must seem somewhat irrelevant, and rather difficult to investigate. These two influences, deterrence and reform, are generally seen as complementary aspects of social control. To 'reformers' however, this issue is central: punishment and deterrence are regarded as repressive, reformation as serving the needs of the individual offender. In these respects as in others, the juvenile justice system and the policy disputes within it constitute a world somewhat apart, the various parts of the system relating more to each other than to the wider society, which they are intended to serve.

There is considerable similarity in the way that these middle class disputes are conducted, no matter what the historical period, and this requires an explanation. The central concept of the reformers is that there is a system of penal treatment which will primarily benefit the offender rather than serve other interests, and that will provide the conditions for a voluntary relinquishment of further offending. Reformative systems, in other words, are nothing to do with punishment. Reformative movements appear in certain social conditions:

... a thriving rehabilitative ideal presupposes a society in which the dominant group possess high self confidence in their definitions of character and their standards of good behaviour, in which resort to the public force to advance and defend these values is seen not only as appropriate but as very nearly inevitable.

(Allen, 1981, p. 11)

Reformative movements, additionally, are seldom based on proven techniques and experience in the field. A large part of their energies is taken up with attacking and damaging existing services, and identifying them with the 'war theory' lobby, interested only in repression.

In general, scientific ignorance has not inspired caution in the devotees of the rehabilitative ideal. On the contrary, the very absence of knowledge has encouraged confident assertions and dogmatic claims.

(ibid., p. 52)

Evanglism reforms the scarcely delinquent

A well documented early dispute illustrates some recurrent tendencies of reformative movements. Carlebach (1970) describes how the Parkhurst Act 1838 established a prison for the 'detention and correction' of young offenders, intended to avoid 'any species of discipline calculated to harden or degrade', provide a judicious course of moral, religious, and industrial training, and avoid any comfort which would weaken the fear of prison in the juvenile population at large, or their parents. The regime developed away from that for adult prisons. Leg irons were soon abolished: diet improved: boys were graded, with incentives for progression through the grades. Within the grades, boys were divided into groups, each with its own staff. Forty hours work, directed at greater self sufficiency for the prison, and eleven hours schooling, were provided per week for each boy. Agricultural training, a preparation for transportation to the colonies, was introduced in 1849. This necessitated work outside the walls, and led 34 boys to attempt escape. A small armed guard was then provided for four years.

But in the late eighteenth and early nineteenth century, reformatory institutions for juveniles had also been developing outside the public sector, under the 'voluntary principle', management by philanthropic committees. The best amongst these, such as the Royal Philanthropic Society's School, had also discovered grading, grouping, incentives, and agricultural training, just as had Parkhurst. Spokesmen for the Voluntary Reform Movement were opposed to state provision in principle: 'Act of Parliament philanthropy is no match for volunteer benevolence' (Clay 1861, quoted by Carlebach, 1970.)

Mary Carpenter, a clergyman's daughter who had opened the first reformatory school for girls, attained prominence in the reformatory movement by writing a scathing attack on Parkhurst in her books 'Reformatory Schools' (1851) and 'Juvenile Delinquents' (1853), alleging that reform there was impossible as 'the heart could not be touched' in the context of a military and repressive regime. Describing this regime in terms of leg irons, armed guards, and fear of escapes in the neighbourhood, she used statistics selectively to misrepresent the condition of the prison (Carlebach, 1970, pp. 48–9). Parkhurst had no control over the number or quality of boys admitted, and had to cope with serious and persistent offenders who had already spent more than a year in the adult prison system, which made 'reform' much more difficult. Reproved in a letter from the Director of Convict Prisons for her 'wholly unfair' attack, Mary Carpenter's peace of mind was not assisted by a riot among inmates of her own reformatory, Red Lodge, which only admitted girls on first conviction and under thirteen. These had to be taken elsewhere with their hands bound.

Mary Carpenter's attack on Parkhurst was, however, successful: the government lost confidence in the institution, and in 1864 it was closed.

Yet Mary Carpenter never succeeded in creating the kind of institution which she had advocated and recommended for so many years ... she began with principles so firmly fixed that nothing that staff or children did could shake her convictions or lead her to view her problems in a different light ... She expected from children that, instead of relying on their own homes and their own parents, they should develop 'new affections and feelings ... which usually either fill an unsatisfied void ... or obliterate what is evil in those already formed and grievously polluted' ... The school must inspire a family feeling so that the child could look back on a 'happy home' [the reformatory school] ...

(Carlebach, 1970, p. 55)

Elements of her belief in the function of reformative residential institutions were to persist for a long time. In 1967 a Rainer Foundation report on juvenile institutions in Sweden commented 'it is difficult to see how they can achieve a lasting reformation of such boys in the short space of nine months or less' and 'the more serious flaw in this approach is the reduction of residential treatment to an interim measure...' (Howell, 1967). The idea that residential regimes should be relevant to the past and future of the offender in the sense of the 'real, as opposed to the institutionally constrained, life of the youngster' (Hoghughi, 1983, p. 244), was relatively unattractive to opinion-formers until recently.

In 1854 and 1866 legislation established a system whereby juveniles could be committed to reformatory schools (after a preliminary period of imprisonment), for from two to five years. This remained an alternative to imprisonment not a substitute for it, and attempts to ameliorate regimes for those juveniles continuing to be imprisoned were set back to the end of the century. The state provided financial support for the reformatory schools under voluntary management. Carlebach explains Mary Carpenter's behaviour in terms of her personality and sex; 'a brilliant, volatile, passionate and arrogant woman' (Carlebach, 1970, p. 40). But her success also bore on the wider issues at stake. One was the proper role of the state, to provide services directly or to financially assist services organised privately. But there was a more fundamental issue too. Mary Carpenter wrote:

Yet let them be treated with respect, with true Christian politeness, and they will give a ready response. Nor let it be imagined an absurd thing to treat these poor little dirty children with respect. Their rags will disappear before those who look at them as young immortal beings: and so many good and beautiful traits of character in them will be revealed to those who treat them with Christian courtesy, that they will learn to respect them.

(Carpenter, quoted by Parsloe, 1978, p. 150, Pearson, 1983, p. 176)

The perception of this statement has varied according to both the ideology and the sex of modern commentators. To Parsloe 'Mary Carpenter was more than ahead of her own times: she was ahead of ours too'. To Pearson 'Mary Carpenter had perfected a technique of looking at the rags of poverty in such a way that they actually disappeared'. Though Britain was then scarcely emerging from the most brutal phases of the industrial revolution 'the urgency of the temporal wants of the labouring classes were diminished in comparison with their spiritual failings'.

But surely what was really at stake here was the gospel of love, ideology of the evangelist sections of the Victorian middle class, which could not be failed, even when sorely tested by juvenile delinquents in institutions. Not only religious love, but parental love, was seen to appertain particularly to the middle classes:

whereas the upper class child that was guilty of a delinquent act was corrected, restrained and trained through that act by its parents in an over-all framework of love and kindness, the lower class child faced one of two dangers. Either its delinquent act went undetected and untreated and thereby acted as a corrupting force on the child, which, by a process of repetition would ultimately turn the child into a professional criminal, or the child was detected in its delinquent act and by being put through the penal processes as if it were an adult, was corrupted by that process towards the same form of professional criminality.

(Carlbach, 1970, p. 42)

There seems to be little role for the working class parent.

Problems of reform
The subsequent history of the Reformatory Schools illustrates persistent tendencies in the post-establishment phase of reform movements.

Rehabilitative ideals have an imminent quality. Once policies are realised, even partially, reformist approbation soon deserts them. This may be to do with the unreal nature of the aspirations themselves, as their benevolence is bound up with a specific version of the contemporary dominant ideology. This creates expectations which are bound to lead to disappointment. The other difficulties in realising these ideals reside in the fact that:

> even under the most favourable circumstances, reformation can never constitute the sole objective of a correctional system, that many other purposes compete with it for realisation.

(Allen, 1981, p. 53)

Among these, one of the most important is the preoccupation of the staff with maintaining their control of the system by processing delinquents with the least possible disturbance to it. In the 1860s reformatory schools were already arousing criticism for admitting children under twelve, who were first offenders: in the 1870s for their penal, restrictive discipline, and for employing juveniles for profit rather than providing industrial training, so that they were reluctant to discharge older, experienced workers. The schools supported the retention of the period of preliminary imprisonment (two weeks in solitary confinement) long after public opinion had abandoned it. Perhaps it helped them and their inmates to see their own work as less punitive. They objected to a departmental committee report of 1896 which recommended, as a matter of basic justice, that children should only be removed from home as a last resort, when there was no other alternative (Carlebach, 1970, p. 78). The numbers sent to reformatory schools reached a peak in the First World War, but subsequently quickly declined, and some forty schools were closed.

> It was clear that courts were ceasing to favour commitment to a school, partly as a reaction to the spread of probation, partly as an economy, and partly because of the general feeling that children should be 'treated', not punished, combined with doubt about the schools' ability to do this.

(Rose, 1961, pp. 154–5)

The other difficulties in realising reformative ideals lie in the punitive and deterrent purposes of criminal justice, with its concern for public order. These logically reassert themselves, as dissuading the general public from offending will show a greater benefit to public order than the success of rehabilitative efforts on the smaller number of detected offenders. The expectation that the principal function of a criminal justice system is to punish culpable behaviour may be shared by most children too.

Paternalism

During the twentieth century, the reformatory schools retained the 'voluntary principle' in their management committees, but were gradually brought under centralised Home Office control as part of the 'approved school' system. The torch of reformative excitement passed to the prison service. The 'Gladstone Committee' (1895) advocated reformative regimes and the borstal system for young offenders, inaugurated in 1907, reached the height of its prestige, and the furthest point of its differentiation from the prison system, during the 1930s. The Prison Commissioner who was its guiding spirit, Alexander Paterson, had experience as a settlement worker, as a probation officer, and as a soldier on active service. Some features of the borstal regime derived from the Royal Philanthropic Society's School, others from the army, and others from prestigious public boarding schools with their 'house' systems and benevolently paternalist housemasters. Emphasis was placed on inspiring and developing responsibility and trust: ideally in 'open' conditions, though it never proved possible to cope with the majority of lads in this way. The system was described as 'educative not punitive' and it appealed directly to the idea that the roots of crime lay in lack of discipline and moral inadequacy, which the staff of university and public school men, and former non-commissioned officers of the armed services, could correct. A few borstals were established by marching inmates across country to build them. There could surely have been no more satisfactory demonstration that even the unruly elements in the population believed in the benevolent paternalism of their social superiors. Exaggerated hopes were entertained of the reformative success of the system. The commissioners looked forward to closing many of their adult prisons, and advised judges that in sentencing offenders to the maximum period of three years, rather than being severe and unkind, they were 'doing the boys and the country the greatest service' (Hood, 1965, p. 25). And also increasing the numbers in custody.

Paterson wrote in 1925 that 'Borstal training is based on the assumption that there is individual good in each, and among nearly all an innate corporate spirit which will respond to the appeal made to the British of every sort to play the game, to follow the flag, to stand by the old ship' (quoted by Hood, 1965, pp. 106–7). Its acceptable 'message' was that the working man should strive to be disciplined and honest, industrious and grateful. And patriotic: the ideal was one of service (Hood, 1965).

The borstal movement improved conditions for juveniles in prison service establishments. Reformative activity relied on discipline, incentives, personal influence and charisma to transcend the conflict between staff and inmates inherent in the administration of custody. To recognise this conflict would be, however, to recognise the limitations of the ideology which gave rise to the reformative activity. The cost of its denial was, in the prisons and borstals holding less reformable inmates, the permanent alienation of the prison officers, faced by insoluble problems of control. The denial could be extended to conflicts which were quite clearly political. When the IRA organised a mutiny at Dartmoor in 1932, the governor was the only member of the service of his grade to have been promoted from the ranks of the uniformed staff. The enquiry blamed him for being insufficiently reformative (Thomas, 1972).

Personal influence

The early twentieth century saw developments at court which were designed to avoid the contaminating effects of association with adult prisoners. A system of juvenile courts sitting on separate days or in buildings separate from adult courts was established by the Childrens Act 1908, which also ended imprisonment for children under fourteen. Separate 'panels' of unpaid juvenile court magistrates, the nominees of political parties, were subsequently developed, and are now the most powerful interest group in the field. To cut down the waiting period before trial, most offences were made subject to summary jurisdiction (trial without a jury), and the development of separate remand facilities which came under local authority control in 1948, avoided the need to commit juveniles awaiting trial to prison or the workhouse.

A range of sentences developed as alternatives to custody. During the nineteenth century advice and assistance had been provided, under the voluntary principle, by court missionaries sponsored by denominational societies. Attempts to legislate for a probation service began in 1886, but reluctance to extend the role of the state in this way frustrated developments for twenty years. The Probation of First Offenders Act 1907 provided for the possibility of continuous supervision for up to three years, but only by strengthening existing missionary activity, and it was to be another thirty years before the probation service was freed from denominational entanglement and temperance propaganda. This longstanding religious connection, together with the service's greater involvement in the adult courts, disappointed influential reformers.

Probation work relied on personal influence on the offender. '. . . the success of this measure depends entirely on the character of the person appointed to act as probation officer . . . It is a task requiring knowledge, patience and experience in dealing with very difficult cases' (Attlee, 1920, p. 39). It never attracted the degree of reformative excitement focused on the custodial or residential sector. While the management of institutions attracted fairly high social status, work with individual offenders and their families did not. Nevertheless, in the 1930s 'more than half of juveniles charged with indictable offences received a probation sentence'. (Pearson, 1983, p. 47). The 1930s, when the working class was well under control, was a 'golden age' of penal reform.

By the 1960s, 'the probation service had some claim to be the leading social work profession in this country' (Jordan, 1971, p. 72); it was also, in 1961, the largest, with 2000 probation officers compared to fewer than 1500 child care officers. Sixty-five per cent of its workers were professionally trained, compared to 25 per cent of child care officers. Policy had focused the service on its professional association rather than a management structure, for financial reasons. Thus 'its officers could boast a remarkable degree of independence and autonomy.' Probation officers shared some of the perspectives of earlier reformers. 'I can think of no professional imputation a probation officer would resent more keenly than that he was in any sense an instrument of punishment' (Watson, 1970, p. 58). Probation officers had developed a way of looking at their contact with clients which divorced it from its context.

Probation literature embodied the psychotherapeutic ideas fashionable in social work at the time. Delinquency was held to be an outcome of disturbance in the individual or in family relationships. Ferrard and Hunnybun (1962) concentrated on the problems of the upwardly mobile. Monger (1964) suggested that delinquency was usually a response to too much discipline in the home, rather than the lack of it. Hunt (1966) justified the use of enforcement by drawing a parallel with the non-voluntary nature of parent-child relationships. The absence of any recognition of conflict wider than personal or family conflict reflected the current general climate of informed opinion. Halmos (1965, p. 18) described the contemporary situation as the age of 'post-political man', when political solutions had been discredited. He claimed that though social workers' therapeutic relationships with their clients were not religious in character, they were equally 'based on faith' and were 'the revitaliser of an otherwise weakening confidence and hope in the nobility of man in our time'.

State Policy in Modern Times: The Fabian Panacea as Conventional Wisdom

This was the period of the post-war consensus, based on Keynesian economic management and Beveridgian state welfare provision. Full employment and the fair economic weather led to assumptions in the dominant sections of both political parties that Labour's post-war 'settlement' had ended class conflict for ever. The Trades Union Movement pursued objectives which were material rather than socialist. It was the heyday of Fabian approaches to social problems, involving the investigation and collection of 'facts', and the implementation of policy by expert officials. These were regarded as unselfish and disinterested. 'The younger generation of today', complained Hayek (1962, p. 97), 'has grown up in a world in which . . . to employ a hundred people is represented as exploitation but to command the same number as honourable'.

The enhanced prestige of economics as an academic subject which resulted from the success of Keynesian economic management reflected on the other social sciences. In the millenarian atmosphere of the time it appeared that a 'science of society' would emerge on the model of the natural sciences, premising the technical means for solving social problems. The social situation was appropriate for the emergence of a reformative movement which aimed to erase both the juvenile courts and the rising curve of juvenile crime. These were the embodiment of moral, social and political conflicts which the reformers wished to be regarded as anachronistic.

Seven years were taken up with the deliberations and legislation arising from the 'indecisive' 'Ingleby Committee', which felt unable to deny the need for both justice and welfare in the juvenile court system. The very next year, 1964, a Labour Party Study Group chaired by Lord Longford issued its report 'Crime – a challenge to us all'. The 'Longford Report' attributed the persistence and increase of crime and the continued need for social workers in the Welfare State era on the failure of the Conservative Party to develop sufficient welfare state provisions on the one hand, and on the existence of personal and family failings on the other. 'Today's offenders are to a great extent "problem people" who have more opportunities to commit crime than ever before' (Longford, 1964, p. 10); '. . . to some extent a product of the society they live in and the deficiencies in its provision for them' (ibid., p. 28). 'Anti-social behaviour in a child may arise from difficulties at home, from unhappiness at school, from physical or mental handicaps or maladjustment, or from a variety of other causes for which the child has no personal responsibility' (ibid., p. 20).

The solution proposed was that the great majority of delinquents of school age should not be perceived or processed as offenders at all, but as deprived children with 'special needs' to be met by psychological treatment, special day or boarding school education, or residential care. They should be treated, in other words, without recourse to punishment.

Juvenile courts would be abolished because 'An appearance on a criminal charge may well aggravate the child's difficulties and be a first step towards a criminal career . . . these children should receive the kind of treatment they need, without any stigma or any association with the penal system.' (Longford, 1964, p. 24). The school, police, or other agency becoming aware of delinquency or maladjustment would instead bring the problem to the attention of a 'Family Service', based on an expanded local authority children's department. With the agreement of the child's parents, the Family Service, 'with the education and health services, will arrange for the child's treatment, if necessary in one of the residential institutions already mentioned . . .' (Longford, 1964, p. 25). Only when agreement with the parents could not be reached would a referral be made to a Family Court, under civil proceedings on the grounds that the child was in need of 'care protection or control'.

The avoidance of stigma, and the exclusive emphasis on residential, psychological and educational treatment, were presumably intended to provide working class families with access to the provisions available to affluent parents with troublesome children: more draconian measures disguised as egalitarianism.

The assumption that working class and middle class parents would be embarrassed or concerned in similar ways may account for the absence of any proposals for dealing with offenders who were not maladjusted: the majority of offenders. The view that stigma was undesirable, and that the role of social workers and magistrates should be limited to investigation and referral to distant experts, technicalised and mystified methods of influencing offenders, emphasising administrative provision above personal influence with a moral component. These ideas are congruent with those of Wootton (1959) a witness who decisively influenced the committee (Bottoms, 1974, p. 327).

The spoils of reform

The Longford Report advertised for political support by tying its proposals to others which would provide professional expansion for various interest groups. The Home Office was to be responsible for the new Family Service, and was to acquire a new Research Council headed by a Director of Criminology whose status would be 'comparable to that of Economic Adviser to the Treasury' (Longford, 1964, p. 11). The child care service was to form the nucleus of the expanded Family Service, which was to establish a localised network of Family Advice Centres. It would expand its own residential provision, particularly that for residential 'assessment of needs' take over the administration of the approved schools and extend their 'closed' (i.e. secure) provisions, and assume responsibility for the handicapped and other disadvantaged groups, then the responsibility of the local authority health and welfare departments and the Ministry of Health.

The child care service had been established in 1948 to provide for children in local authority care through parental incapacity. It had experience of the approved school system where one third of the inmates were non-offenders in local authority care. In 1963, legislation arising from the Ingleby Report had made it responsible for work, some of which had previously been undertaken by the probation service, intended to prevent the need for children to be received into care or brought before the juvenile court. Unfortunately this involvement with children who had not yet committed offences seemed to be associated with rising numbers of receptions into care rather than the reverse. But the 'crime control' and 'public defence' potential of this 'preventive' policy was perhaps unlikely at that time to have been the reason for support from police sources for the Longford proposals, though later there were claims that the police should be represented on local authority children's committees. The Report promised to 'strengthen' the force. It was absolved from efforts to redevelop beat policing, and pressed instead to place reliance on technical methods: 'we urge a more imaginative development of the resources available – for instance, the 'team policing' method of transporting mobile squads of men unexpectedly from one precinct to another and the use of walkie-talkie radio.' Beat patrolling was condemned because of the effect of its monotony on recruitment (Longford, 1964, p. 32).

Universities were also going to benefit from the expansion of social work training and from the expanded graduate intake into a police force with enhanced pay and conditions (Longford, 1964, p. 33 and 67).

Once the Labour Party was returned to power, parts of the Report were translated into a White Paper 'The Child, the Family and the Young Offender' (Cmnd 1965). This now envisaged that referrals from the police and others would be made to 'Family Councils', rather than to the Family Service. Family Councils would be made up of social workers and other experts. They would work by agreement with the parents, except that even when parents disagreed, they were to have the power to refer a child to an observation and assessment centre for a report on 'the type of treatment likely to be successful in his case'.

The Council would enquire into each case and either take no action by leaving the matter to the parents, arrange compensation from the parents to the victim, arrange supervision (not mentioned in Longford) by a child care officer, or send the offender for residential training. Attendance centres and detention centres would be retained, junior approved schools would merge with general child care provision and senior approved schools would merge with borstals into a new system of 'youth custody centres' and 'young offender institutions'.

Interest and ideology
Opposition came from interest groups who would be deprived of their roles: lawyers, magistrates and probation officers. They emphasised the experience and the valuable aspects of the services to be replaced (Jarvis, 1966, Cavanagh, 1966). Others stressed the practical difficulties inherent in proposals which tried to deal with offending while appearing not to do so.

A young person cannot be an offender, he has to be 'a child under sixteen who has done an act which is an offence in the case of an older person'.

(Scott, 1966, p. 109)

The media expressed fears which demonstrate some of the permanent political interests between which any system of delinquency control is balanced: the threat to civil liberties in the removal of court proceedings: the fear that Family Councils would intervene in families to an unwarranted extent: and conversely that they would be too 'soft' (Kahan, 1966) and that the citizenry would then take matters into its own hands (Cavanagh, 1966). There were fears of losing control of delinquents: 'By the time a constable has shouted "Stop thief! or I will refer you to the Family Council" any delinquent worth his salt will have blown a raspberry and disappeared' (Montagu, 1965). It would also be difficult to keep track of the problem as a whole, and the measures taken to deal with it; as a supporter of reform later stated:

Another group who may be in trouble are those research workers who like to measure the success and failure of social work help and residential treatment against the reconviction rate. If most children are dealt with informally, the reconviction rate won't help much. We ought, however, to help research workers to find new and more valid indices against which they can measure our performance.

(Bilton, 1968)

The major issue of high principle was the alleged threat to 'equality before the law' if the offender did not have the right to be tried on the basis of his actions rather than his family background. To some extent it must have been the naked character of this threat which so upset the legal profession, as existing practice already took cognisance of family background in the exercise of police discretion and in sentencing with the help of written reports. Did the clash of 'principles' reflect little more than a squabble over the division of labour in society, and the choice of moral vocabulary, among some of society's more powerful groupings? There would have been a greater meaning had delinquents and their parents been certain to appreciate that they were being spared the stigma of criminality, being treated and not punished. This never seemed likely, as the Family Service were to undertake functions previously carried out by police, probation, courts and residential and custodial services, which were irreducibly concerned with conflict, social control and public order. It was claimed that the fact that parents did not have to agree to juvenile court decisions was a positive advantage to family relationships:

... it may do little to alter practice ... it is pretty much the same type of child who comes under supervision or is taken from home in Scotland, Denmark or Sweden, as had these experiences in our juvenile courts ... To have a child who commits an offence is not the end of the world for lower-class families, it is a hazard lying in wait for all youngsters reared in poor, urban areas . . . If he has to appear before a juvenile court it may be less of an affront from their [the parents'] point of view that he appear for law-breaking, an episodic event, than to have him described as in need of care, protection and control, a continuing state of affairs.

(Lowson, 1975, p. 70, p. 75)

. . . so long as force of any kind is used to commit children to treatment programmes, such programmes will be regarded by the children as to some degree punitive. Children cannot be so easily bluffed as some reformers would like to believe . . .

(Mays, 1975, p. 3)

The controversy over reform in the 1960s also bore on wider issues to do with the proper role of the state. The 'justice' and 'welfare' ideologies into which the opposing arguments have subsequently been systematised by Parsloe (1978) and others have close connections to *laissez faire* and Fabian ideologies of social policy. The justice/*laissez faire* model of juvenile justice is concerned to limit the extent of state intervention. It tends to see most offending behaviour as rational and calculating, for which the offender should be held responsible. It regards proof of a criminal offence as the sole justification for intervention and the sole basis for punishment. The offences and punishments should be clearly and specifically defined by law.

The welfare/Fabian model assumes criminal behaviour to be only an outcome of a wider problem of social, economic or biological disadvantage, so that any state intervention should be aimed at alleviating these disadvantages as much, if not more than, punishing the offender. With regard to the individual offender, intervention should be directed towards expert assessment and treatment of his 'needs'. Though the perception and classification of such needs remains obstinately subjective, they are generally described in scientific or 'medicalised' terms. To be effective, treatment should ideally be voluntary: but failing this it will be enforced. Individualised treatment requires discretionary decision making by the treatment authority, and hence intervention needs to be indeterminate and its duration based on the progress of the individual.

Whilst interest groups may adopt one of these ideologies to further their position, to advocate that 'justice' or 'welfare' 'should' form the basis of juvenile justice policy is essentially futile, as the relative autonomy of the many decision makers in any system exposes them to the pragmatic concerns of public order, retribution, reformation, social defence, and so on, however the means to these ends are currently labelled. The ever-changing exigencies of the problem require a flexible and temporary balance between these interests, and since the interpretation of most juvenile justice decisions is a relative matter, the decision makers are beyond the reach of ideological monitoring or control.

Changing academic perceptions
The reformers of the 1960s, however, presented their proposals as rational and technical rather than ideological or political: part of the slow march of progress (Kahan, 1966). They were supported by a substantial weight of then respectable 'positivist' criminology which located the causes of delinquency in the deficits of deviant individuals, their biological inheritance, early upbringing, or imperfect socialisation. This inferred that delinquency could be largely prevented before it occurred by the avoidance of circumstances likely to separate mothers and young children, and by therapeutic family counselling.

But during the 1960s, sociological conceptualisations of the problem became prominent, which located the reasons for delinquency and crime in the nature of society itself. Offence behaviour could be a rational response for those whose access to legitimate goals was blocked by competition and inequality. They might thus compensate themselves materially, hit back at the society which had rejected them, or establish separate status arrangements in which they could compete (Merton, 1937, 1957; Cohen, 1955; Cloward and Ohlin, 1960).

Attention also shifted to the role of the control agencies themselves in creating or at least amplifying social problems by labelling as deviant, behaviour which was contrary to powerful interests. Deviance was perceived as a property conferred upon, rather than inherent in, behaviour (Becker, 1963; Lemert, 1967). Labelling theory inferred that processing individuals as delinquents tended to powerfully reinforce a delinquent sense of identity.

The new climate of ideas was a largely successful challenge to 'positivism', and would in due course call into question the advantages of the proposed reforms as little more than an exchange of punitive labels for therapeutic ones, while the processes at work remained much the same. But the immediate effect was strongly libertarian. If delinquency was nothing more than a construction of the control agencies, then 'social control' was the problem, and the term came to be used perjoratively. More equality in society, and less control, could abolish delinquency; the way to stop 'taking and driving away' offences was to give the culprits cars.

Reform for all
Opposition to the 1965 proposals had been successful. But three years later similar proposals were advanced in a new White Paper, 'Children in Trouble', (Cmnd 1968). This had the same ideological 'message', that families were dependent on the ministrations of expert officials for the

good behaviour of their children. But they incorporated much more of the contemporary philosophy of social work. Police and social workers were encouraged to meet needs informally, but this time the juvenile court was to be retained. Bottoms (1974) has carefully charted the many contingent factors leading to the acceptance of these proposals. There was a conjunction of interests and ideology between the Labour Party and key social work personnel. The plans for a unified social services department, and a unified professional organisation for social workers, were now well advanced. Support at the Home Office was strong. Probation officers were debilitated by internal divisions over whether to join the new organisation, and few magistrates may have realised the magnitude of the changes to be imposed on their courts. For a child under 14, the commission of an offence would cease to be, by itself, a sufficient ground for bringing him before a court. Where proceedings were necessary, these would be brought under the care, protection or control procedure. Older children could be either prosecuted or brought under this civil procedure. The existing penalties of discharge and fine were to be retained, but supervision replaced probation and could be made partly residential or more demanding by the insertion of 'intermediate treatment' requirements. Care orders would be the only residential order, the disposition of provisions much as in the earlier proposals, save that detention centres would be incorporated in the general range. Attendance centres would be incorporated into inter-mediate treatment. It was hoped to accommodate many delinquents in children's and foster homes but it was recognised that a 'substantial minority' would require institutional care, and 'These proposals will not diminish the need for residential facilities'. (Cmnd, 1968, p. 12).

The arrangements for dealing with identified delinquents were only part of the government's strategy:

The Home Office children's department wanted the White Paper and any subsequent legislation to deal with delinquency not only through the judicial system, but in the context of preventive work, with community development as the means of promoting social growth and reducing anti-social behaviour.

(Cooper, 1983, p. 93)

Whether the community development projects and the community work aspirations of the new unified departments ('Seebohm Report', S.2) lay outside the province of social control or were an extension of it is a moot point. Intermediate treatment was also to be provided for this 'preventive' sector, for children 'legally aged 0–18' (Cooper, 1970). Divorcing it from the judicial control system made it a focus of reformative excitement.

D. H. Morrell, the Assistant Under-Secretary of State responsible for both the juvenile justice legislation and the community projects (*The*

Times, 1969) celebrated success by asserting that the new work would bring new social status to social workers: 'You are therefore creating a great profession – perhaps, one day, *the* great profession'. (Morell, 1969).

Aftermath: The Fragmentation of Wisdom

The 'Longford Report' had opined that 'a new spirit must inspire the services at all levels' (p. 64) but the power struggle poisoned relationships between the services for two decades. The juvenile courts and probation service had been pilloried; they had regarded themselves as humane and progressive parts of the justice system. Now the system of which they formed a part was portrayed as unnecessary, repressive and ridiculous. The reformers were equally outraged by criticism:

It is very disturbing that while pages have been splashed with emotional verbiage about the depraved, about non offenders in approved schools and just about any mud that can be slung at children's departments, the Lords debate was largely ignored. I accuse the national dailies of being irresponsible and biased. I suspect that the magistrates, or some of them, have been the instigators of this scurrilous campaign. It is a good job that we have had some first rate ministers and civil servants at the Home Office . . .

(Smart, 1969, p. 15)

Very little of the Children and Young Persons Act 1969 has subsequently been implemented. After the first part had been implemented in 1971, 'a serious magisterial revolt took place' (Bottoms, 1974, p. 335). What was already implemented, has subsequently been amended. Subsequent to the Act:

The over-expansion of all juvenile justice provisions meant that at each stage facilities, whether community-based or institution-based, were 'recruiting' clients, with consequent shift of the old approved school population to custodial institutions, truants and minor delinquents shifting from supervision to care, and the new community programmes such as intermediate treatment finding a client group among those deemed, often on very spurious grounds, at risk of delinquency rather than actually delinquent.

(Hudson, 1984)

The proportion of children under lock and key has now returned to pre-1907 levels (Millham, Bullock and Hosie, 1978). It is difficult to say what effect the Act has had on these developments, as the proportion placed on probation was falling, and open institutions were finding it increasingly difficult to contain their charges, before 1969. By weakening the authority of those administering care and supervision sentences compared to those of their pre-1969 equivalents, the Act may have contributed to the decline in their use. Perhaps larger factors are also at work, such as a decline in the importance attributed to the influence of individuals in favour of the influence of the social environment. Or society may have become less tolerant of delinquency. Or there may be stronger feelings of class conflict.

The age of 'post-political man' has ended, with the passing of the post-war consensus and the restoration of overt class warfare to the centre of the political arena. In criminology, Marxists emphasised the contribution made by class conflict to delinquency (Taylor et al., 1973). Others (Hirschi, 1969; Box, 1971) undermined the view that delinquency is behaviour which is sufficiently distinctive to warrant expert explanation and understanding in terms of something exceptional. Instead they suggested that society provides some individuals with 'more to lose' in terms of status, relationships, etc., through committing offences, than through deciding not to do so. The others may offend if an opportunity presents itself. This changed climate of political and academic thought has lessened the extent to which it can be denied that social control is a necessity of social life. Labelling theory is somewhat marginal to policies whose main object is to maintain public order. If processing delinquents for, say, residential burglary, may reinforce their delinquent identities (though empirical supporting evidence is limited), are we to infer that without such processing there would be more such burglaries, or fewer? This is now the question for policy (Walker, 1974). Evidence of 'self-report' studies, in which juveniles record in confidence offences for which they have not been detected, has shown that the serious and persistent offenders are those most likely to get caught. Juveniles from the most deprived section of the population are over-represented among them. So official statistics are not just a reflection of action in law enforcement (Rutter and Giller, 1983, pp. 26–31).

Sociologists had ridiculed the long years of 'positivist' research into the distinctive characteristics of offenders, which had yielded so few clear and unambiguous findings. Their own work now came under attack from criminologists emphasising the very varied range of activities regarded as crimes.

... not all criminologists have reasoned ... to the common sense and harmless conclusion that there must be more than one kind of crime. Instead, they have arrived at the incredible inference that there must be a single explanation of crime, if only it could be found and formulated ... those who have reasoned in this way have all been sociologists. 'Grand theory' has the sort of prestige among sociologists of deviance which Grand Opera has in the world of singers.

(Walker, 1974, p. 48)

As Croft (1980, p. 2) states; '... it is difficult to point to any single theory of criminal behaviour which is acceptable for incorporation in practical policy'. Reviewing a decade of research, Parker and Giller (1981) conclude that work on reducing the opportunities for crime provides the only apparent, if limited, method of advance.

Less is now expected of research and analysis of the 'facts' of crime:

... so many of the issues at stake are as much political and moral as scientific ...
Criminological research has not solved the problem of crime and, in so far as
research is an element of technological management, such management ... has
been a failure ... The issue of power in the control of crime, who uses it and
how: and its effects on those it attempts to constrain, cannot be ignored ...

(Croft, 1981, pp. 3, 4)

And nothing is now expected of reformative services as regards their
effect on recidivism. '... penological research carried out in the course
of the last twenty years or so suggests that penal "treatments", as we
significantly describe them, do not have any reformative effect,
whatever other effects they may have'. (Croft, 1978, p. 4).

This applies as much to institutional as to non-institutional treatments. While it is possible to affect the behaviour of those actually in
residential treatment, no long term effect is discernible after release.
These findings, valid for all countries where research has been rigorous,
could be fatal for the principle that for reformative purposes, courts are
justified in passing sentences which involve greater intervention than is
warranted by the gravity of the offence committed.

Policy for the 1980s
In what circumstances does the government formulate its policy? It is
first necessary to admit three essential limitations on government
influence. The first is the relative autonomy of decision makers at key
points in the system.

... (the government's) difficulties are obvious. One is lack of control or even
influence at so many key points: the amount of crime committed and reported to
the police, and the response to it of the police and the courts.

(Moriarty, 1977, p. 143)

The second is the relative unimportance of crime as a problem
compared to, say, economic problems. 'As desirable as it may be to put a
stop to crime, the world cannot be put to rights on that account alone'
(Croft, 1980, p. 1). If, for instance, research was to show that
commercial advertising created a demand for consumer goods which
not all its 'target' population could satisfy by legitimate means, it is
unlikely that advertising would be restricted for that reason.

Croft has advanced a conceptual basis for a policy of crime reduction,
based on Home Office and other research. Reduction can be achieved by
'proper supervision' of children by parents within the home and outside
it: schools where discipline is similarly firm: neighbourhoods where
multiple disadvantage is reduced to the minimum and opportunities for

crime are limited: community influences and example: and increasing the risks of being caught. But the most that the Home Office can do to implement these ideas is to try to ensure that crime reduction has a place in the thinking of politicians, administrators, professionals and citizens with many other concerns.

The third limitation on government action is the continued tightness of financial resources, particularly for programmes which lack political support. This is but one factor in the 'increasing intervention by Parliamentary Committees in an area hitherto left to other kinds of advisory bodies, and a corresponding decline in the influence of Departmentally appointed committees' (Walker and Giller, 1977, p. iii). 'The politicisation of penal policy issues could well encourage the development of crude policies and the raising of expectations which, given the intractable nature of the crime problem, no Government could fulfil' (Moriarty, 1977, p. 133). The powerful All-Party Parliamentary Penal Affairs Committee brings together Members and Peers with specialist knowledge and interests in the field, and tries to counteract such tendencies, but nevertheless legislation is a risky business: the 1982 Criminal Justice Act was affected by somewhat impracticable amendments by a back-bencher in the Commons (S.20, 21) and by a Peer identified with particular professional interests (S.1).

There is no scope, in the area of Home Office responsibility, for the flexible switching of resources from custody into the non-custodial sector. Overcrowding in youth custody is such that there would have to be an unrealistically large reduction in numbers there before any substantial saving in the financial costs of custody was achieved. Any extra community-based programmes have, therefore, to be funded out of new resources, or from the DHSS, which was given responsibility for local authority social services.

The central government departments now tend to emphasise the relative autonomy of the services, and their own role in scrutinising their claims for additional resources, a more distant relationship than in the 1960s (Moriarty, 1977). There has actually been increased investment in intermediate treatment, and in the probation service. Perhaps belief in the power to reform delinquents is an integral part of the middle class identity.

Predictions
What could be predicted for policy during the late 1980s? The climate of informed opinion, and political circumstances, favour a slight tilt towards the 'justice' ideology; reformative ideals are likely to play a peripheral rather than a central role. Nor is the Thatcherite assertion of dominance over the working class yet sufficiently consolidated to provide the conditions for a reformative surge. By changing the

detention centre regimes in a more punitive direction, the Thatcher Government sent off its ideological 'message', and in that way the problem served the government's purpose. No particularly important initiatives with regard to the continuing management of delinquency appear to be in prospect, though a small specific move in a repressive direction, with few resource implications, takes place each summer in anticipation of the Party Conference. The recent introduction of regimes of enervating work may be intended to reconcile young offenders to long-term unemployment.

On present form it seems unlikely that the government will seek to bring the benefits of competition to the criminal justice area: for instance, by restricting the police to protecting the property of the poor, and leaving the better-off to buy security on the private market. Nor are there any proposals to introduce punitive equivalence between different types of sentence, giving the offender the choice of serving either a short period in prison, a long period on supervision, or a medium term of some more rigorous community activity. Instead the magistracy are regarded as the only market, and community-based programmes of ever more restrictive supervision are devised in attempts to interest them in non-custodial sentences (Ely, Swift and Sutherland, 1985).

What of the erstwhile followers of the welfare ideology, interested in expanding the relevant services? There is wide support for 'civilising' the criminal law in the sense of making delinquency less a concern of the state and more an issue between offender and victim, emphasising reparation and reconciliation. It seems quite feasible to deal with a proportion of delinquents in this way, though it is not yet clear what new bureaucracy will be required for the task. Possibly lawyers will play an important role: though funded by the state through Legal Aid they do not have the appearance of being employed by it.

There is also continued advocacy of technological management: the expansion of management information systems for social services, presented as a means of influencing decisions in the justice system. In addition, there is hope for expansion in services which can be presented as transferring offenders out of the residential and custodial sector into non-residential programmes. Reformative excitement centres on Inter-mediate Treatment, expected to do this among its many other functions. Instead of using IT as the 'penologists' stone', it is now being clawed back from generalised, preventive programmes to the control of serious offenders in the community. The DHSS is providing 'new money' for intensive IT, provided that it is managed on the 'voluntary principle'. As this happens, a historical process repeats itself: as schemes face up to the reality of controlling delinquent behaviour, and assume the character-istics needed for this task, they lose the sympathy of reformers (Pitts, 1979).

The curiously named group New Approaches to Juvenile Crime (McCabe and Treitel, 1983), advocate the replacement of juvenile court proceedings for children under 14 by panel hearings on the Scottish model. These probably do have technical advantages in easier communication with offenders and parents. Independent officials called reporters, part of the Scottish tradition of independent prosecution, determine referrals to the panels and reduce the numbers of offenders entering the system.

This somewhat paradoxical advocacy of measures to expand the bureaucracies in order to restrict the extent of the system and the scope of intervention are justified to reform interests through retrospectively presenting the policies of the 1960s as moves towards non-residential and non-custodial treatment. (Taylor, 1978; Thorpe et al., 1980; Tutt, 1982; Hudson, 1984).

Finally, we can review Taylor's (1981) Marxist ideas for juvenile justice in the 'transitional stage' leading to socialism. 'Liberal' professional services will be abandoned as not democratically accountable, non-residential programmes will also be attacked as favouring delinquents over non-delinquents from the same area (the 'least eligibility' principle). Offenders, described as 'violent activists of the racist and fascist right' will be obliged to undergo retraining in racial and sexual relationships in community homes. Their sentences will be indeterminate, serving the legitimate need for working class retribution. Release will be determined by the committees of working class people who will manage the institutions. These proposals would place power over the local juvenile justice system in the hands of previously underprivilieged groups, workers, blacks, and women. They show a convergence of rehabilitative and social defence interests, reminiscent of systems in existing socialist states.

In conclusion it may be suggested that no government can change the content of juvenile justice policy, which is devoted primarily to the maintenance of public order, in no matter what form the provisions are set. Public order also requires however, that within these constraints, administrators perpetually attempt the construction of a paradox: sentences which provide the potential for juvenile offenders to develop and grow, and form an accommodation to society. The development of such sentences is damaged by political and occupational interests which use policy to express or impose unitary ideas of social conflict or social consensus.

6 Unemployment and Inflation
John Baldock and Stewart Miller

Most of the problems described in this book arise largely as difficulties in personal and family life. It is argued that they are *social* problems to the extent that their gravity and their origins in social relations make them matters of public concern and collective action. But the label 'social problem' is also attached to broad, self-evidently public matters, some of which, for instance, are also describable as 'economic issues'. The matter which looms largest in the public mind as a social problem of the 1980s is mass unemployment. There is widespread agreement that in its consequences it is both a private trouble and a public issue of serious dimensions. But there is fundamental disagreement about how far its causes and its remedies lie in the public domain. In particular, the desirable public good of high employment appears to be in rivalry with another: low inflation.

The links between jobs and prices, and the choices associated with them, have become the basis for much political debate and social conflict. This is both an institutional battle, between the significant organised interests in society, and an ideological one. It pervades every aspect of social life: Parliament, where a government defends its financial achievements against an opposition that points to the human misery that persists; the public services, where the guardians of cash-limited resources impose rationing on the needy; industry, where the search for competitiveness has required a ruthless pruning of jobs; academe, where monetarist and Keynesian engage in mutual contradiction; and the family, where conflict often exists between the interests of men and of women, of parents and of children, and where the getting and keeping of a job is sometimes seen as a test of personal worth.

We do not attempt in this chapter a technical analysis of unemployment and inflation such as can be found in Snowdon and Osborne's article, 'Inflation and Unemployment' (1982). We consider rather the impact on social politics in Britain of the two phenomena seen as social problems, largely in a kind of contest with each other for prior treatment; at times, indeed, serving as the flagship issues of opposing ideologies. This is a conflict which has been about the aims and extent as much as the mechanics of economic regulation, and, crucially for our interests, about the responsibility of the state for the welfare of citizens. Far from being exceptional, save in its scale, this conflict has to be seen in the context of a crisis of liberal democracy which has been characterised by parallel clashes over social and political issues – crime and defence policy are other examples – and which has proved long and intractable. It is, moreover, a political crisis which has been reflected in social science analysis and argument. Researchers and other scholars have pitched in with a rare will, lending support to one or other of the contending policy approaches, or, frequently, damning them for ill-considered meddling. Whatever the role of social science in relation to these problems, it has not been to provide guidance as to their resolution which is generally accepted as authoritative.

In order to reach some kind of understanding of unemployment, inflation and their interrelation, we shall explore the recent history of the two phenomena and some concomitant issues. This will bring us to the responses of government and the paradoxes these present; and finally to a consideration of these two problems and their attendant solutions in terms of the ideologies they represent.

Recent History

For much of the 1950s or 1960s, it might well have seemed almost eccentric to write about either unemployment or inflation as current major British problems. The social scientist interested in the impact of economic problems and policies on social politics would probably have selected the balance of payments, the exchange value of the currency, or the combination of the two, as the economic disruption whose intrusion into social policy making was most salient. Governments were continually caught up in the struggle to keep the flow of goods and services in and out of the United Kingdom as profitable, or as little unprofitable, as possible, while maintaining the value of the Pound Sterling in the manner prescribed by the now defunct system of international exchange rate controls – and by the perception that that value was a matter of national prestige. This was the era both of two-party dominance of the electoral system and of a considerable degree of bipartisan consensus as to the limits beyond which such key indicators as unemployment and the payments deficit could not be allowed to go.

This implicit agreement about both the broad objectives and the techniques of economic and social policy has often been referred to as 'Butskellism', after the Conservative R.A. Butler and the Labourist Hugh Gaitskell, the two Chancellors of the Exchequer whose policies best exemplified it. It is also sometimes described as a product of the 'the post-war settlement' between labour and capital, since it marked a sharp break with the inter-war period when the interests of the working class, in high wages and high employment, had been seen as being in direct conflict with the interests of industrial and financial capital, in 'sound money' and low wage and tax costs (Jessop, 1980, pp. 28–9). In the 1920s and 1930s the models of economics which found acceptance in government had offered no policy technique by which the state could arbitrate between these contradictory forces. The weakness of labour, especially after the General Strike of 1926, had meant that the interests of capital tended to predominate.

The immediate post-war years saw not only a shift in the political balance, reflected in the election of the first ever majority Labour Government, but also the general acceptance in Whitehall of the ideas of the economist John Maynard Keynes. These, in a most fortunate and timely way, appeared to offer relatively non-interventionist fiscal techniques by which governments could strike a fine balance between the interests of capital on the one hand and, on the other, the labour movement's now undeniable insistence upon full employment and extensive welfare services. The key to the new strategy was the management of the government deficit. The latter could be expanded through increased public spending, reduced taxation, or both, when total demand was too low and resources lay unused, or contracted through spending reductions and higher taxation when demand appeared to be exceeding the productive capacity of the economy and to be generating inflation and excessive imports.

It ought to be admitted, of course, that this interpretation of the heyday of demand management is indeed *only* an interpretation. There is an alternative, which has been summarised succinctly by Samuel Brittan:

> The truth is that, for most of this period, neither the U.K. nor most other countries pursued demand management policies directed at full employment. The language of such policies was often used. But so long as the Bretton Woods system of exchange rates fixed against the dollar prevailed, the overriding aim was to maintain the currency parity ... As Mr. Nigel Lawson ... has written, 'During this period foreign exchange crises served as a proxy for monetary disciplines.'
>
> (Brittan, 1981, p. 32)

Moreover, if governments were indeed able to strike a technical and consensual balance of the kind we have described, it was certainly only during a brief golden age – until the mid-sixties. It was an era of relatively full employment, high profits and growing welfare expenditure during which Harold Macmillan felt able to tell the British electorate, 'You've never had it so good.' But Keynesian techniques were never so successful as to fine-tune the economy into a state of steady growth. This was also the era of 'stop-go' policies. The commitment to full employment and high demand meant the economy tended to overheat, suck in imports, inflate prices and threaten the exchange rate. Demand would have to be reined back, only to be whipped on again a little later to prevent unemployment. The oscillations involved in these cycles tended to become more violent, and the metaphor of 'fine-tuning' less and less appropriate (Jessop, 1980, pp. 31–2). Nevertheless, the range of the acceptable remained fairly narrow: for more than two years after assuming office in 1964, Labour struggled heroically to avoid a degree of devaluation of the pound at which scarcely an eyelid would have been batted ten years later; and the consequences for British democracy if unemployment were ever to reach the figure of a million were conventionally presented as dire.

Two of the initial objectives – a 'healthy' pound and a 'healthy' trade balance – were often at odds with one another, since a highly-priced currency does not help a country to sell its produce abroad, while it does help its citizens to buy 'foreign'. This added to the spice in the situation, and to the general obsession with these issues. It was generally felt that massive nationwide unemployment was a problem of the past – although regional unemployment was a matter of concern – and, while rising prices were bemoaned as damaging to standards of living and the competitiveness of British goods abroad, and the government occasionally tried to control them through 'price freezes', serious inflation was thought of as a problem of less stable societies than the British. That this perception became impossible to sustain in the 1970s is shown starkly in Table 6.1.

There are a number of fairly obvious features to this table. The rate of change in the retail price index (RPI) shows two peaks of inflation of spectacular dimensions for a developed nation in the post-war period, and a sustained level through the seventies and early eighties which is in marked contrast to that of the preceding period. This is accompanied, against all expectations from that earlier time, by steadily rising and ultimately massive unemployment. Wage increases in cash terms peak with price inflation in 1975 and 1980, and generally run higher than price rises, except in the aftermath of both peaks. Gross domestic product (GDP) tends to grow modestly if unevenly, peaking just before price and wage inflation.

There is of course more than one way of interpreting these figures. The period since 1950 can be seen as one of slow (by international standards) and declining economic growth, accompanied in latter years by inflation and unemployment whose rates of increase accelerated together in the 1970s. That inflation moderated in the 1980s seems to have been at the cost of even higher levels of unemployment. On the other hand, it is possible also to discern in the picture what was, for a while, exceptionally high growth by all past standards. Moreover, wage increases generally exceeded inflation by a considerable margin. The historically low levels of unemployment in the 1950s and 1960s were followed by a return to what can be seen as much more 'normal' levels at

Table 6.1 Key economic indicators, 1951–1985
(Percentage change on 12 months earlier unless otherwise stated)

	51-60	61-70	71	72	73	74	75	76	77	78	79	80	81	82	83	84*	85*
	Average annual rate																
i) Unemployment excluding school-leavers																	
%	1.4	1.9	3.3	3.6	2.6	2.5	3.9	5.2	5.6	5.5	5.1	6.4	10.0	11.7	12.4	12.4	12.4
No. millions	0.3	0.4	0.8	0.8	0.6	0.6	0.9	1.2	1.3	1.3	1.2	1.6	2.4	2.8	3.0	3.0	3.0
ii) Retail Price Index % change	4.1	3.8	9.4	7.1	9.2	16.1	24.2	16.5	15.8	8.3	13.4	18.0	11.9	8.6	4.6	5.1	5.3
iii) Wage Rates % change, in cash	5.4	6.1	12.9	13.8	13.7	19.8	29.5	19.3	6.6	14.1	15.0	18.0	10.0	6.9	5.6	8.0	9.0
iv) GDP % change	2.5	2.7	2.3	1.3	7.7	-0.7	-0.8	3.7	1.7	2.9	1.7	-2.4	-0.9	2.3	3.5	2.8	2.3
v) Total Govt. Expenditure in cash % change	7.1	9.2	12.4	12.3	15.9	28.3	31.4	13.4	5.8	16.2	18.5	21.8	12.0	10.3	8.2	5.0	4.5

Sources: i) Dept. of Employment Gazette, HMSO
ii) Economic Trends, HMSO
iii) Weekly rates, manual workers, all industries and services, Economic Trends, HMSO
iv) GDP at factor cost, expenditure based, Economic Trends, HMSO
v) Economic Trends, HMSO
* Estimates: *Financial Times* average of forecasts, 26.6.84.

a time when the percentage of the population of working age and the total numbers in work have been at record levels.

A third point should be mentioned here. The statistics in the table are themselves open to dispute, redefinition and recalculation. Should we measure unemployment in terms of the monthly stock of people registered as available for work (as is done in Table 6.1) or should we take account of the flow of people out of jobs and into other jobs and the length of time between the two? What about the people who fail to register, perhaps because they see no point, but who might do if the economy picked up? In the case of inflation too, the official RPI is just the measure of change in one particular 'basket of goods and expenses'. It is a carefully considered one and reasonably relevant to most people, but it must be remembered that people in different circumstances and on different levels of income may face very different combinations of costs. For example, those with mortgages may experience a reduction in their housing costs (repayments) at the same time as council tenants see a rise in theirs (rents). Those in the countryside are more vulnerable to increases in petrol prices, those living on their own to increases in heating costs.

If the facts of the period are open to more than one interpretation, they are subject to an even greater variety of explanation, from which we wish to point to two types. The first of these is the Keynesian. Here, the 1950s and 1960s are seen as the era of the managed economy, when manipulation of the level of demand kept a degree of balance between key variables – chiefly inflation, unemployment, the value of sterling and the balance of payments – within a range of variation and trade-off which was politically acceptable, even if the details were controversial. Keynesians would tell us that in the 1970s the range of variation increased, largely because of the external shock of oil price increases and the impact of world recession, but that the effect of these was exacerbated by deflationary economic policies after 1976. To the monetarist, on the other hand, what we have seen is a period of natural growth handicapped by expansionary monetary policies, more often implicit than explicit, which slowed the restructuring of the economy and led to a progressive loss of competitiveness and rising inflation and unemployment. So, in this account, the two contrasting periods do not present so much two different stories as two parts of a tale of complacent folly and its awful consequences.

In both of these accounts, be it noted, the ideas of economists have the status of significant and independent causal factors: the wisdom or foolishness of economic advisers has been reflected in governmental decisions, with substantial effects on the real world (Mishra, 1984, pp. 12–16). Academic success among economists has sometimes been measured partly by the frequency of their trips to Whitehall, and for much of this period most of the notable, and almost all of the influential, British economists were Keynesians of one hue or another. So when, in the 1970s, the peaks of inflation and the troughs of unemployment became increasingly steep, and began to overlap and even coincide, commentators began to speak of the crisis as the failure of Keynesianism. Butskellite policies were agreed by both left and right to have failed (Heald, 1983, p. 257; Roper, 1982, p. 36). Whatever the rights and wrongs of the technical debate, the implications of this perceived failure were clear. Either some new method had to be found to keep inflation, unemployment and other key variables within acceptable limits or the unwritten political concordat delimiting the acceptable would have to be broken.

Incomes policies, compulsory and voluntary, constituted attempts at new ways of achieving the old objectives. But as our introductory chapter points out, policies stand a much reduced chance of winning widespread support in so far as they directly and adversely discriminate against the interests of particular social groups. The record of income policies is an interesting and ambiguous one, both technically and politically (Brittan and Lilley, 1977). Here it is sufficient to point out that the opposition of organised labour meant that such policies could not be sustained with sufficient success and support for the governments that used them to win re-election. One way or another, an incomes policy was an election-loser, the severest weakness a policy can have. It is the second type of solution to the crisis of Keynesianism, a redefinition of policy objectives, that has been prosecuted since 1979.

Breaking the consensus: new attitudes and new policies

We stress again that not the technical economic arguments, but rather the reorientation of perceptions and the redefinition of the social problem are our concern. In short, inflation and unemployment were no longer defined as equally unfavourable indices of economic performance. Primacy was given to defeating inflation, both logically as the variable amenable to manipulation and upon which, it was argued, unemployment ultimately depends, and morally, as the greater evil for British society. Unemployment received scant attention in the Conservative Party's 1979 manifesto. Where it is referred to, the object is to define it as a secondary problem, or to redefine its significance:

When (the state) spends and borrows too much, taxes, interest rates, prices and unemployment rise.

Too much emphasis has been placed on attempts to preserve existing jobs. We need to concentrate more on the creation of conditions in which new, more modern, more secure, better paid jobs come into existence.

(Conservative Party, 1979, p. 8, p. 14)

It would greatly suit the presentation of this argument if the Labour Party had chosen to offer the electorate the reverse of the Conservatives' definition of the problem – its mirror image – and the electorate had made a clear choice between the competing perceptions. But the result of the 1979 election seems to have been affected by a popular reaction against the industrial relations problems which plagued the Labour Government's attempts at an anti-inflation strategy, largely forced on it by the International Monetary Fund; there is little evidence that Conservative policies appeared very attractive to voters (Butler and Kavanagh, 1980, p. 340). In the early 1980s the Labour Party did strive to offer an alternative economic strategy to that of the Conservatives; but the party was so beset by internal conflict when the opportunity to present this strategy arose in the General Election of 1983, and so intrusive was the effect of factors outwith the economic field altogether – chiefly, of course, the famous 'Falklands factor' – that the result of that election is also of little use in discerning the public view of unemployment and inflation as competing social problems. Indeed, that result was a victory – albeit without anything like a popular majority – for a singlemindedly anti-inflation government in the face of an evident popular opinion that unemployment was the prime social issue (Crewe, 1983).

The observer can discern something of the public's views on these matters from the results of opinion polls. We see three main points emerging from the information this source provides. Firstly, in post-war Britain there has been an exceptional tendency (compared with the United States for example) to see the problems of the country in economic terms and to judge governments by the performance of the economy. Hence economic issues have always topped the polls except for a brief period during the Falklands crisis (de Boer, 1983). Secondly, for a period in the 1970s inflation, rather than unemployment, came to be seen as the key problem. During 1980 a switchover occurred, unemployment replacing inflation as the most mentioned problem. However the Thatcher Government seems to have managed to decouple itself from responsibility for unemployment, in the public mind, to an unusual degree (National Opinion Polls, 1976, 1982). It was not so much that the public had faith in the Conservative Government's economic policies. Most, including Conservative voters, did not. Rather, many years of worsening economic performance appear to have induced the view that high unemployment and inflation were a permanent part of economic life (Harrison, 1984, pp. 47–50). Thirdly, the public seem to have little knowledge of the true rate of inflation, even when high, and little understanding of its implications. On the other hand, the polls show that the public have a relatively sophisticated understanding of unemployment: the numbers involved, its incidence amongst different occupational groupings and in different parts of the country (National Opinion Polls, 1975, p. 12).

What is the significance of these patterns of public opinion? It is helpful to consider them in terms of some of the general characteristics of social problems outlined in Chapter 1 of this book. There we distinguished between social problems as matters of fact and as matters of opinion. A distinction was also drawn between those issues which are seen primarily as problems of universal morality or of a technical nature and those which appear as sharp conflicts of interest between different social groups or classes. It is clear that problems which are perceived as belonging to the first group are the more likely to produce a sustainable consensus about what should be done. Chapter 1 also contrasted those perceptions that are rooted in people's own experience with those that they learn from the media. In the cases of unemployment and inflation is not immediately clear which categories are most appropriate. On the one hand it can be argued that both have had real and profound effects on people's lives. On the other hand it is possible to demonstrate that the majority of people have escaped most of the direct consequences of both. Those in work or dependent upon state benefits have more often than not seen their incomes rise faster than prices (Table 6.1 above; Upton, 1980, Table 4). Moreover, the many in our society who are debtors rather than creditors did rather well out of inflation. During the 1970s the large proportion of Britain's householders who were buying their homes on mortgages saw the burden of their debt rapidly eaten away while the value of their asset grew by leaps and bounds. People's relative ignorance about inflation perhaps reflects their relative immunity to it, even if they do not quite see it that way. Unemployment too, while much more widespread in the late seventies and the eighties than in previous post-war decades, remained a fairly concentrated phenomenon affecting the unskilled and the young (Disney, 1979) and largely avoided by the bulk of the population.

At the same time as inflation and unemployment have achieved their present notoriety, another, perhaps more significant post-war economic trend has disappeared without fanfare. Economic growth is agreed by most social historians to have been the most powerful and widespread economic source of change in the last forty years. During the 1950s and 1960s the slow drip of two or three per cent annual growth transformed the material conditions in which most people lived (Toland, 1980). Had Britain been able to sustain its 1973 growth rate throughout the subsequent decade it would have ended it some 25 per cent richer than it actually became. Yet economic growth and its demise in the late seventies was hardly ever mentioned to pollsters and in turn, therefore, was hardly ever asked about by them.

Should we therefore regard the persistent dominance, in the public mind, of unemployment and inflation as the major social problems as a creation of the media? Have the minority who are adversely affected by inflation – substantially, those few who own or control large financial assets – successfully wielded a disproportionate influence? In the case of unemployment it may be fear amongst the majority in work that the problem will spread still further that explains the high levels of public concern over a problem which still leaves most unscathed. Indeed it is sometimes argued that it is the disciplining effect of this fear that the powerful most wish to exploit. There is a high level of popular agreement that, while unemployment is the main problem for Britain in the mid-1980s, it is unlikely that the present Conservative Government or any feasible alternative can substantially reduce it, and indeed only a minority are prepared to blame government policies for the record numbers without jobs (de Boer, 1983, pp. 438–9). This is the decoupling effect mentioned earlier. The problem has been separated from government responsibility, allowing the re-election of Mrs Thatcher's Government in 1983 despite a level of unemployment that would have ensured defeat in any of the previous three decades. The assumptions that have produced this outcome – whether those of the public, most experts or many politicians, and whether justified or not – are really quite novel. As recently as 1975, the number of people out of work was below a million. Today there is widespread belief that unemployment of more than three times the 1975 figure, and eight times that of the early fifties, is an ineluctable and permanent feature of the British economy, and that government employment policies, where they exist at all, must necessarily be limited to minor make-work programmes (Hill, 1983, pp. 253–4). Given the relative recentness of good times, this widespread pessimism, shared by left and right for similar reasons, is really quite remarkable.

The innovatory achievements of the Conservative Government since 1979 have been, firstly, the adoption of a theory denying that economic policy can have any direct influence on unemployment, and, secondly and more importantly, the conversion of a substantial proportion of the electorate to such a view; or at least to the apparent suspension of their objections to it. It might even be argued that, in a sense, unemployment has ceased to be a *social* problem. Definitions of social problems often build in the possibility of some concerted, deliberate and rational policy solution, or at least amelioration. That is what makes the problem 'social'. If the reduction of unemployment can no longer command a realistic degree of priority as an object of policy, has it not by definition lost its designation as a social problem? Certainly the post-1979 insistence that government can and should tackle the 'evil' of inflation but cannot and should not engineer more than a limited amount of job-creation marks a significant break with previous conceptions of government's role and policy priorities, however unsuccessful policies based on such conceptions may have been. It is inflation that has, *effectively*, won the title of universal moral and technical problem; this despite the possibility that its effects on the real economy may on balance have been positive and that its distributional consequences are not essentially inegalitarian (Piachaud, 1978). Unemployment, on the other hand, undeniably a source of massive individual deprivation and collective loss to the nation's income, is successfully presented as economically necessary and accepted as technically intractable, only a decade after an era in which deliberately-engineered full employment contributed to the greatest increments to welfare in the nation's history.

State Policy Choices: The Primacy of Inflation Versus the Primacy of Unemployment

The degree to which government is seen (or at least presented) as having a vital responding role to play in relation to unemployment and inflation depends on perceptions of the two problems. In particular, the view that inflation is the greater evil tends to be accompanied by a judgement that government has a relatively modest function in economic and social life – indeed, the more modest the better, since it is largely government interference in what ought to be the open market that is thought to cause inflation. That is, we are told, because government both seizes (through taxation) and borrows money which ought to be available as cheaply as possible for investment purposes, and so pushes up interest rates and other costs.

In this view of the world, unemployment is almost a mere by-product of inflation and other disorders, and its amelioration will follow the setting to rights of the relationship between government and the more legitimate users of money. Indeed, recession with concomitant unemployment is likely to be of benefit to a country suffering from inflation:

If the Friedman-Hayek view is accepted, the policy issue is determined by a balance of the gains from a *permanent* reduction of inflation against the losses from a *temporary* waste of resources.

(Stapleton, 1981, p. 7)

This view, characterised here by the names of two of its leading proponents, seems indeed to have found acceptance in recent years. Mr John Biffen, then Secretary of State for Trade, was reported, in August 1981, to have found consolation in just such a view of unemployment, which he urged on fellow Conservatives:

Though harsh in terms of long-term misery, he said, high unemployment had brought some significant advantages to the country as a whole . . . they included a reduction in overmanning, a sharp fall in the number of strikes, a lower level of pay settlements, and the halving of the rate of inflation from its peak of just over 22 per cent.

(*Guardian*, 11 August 1981)

There is thought to be a minimum level of unemployment which prevents wage rises, which are always affected by expectations of inflation, moving ahead of the rate of 'real' growth in the economy. And even if unemployment is seen as regrettable, there is no hope of checking it in the long run by artificially creating jobs and bringing it below its natural level in the short term, because this will raise the cost of labour and enhance the general disincentive to employ it. Here, it is not accepted that there is any kind of genuine trade-off between inflation and unemployment, because they are not in counterposition, nor of the same order: they are, respectively, primary and secondary aspects of the problem of economic disruption or imbalance (Snowdon and Osborne, 1982, p. 16).

On the other hand, the opinion that unemployment is the primary evil tends to be placed within a view of the world in which government *rightly* looms much larger. Here, the state *ought* to have the capacity and the will so to order relationships in the marketplace that the supply of jobs reflects the demand for them, and it must be forever applying such adjustments both to its own and to others' economic activity as will keep this balance intact, or restore it when it has been lost. There are levels of inflation which may acceptably, or even helpfully, accompany such a process. Once mass unemployment is defined as an unacceptable burden, then the costs of remedying it become acceptable by definition. Michael Foot argued in the 1983 Labour Party manifesto that 'if nothing can be done about unemployment, nothing truly enduring can be done about anything else' (Labour Party, 1983, p. 5).

Thus there is much more scope in a 'primacy of unemployment' model than in a 'primacy of inflation' model for seeing the social effects of economic disruption as social problems, requiring collective action. This is not merely a matter of ideological consistency. Full employment is thought to generate more taxes and fewer expenses than unemployment in an economy. 'Any given level of generosity in the tax/transfer system is much less costly when there is a macroeconomic commitment to full employment,' observes Heald (1983, p. 259). Poverty, deprivation and idleness can more easily be taken on board as collective responsibilities by commentators and politicians holding this kind of view than by those principally concerned with inflation, for whom such other problems require an overlay of personal morality or threat to order before the residual, 'policeman' state can properly become involved. As Roper puts it, 'This debate thus poses the fundamental issue of whether state management of the economy is effective or whether it must inevitably threaten both economic efficiency and political liberty' (Roper, 1982, p. 27).

This is, of course, to deal with what are relative biases of approach in terms of ideal models, and few issues are actually decided on such a basis. (Mr Biffen, for instance, in the speech quoted above, was at pains to qualify his enthusiasm for unemployment by suggesting that the government needed not only 'the stamina to stick with the policy' but also 'the compassion to temper its sharp and personal effects'.) But such differences in emphasis are enormously important, both for those affected by the changes that it is within governments' power to make and as part of the game of adversary politics.

We ought not to exaggerate the extent to which, even in recent years, British governments of different hues have effected, or indeed attempted, economic and social action in radically different directions. Rose (1984) draws attention to the continuities imposed on successive governments by circumscribing factors, of which secular trends in the economy constitute one of the most powerful and constricting. He contrasts, on the one hand, the rhetoric of parties in office, in opposition and at elections with, on the other hand, the actual content of policies as well as their outcomes. This strikes us as less characteristic of the 1980s than of the earlier part of the period (from the 1950s) which Rose examines; although even the Thatcher Government has found how difficult it is, for instance, to make actual reductions of expenditure in areas of manpower intensive services, automatic entitlements, or needs enhanced by demographic factors. But there is no gainsaying the increasingly strident level of rhetoric which has characterised the relations between the major political parties in the past ten years or so; and, if the power of parties in office to radically change the direction of the economy or even of policy is half as limited as Rose suggests, that rhetoric can be seen as almost as important as policy action itself. Certainly, this is the case in the matter of gauging perceptions of social problems, relative priorities and degrees of consensus or conflict.

It would be a mistake, then, to conclude from the coincidence of unemployment and inflation in recent times, or from the practical impossibility of entirely ignoring one while acting on the other, that the tension between the two forms of economic disruption as problems of policy was merely a theoretical one. Far from it: the famous 'Philips Curve', which economists adopted to describe the trade-off relationship between unemployment and inflation, and therefore between policies to combat one and changes in the other, has continued to portray vividly the policy tensions of governmental decision making, even if its power of quantitative prediction has waned. The British in particular are prone to seeing the problem as a stark choice between one evil and the other, which need not be the case. Heidenheimer et al. point out that the single minded pursuits of Keynesianism and monetarism are not so much unavoidable alternatives as two possible strategies among many open to Western governments. These writers suggest that 'singleminded Keynesianism' and 'singleminded monetarism' – to the extent that either is practicable – seem to suit the characteristic, arms-length, British approach to governmental action in the economy:

Both approaches place total emphasis on governmental control over key economic aggregates – general levels of total demand in the former, and particular measures of money supply in the latter. Concentrating on these 'key levers' excused British officialdom from any deep involvement in the details of industrial production and finance.

(Heidenheimer et al., 1983, p. 141)

However, this reluctance to manage in detail does not extend to the public service sector, which is dominated by social services: the Welfare State seems to be an enterprise which British government feels it can manage properly and without distaste.

The electoral system may also have helped to create rigid patterns of policy response. Heidenheimer and his colleagues (1983, pp. 153–4) attribute the unanimity with which Western governments shifted radically towards anti-inflation policies in the 1970s to the much broader constituency affected by inflation than that hit by unemployment. Given the coincidence of both problems, governments felt they could pursue the short term interests of larger sectors of their electorates by giving priority to the anti-inflation drive. The British electoral system of 'first past the post' tends to institutionalise this factor. As north and south of the country have followed different economic paths so the votes of the unemployed and their neighbours have become less and less important to the Conservative Party. In 1979 the Labour Party won in 95 out of the 100 constituencies with the highest levels of unemployment. In 1983 the Conservative vote amongst the unemployed fell a further ten per cent (Ross, 1983, p. 81).

Conventional Wisdom: The Social Consequences of Economic Policies

The central battleground in the struggle between the two emphases of policy has been the field of public expenditure, and it is mainly the centrality of social spending in that field that has trapped the providers of social welfare in the thick of the fighting. Public expenditure can be seen as a tool for stimulation of demand, and indeed direct job creation, as well as the means of relief of the individual and communal depredations of unemployment. On the other hand, it also figures as the generator of inflation, and the rapacious rival of productive investment. Little wonder, then, that the politics of economic policy are frequently fought out around spending decisions, and particularly those on social welfare spending. The unemployed and the growing cost of their maintenance constitute a central issue here.

The particular arrangements for social security are subject to constraints imposed as the requirements of economic strategy. Some economists are prepared to argue that a good deal of unemployment is voluntary, and encouraged by state benefits for the out-of-work. Professor Patrick Minford has written that his own analysis 'suggests that every 10% rise in real social security benefits relative to the marginal product of labour raises unemployment by about half a million' (Minford and Peel, 1981, p. 15). His remedy is 'a series of cuts in social security benefits available to the employable.' This would have the effect of lowering wages and thereby encouraging the creation of jobs. In consequence, 'those who remain unemployed will be worse off, but their decision to remain unemployed will be a voluntary one' (ibid.). While this is not a logic explicitly adopted by the Thatcher Government it is consistent with the decision to cut unemployment benefit by abolishing earnings-related supplement and taxing all benefits. Professor Minford's basic assumption is that 'people use information efficiently in pursuit of their own interests' (ibid., p. 1). The Tory philosophy is: 'We want to work with the grain of human nature, helping people to help themselves' (Conservative Party, 1979, p. 7).

It is this logic, rather than the undoubted attempt to save money, that most convincingly explains policies reducing benefits for the unemployed. The sums involved are too small to count as important economies. Indeed once a government is convinced that the fruits of full employment will not issue from the expansion of demand then the costs of maintaining the unemployed do not constitute an overwhelming financial burden. In its outline of the primary considerations likely to affect decisions about public expenditure in the 1990s, the Thatcher Government indicates the relative unimportance of these costs. In explaining the growth of social security expenditure it points out that, amongst other things, it has been affected by:

... the recession, leading to significant increases in spending on unemployment benefit and supplementary benefits; in total, expenditure on the unemployed has increased in real terms since 1978–79 from £2.2 billion to £5.9 billion and now represents about 17 per cent of the social security programme, or 5 per cent of the public expenditure planning total.

(HM Treasury, 1984, p. 8)

In other words, if costs are defined in this way, the financing of the increase in unemployment between 1978–79 and 1983–84 has required an extra £3.7 billion or only 3 per cent of public expenditure. The savings achieved by cuts at the margins of this expenditure, therefore, have been very small indeed.

However, the policy debate is not essentially about the numbers involved, whether they be numbers of people or numbers of pounds, but about how these numbers are to be evaluated. The perspective attributing primacy to the costs of unemployment gives weight to other aspects of the problem, for example the income levels of the unemployed. From income data provided by the Family Finances Survey, Bradshaw and his colleagues compare the incomes of the unemployed with those of the lowest paid in employment, and conclude that:

the unemployed as a whole are considerably poorer even than very low wage earners. The long-term unemployed are living on just over half (57 per cent) of the gross income of the long-term employed . . . As would be expected, the income differential between the employed and the unemployed is smaller for disposable than for gross income, but even so the long-term unemployed have only two-thirds of the mean disposable income of the long-term employed.

(Bradshaw et al., 1983, p. 441)

Expenditure patterns suggested that the difference was not compensated for by substantially lower unavoidable costs (ibid., p. 445). And *The Economist* reported in June 1984 that evidence of the income effects of unemployment in OECD countries was embarrassing at least two member states sufficiently for them to take drastic action:

Whitehall is using its muscle to suppress an international report on the poverty created by long-term unemployment in Britain and other industrialised countries. British officials are comforted that the American government has joined in their efforts to delete a whole chapter of The Employment Outlook, published by the Organisation for Economic Development and Co-operation (OECD). They are now almost certain to get their way.

The study draws on the work of a British academic, Mr David Piachaud, of the London School of Economics. His analysis leads to the conclusion that unemployment causes real poverty, especially if it last over six months.

(*The Economist*, 16 June 1984)

The study is said to show replacement ratios – the proportion of income in work provided by the social security and tax systems to those out of work – in OECD countries ranging from about 65 per cent, for a married couple of earners, one of whom has been unemployed for less than six months, down to 35–40 per cent, for the same couple after more than twelve months, and for single people (ibid.).

It is difficult to disagree with the argument of Bradshaw and his colleagues that British social security policy, the broad outlines of which were laid down after the Second World War on assumptions of full employment, has failed to cope with the income implications of the unemployment problem. There is no provision in the social insurance system for long term unemployment, so there is enormous dependence on means-tested assistance (Supplementary Benefit), which also

discriminates against the long term unemployed by k
relatively low, short term rates, regardless of the d
condition.

These patterns of provision are the outcome of a p
which logic and ideology are, as always, inextricably
security, like other kinds of public expenditure, was use
regulator in the days of 'demand management', this h
less the case in more recent years, even if the mechanism has been a
different one. The current use of income maintenance arrangements for
economic purposes is against inflation, at the levels both of macro-
economic and of micro-economic strategy. At the macro level, the
limitation of the income maintenance responsibilities acknowledged
helps, if only a little, to keep down public expenditure and public
borrowing; and at the micro level, the maintenance of differentials
between the living standards of those in and out of work is intended to
keep the incentive to enter the labour market high without the costs
involved in high wages. The first of these strategies is evidently a case of
the response perceived appropriate to one problem (inflation) restricting
that to another (the income difficulties of the unemployed). The second,
and we would suggest the more important strategy, can be seen as one in
which the responses to both problems (unemployment seen as a
problem of personal incentives; and inflation as the product, in part, of
excessive governmental interference) coincide happily.

Unconventional Wisdom: Unemployment, Inflation and Ideology

Conceptions of what 'social problems' are frequently contain some or all
of three key ingredients. Firstly, there should be established evidence to
indicate that the problem adversely affects the lives of substantial
numbers of people, either in its causes or its effects or both. Secondly,
there is a duty upon the state to do something about the situation.
Thirdly, it is implicit that those conditions which have the status of
social problems are perceived as such by a large number of people,
possibly a majority in a society. It is arguable that these ingredients are
simple derivatives of three fundamental values of liberal democracy:
commitments to (a) the rational search for policy solutions, (b) the state
as servant rather than master, and (c) the paramountcy of majorities
(subject to some provision for the protection of minorities). This is why
social theorists whose conception of society is at odds with liberal
tradition find the concept of a social problem an uncomfortable one. If
'social problem' is a loaded concept then the loading does appear to
cluster round the presumptions of liberal democracy.

Inflation and unemployment fit easily into this framework. We have
witnessed their 'popularity' as social problems in recent times. Their

tion has been complicated by crucial divisions amongst those who
re expected to supply rational explanations, the economists. The
construction of policies to deal with the two problems has become a
matter of basic dispute between government and its opposition.
However, that unemployment and inflation have given rise to such
fundamental conflict may be seen as a symptom of crisis or at least
instability in liberal democracy itself. A mature polity of such a kind
draws much of its strength from a degree of agreement on the role of the
state and the maximum and minimum limits to its legitimate intervention. This agreement is the product of a long historical process
which, in Britain and elsewhere, has been characterised by a progressive
growth in state action beyond the minimal functions of the state which
provided for common defense against enemies and maintained law and
order within its boundaries.

The critical item of agreement for our purposes has been that to
guarantee certain standards of living for citizens. Its basic manifestation
has been the post-war consensus supporting the Welfare State and the
management of the economy in such a way as to ensure full employment.
It is a measure of the new and greater political uncertainty of the
1980s that not only this relatively new agreement but also those concerning the old-established activities of states are now contested. There
are sharp divisions in our society about how it should defend itself and
whether the existing policies provide much protection at all. There is
considerable disagreement and uncertainty about the degree to which
the criminal justice system offers protection to the law abiding citizen
and helps limit crime. And, similarly and no less bitterly, whether or
not the state can or should manage the economy and guarantee certain
forms of welfare is once again a central political issue. In each case too
the experts who previously seemed to provide a rational link between
public concern about problems and agreed policy have fallen out and are
in disarray.

If defining difficult issues into the form of social problems is typical of
liberal democracy, and progress in agreeing policies to deal with them is
a measure of its strength, then perhaps the re-emergence of these issues
as the grounds of major conflict may signal its weakness; and a parallel
point may be made of social science approaches to such phenomena as
unemployment, inflation and the range of 'social problems' in such
societies.

Much of this chapter has been essentially a descriptive account of the
policy choices made by British governments in response to the issues of
unemployment and inflation. This narrative has been set within a
framework which delineates different conceptions of the 'problem' and
the priorities these generate. In this last section we consider how far it is
possible to analyse this process of choice and to distinguish any general

patterns, particularly patterns that are shared with the life histories of other social problems.

The pattern of choice in economic policy making would appear to be determined by three sets of factors. Firstly, governments are bound to take notice of the theories and predictions of economists. Their influence has become institutionalised in the form of various academic orthodoxies, such as the 'Treasury view' (essentially the prevailing perspective of professional civil service economists) and, more recently, in the almost mechanical form of the 'Treasury model', a computer-based simulation of the whole economy. All these sources tell politicians what is likely to happen to various parts of the economy as a result of a new policy. For example, the Treasury model will predict the consequences an increase in public spending will have upon the level of demand, the volume of imports and exports, the value of the pound, the level of unemployment, the rate of inflation and the pace of economic growth. It makes clear instantly what are the predicted trade-offs between potential policy decisions. Of course forecasting is inherently an uncertain business, but the accuracy record of Treasury economists and advisors is sufficient to make their views very potent (Kennedy, 1982, pp. 30–6).

Secondly, policy choices are constrained by what is believed to be politically feasible and acceptable. Politicians and governments seek re-election. In addition, they are vulnerable to the protests, even the vetoes, of powerful groups in society which may believe their interests to be threatened. In the last resort, governments may have to reckon with the possibility of insurrection in the streets. This is rare in Britain but not an unknown consideration in policy making. Glynn and Booth give an example from the critical period after the First World War:

> ... orthodoxy was neither so monolithic nor so pervasive, that it prevented expansionist policies from being discussed and even implemented. Thus, early in 1919 we find that arch-apostle of orthodoxy, Sir Auckland Geddes, arguing in Cabinet: 'Inflation is absolutely essential. This policy which has been urged of getting rid of it is unsound. We have to keep up inflation'. 'Inflation' consisted of encouraging private and public sector enterprises to borrow. It was essential because *inflation maintained employment in the short term* at a time when the Cabinet was deeply suspicious of the revolutionary potential of ex-servicemen; Ministers feared the political consequences of rising unemployment.

> (Glynn and Booth 1983, p. 339; emphasis original)

However, political threats do not only come from 'mobs' on the street. Between 1964 and 1970 the economic choices of Harold Wilson's Labour Government were very much constrained by (as he called them) 'the gnomes of Zurich' – the men who controlled international currency flows and who might instigate a 'run on the pound'. In 1973 the crisis of the 'three-day week' demonstrated to Edward Heath's Tory Government that it could not maintain its incomes policy in the face of determined union opposition, particularly from the National Union of Mineworkers. James Callaghan's Labour Government had to bow to the dictate of the officials of the International Monetary Fund in 1976 in order to finance the debts generated by rapid increases in public expenditure.

All these cases are examples of the failure of government control to prevent the fluctuation of economic variables beyond an acceptable range. As has already been remarked, we would argue that the re-emergence of unemployment and inflation as divisive social issues is part of a process by which such failure has become increasingly common. At the height of the post-war Butskellite consensus, only fully enjoyed by the Conservative Governments of 1951–64, the great advantage economic policy makers had was that they were able to keep all the key variables within the bounds of political acceptability. In that sense they did not have to choose between effects on these variables except at fairly narrow margins. In particular from our point of view, both unemployment and inflation – the latter represented as a balance of payments problem – could be kept simultaneously at what were seen as tolerable levels. (Although even at that time regional unemployment was far from negligible except, it seemed, in terms of national politics.) These halcyon days slipped away, and by the mid-seventies the choice was, in practice, between one social problem and another: too much inflation or too little employment. Now this, of course, raises the question of what is too much or too little. How are politicians to gauge the limits of the politically acceptable? This range can only be known precisely after the events, when governments have fallen, or at least run into dire trouble. Ralph Miliband (1973) is one of the most explicit in arguing that Labour Governments in particular have been prone to misjudge and exaggerate the constraints on political room for manoeuvre. They too easily fell prey, he argues, to an 'establishment' ideology: a construction of the economic and political limits that amounted almost to a false consciousness (ibid., p. 244).

This brings us to the third determinant of economic policy choices: ideology. It is however not merely one amongst three but of a different and more difficult order altogether. For ideology penetrates both of the first two factors we have mentioned. Economics is not yet, if it ever will be, a neutral value-free science; it is inevitably shot through with the political preferences of its practitioners. Equally, the perceived limits of political choice faced by governments are built on ideological founda-tions. How then are we to analyse the impact of ideology on the ways in which inflation and unemployment have been tackled? For it is this issue, rather than the substantive one of how unemployment and inflation are to be tackled, that we see as crucial to the concerns of this book: the critical understanding of the concept of 'social problem' and its limitations, and the processes by which conceptions of phenomena as 'social problems' are formed and acted on.

Can we afford to presume that students of social problems have a special perspective that allows them to stand back from the fray and form particularly objective judgements for the enlightenment of others? We would argue not: we are all (to use a phrase Weber once applied to Marxist analysis) aboard a taxi from which some of us cannot just alight at will. If ideology affects those we study then it affects us too. However, we can extend our understanding by being constantly aware that we are all aboard the same taxi and by attempting to analyse the nature of our journey.

Much of our discussion so far has been confined more or less within the limits both of a conventional, Weberian approach to the under-standing of social phenomena, and – at least by implication – of an equally conventional, social democratic approach to social politics. The first of these stresses the *perceptions* of social actors as crucial to the definition and understanding of social phenomena, including social problems; phenomena are social problems to the extent that they are perceived as such. The brand of social criticism favoured in the second, social democratic approach tends to concentrate on the realm of the immediately feasible, given the constraints of the existing socio-economic system; here, indeed, phenomena are social problems to the extent that it is feasible to achieve a better working of the system by acting against them.

But there is more to social analysis than this, particularly when we consider the societal processes of which the conflict around unemploy-ment and inflation is one example. If there are contesting views of which of two or more social problems ought to command priority, or of the processes by which an economy has run into trouble, there are equally contending theories about the ways in which labels like social problem are attached to phenomena, about the meaning and validity of this particular label, and about the nature and characteristics of the society that experiences these problems. It behoves the student of social science to be aware of this contention.

Of the many perspectives in which one can view the emergence of such phenomena as unemployment and inflation as social issues, we would suggest that there are two, or rather two types, to which one ought to pay particular attention. The first of these views is, essentially, the one we have inclined towards so far, and its vital characteristic is its *relativism*. In this analysis, the rivalry between the 'primacy of unemployment' and the 'primacy of inflation' approaches to economic disruption and its social implications is a crucial one, but also typical of social interaction. Society is seen as comprising numerous and changing coalitions of its members. Each group tends to pursue its own interests defined according to its own interpretation of the social world – its own 'construction of reality', to use a well-worn phrase – and will attempt to establish that interpretation and those interests at the expense of those which threaten them. Rival views of social issues (such as unemployment and inflation) are locked in ideological struggle, the outcome of which is of vital importance both for the understanding and for the very future of society. Precisely because the perceptions of social actors – the way people see the world, rather than some kind of objective truth about it – are critically important, which view 'wins out' in social struggle is the deciding factor for the social scientist as to what is *really* a social problem. 'Social problems are what people think they are' (Fuller and Myers, 1941, p. 320).

If it is inflation that attracts social concern and political action, then inflation has the status of 'social problem' for the purposes of describing, interpreting and understanding society. If it is unemployment, then that is a social problem; if both, both are. If neither attracts such attention, there is no special authority that the sociologist, for example, can call on to support the application of the label as an appropriate, objective description of these phenomena. This need not disable him or her as a political actor, campaigning for the recognition of unseen problems; but only a broad social response, and no amount of social science expertise and authority, can confer such recognition.

The acceptance of this discipline by the social analyst interested in the study of social problems will, inevitably, determine the bias of his subject matter towards those potential social problems whose perception as such fits the conventions of current social politics. In the context of late twentieth-century capitalist society, this has tended to coincide with the view of the world we have described, loosely enough, as social democracy. By this we mean the kind of middle-of-the-road approach to social politics favoured by the supporters of Butskellism, and, apparently, by a substantial proportion of the British electorate for much of the post-war era. Both the construction of the Welfare State and many of the limitations imposed on it, from its birth, by cautious approaches to economic management fit into the picture of social democracy.

The other perspective we have alluded to is in marked contrast. In a *materialist*, (particularly Marxian) context this struggle between rival perceptions is itself no more than an indication of capitalism's essential contradictions and the impossibility, in the long run, of the simultaneous pursuit of private enterprise, state participation and individual welfare. The primacy of one social problem or another is merely a characteristic of a particular formulation of the optimistic view that capitalism can be rendered satisfactory by adjustments: the triumph of ideological hope over material experience.

For many social scientists, then, unemployment and inflation are contrasted disorders – problems – of essentially, or at least potentially, sound economies; for others, unemployment is a secondary and inflation a primary flaw of economies in which the market has been polluted by state intervention. To the Marxian analyst, these very ideas are themselves products of their socio-economic environment. It was indeed Marx who coined the term 'ideology' to describe, as Ian Gough puts it, 'the set of ideas about a society generated by that society'.

All societies (Gough goes on) generate beliefs and concepts about themselves which are contradictory. At one level the leading ideas correspond to the reality of that mode of production, yet at another level they are distorted because they present that particular mode of production as eternal. The false appearance generated by ideologies stems from their failure to explain history as a succession of qualitatively different modes of production. Thus much writing by economists on exchange or by sociologists on industrial society assumes the present forms of capitalist society. Sometimes this is contrasted to a previous 'simple' or 'primitive' stage of history, but there is no perception of capitalism itself as a historically specific stage.

(Gough, 1979, p. 24)

One of the most important consequences of the present crisis in capitalist economies, then, has been critical damage to the ideological consensus built by the past successes of the post-war mixed economy. Critics of that system and the truce between capital and labour on which it was partly based will see this as no bad thing. The present antagonisms of social and economic politics can be seen as much more accurately reflecting the true relations of an essentially capitalist system, and, potentially at least, productive of ideologies closer to the objective facts of life in such a system.

Capitalism has survived crises scarcely less serious than the present one. It will probably adapt in such a way as to survive again. What will be interesting, in terms of our present concerns, will be whether part of that adaptation will include an acceptance in the dominant ideology – and therefore in received opinion – of unemployment and inflation as continuing facts of life, with or without the status of 'social problems'.

7 Reconstructing Social Problems: Policy Failure, Ideology and Social Knowledge

Nick Manning

In Chapter 1 we showed that the social problems literature ranged along a dimension which at one end emphasised the extent to which the social conditions themselves were felt to be detrimental to human well-being; at the other end of the dimension the values and attitudes of those offended by the social conditions were stressed. As the key points of definition of a social problem, these positions stress respectively an objective and a subjective approach to social reality. Yet we argued that each suffers from weaknesses, which in turn are the strengths of the other. Objective study of detrimental social conditions presumes a consensus of public judgement, or arrogantly posits what the public should be concerned about. Subjective study of public concerns on the other hand has no way of sifting the important from the trivial, or of resolving ambivalent attitudes or conflict about the significance of social issues.

This tension between a spurious objectivity and complete relativism was partly produced as a result of the static nature of this traditional debate in the literature about whether social problems were 'really' one or the other. The dynamic and historical view suggested by Spector and Kitsuse (1977) was an attempt to sidestep this sterile debate by including both the objective social conditions in their model and the resulting subjective sense of grievance that motivated people to register a claim in the political system. Yet, we argued, this proposed solution had its own limitations. First in its own terms it did not suggest much more than a traditional pressure group model of politics. It had little to say about the nature of that political system, nor about the process through which grievance claims are publicly debated. We therefore discussed the general way social problems enter the life of the modern state, and the influence of the mass media on this process in order to fill out these gaps in Spector and Kitsuse's model.

However, a second limitation is that there is still the question of the relationship between social conditions and people's ideas about them as social problems. Spector and Kitsuse's solution was essentially contingent: *if* people found social conditions offensive, and *if* they could construct a legitimate grievance claim, and *if* the state responded, then something might be done about the social problem. We suggested that these contingencies could be understood through the notion of ideology. We drew on Mannheim's (1960) ideas to suggest that people perceive the world according to their own interests, so that there is a bias in the way social problems are understood. Clarke (1975), we noticed, had suggested that modern social problem beliefs tended to focus on the *individual* (rather than the group or collectivity) and on the individual's misfortune as *natural,* that is without being the responsibility of anyone. This was commensurate therefore with a technical, depoliticised response to social problems which Haines (1979) argued involved the enclosure of previous conflicts into a definition of the problem in which the professional expert becomes the judge of the solutions available to the original problem.

Armed with this extended model of social problems we proceeded to examine, through a series of concrete examples in the following chapters, whether we had achieved a satisfactory understanding of the general features of social problems in modern society. The case studies amply illustrate our argument that social problems cannot be reduced to either an objective appraisal of social conditions or a purely subjective contest between competing perceptions. In each of them we see a variety of perceptions in conflict, or different perceptions appearing over time; but each viewpoint is not detached or freefloating, rather it is constructed upon the available evidence about the social conditions in question. In tracing the history of each problem the case studies have also demonstrated the influence of the mass media; and a consistent ideological tendency, in the processing of grievance claims by official agencies, to reduce problems to the administratively or professionally manageable. In other words we cannot understand those problems without a dynamic view of their history, their portrayal in the media, and the ideology of administrative and professional management within official state agencies.

Perhaps, at this rather general level, we should not be too surprised that we found what we were looking for. However, in addition to reassuring ourselves that we were looking at the right institutions and processes for an understanding of social problems, we also want to know what else the case studies have shown us. Objections may be raised that by definition case studies are about a unique cluster of events from which any generalisations cannot be drawn. Yet by using them together as a small sample for comparison we can begin to detect common and disparate elements. In the rest of this chapter we will explore some further issues which our comparison of case studies has raised.

Some Unresolved Issues

The case studies together raise a number of questions to which they suggest a range of answers. The issues in common can be grouped into three questions:

1   Why do social conditions become social problems for which a solution can be expected?
2   Why is the modern state the major site for the solution of perceived problems?
3   Why do people continue to support state intervention when it repeatedly fails to solve social problems?

Starting with the third question, the most obvious common finding from the case studies is the failure of state policy to provide effective solutions to social problems. This is particularly ironic since a major influence on the emergence of a successful social problem is the availability of a promising solution for it – in many cases the solution determines the problem rather than vice versa. For example, the emergence of women's refuges as a solution to the problem of battered women was intimately connected with its emergence as a legitimate problem in the first place. Green (1975) has suggested in this respect that social problems frequently emerge when social conditions are getting better and when the possibility of a final solution seems near.

A second finding is the tenacity with which policies and their justifications are retained despite their apparent failure to work. For example, the ineffectiveness of penal measures, of the treatment of mental illness, and of the combatting of racial disadvantage, have been a clear theme in our case studies; yet the continued support of these policies is quite normal. In a review of the way in which government intervention frequently leads to a worse rather than a better outcome, Sieber (1981) suggests that much intervention is regressive and ironically leads to 'fatal remedies'. While the typical reaction from the right is to 'do nothing', and from the left is to 'change everything', he suggests that the most frequent effect is for policy makers to redouble their efforts at rational problem solving by taking more variables into account in order to try and control adverse effects. While computers will sustain such attempts in evermore complex models, it might be more interesting to answer the question which he only raises at the end of his book, but fails to answer: 'What makes it possible to sustain actions that have reverse consequences?' (Sieber, 1981, p. 201).

The answer to this question, and the others at the beginning of this section, requires a restatement of how social problems arise on the agenda of the state in modern societies. To say the least, we must concede from Chapter 1 that the notion of 'social problem' is problematic: there are uncertainties over its definition; it is peculiarly subject to ideological assumptions; and it may, therefore, represent the politically or administratively legitimate tip of an iceberg of deeper social grievances. Yet it is difficult for the social scientist to stand outside these issues and bring an intellectual neutrality to the area. Such a solution suggested by Max Weber (1949), has been a considerable influence in social science. It has to a certain extent gained the sociologist respectability, yet at the same time there has been a growing dissatisfaction with the notion. The main criticism has been that a neutral sociology in fact masks an accepting sociology – one that is uncritical of the society in which it exists, and therefore, one which in effect approves of current social arrangements. As Gouldner (1963) puts it, 'one meaning of a value-free sociology is that thou shalt not commit a critical or negative value judgement – especially of one's own society' (p. 43). He feels that many social scientists have surrendered their critical impulses in return for a measure of autonomy and social support.

In the social problems field the Manis (1976) approach of gathering social facts evidently subscribes to a notion of objectivity. Yet even Green's (1975) more responsive questioning of the definition of social problems follows suit. For example the idea of value conflict, that a social problem appears where there are conflicting views of a social condition such as poverty, attempts to place the sociologist outside the conflict in a neutral position. He is saying in effect that group X (perhaps a political party) and group Y (perhaps the unemployed) view poverty in different ways, and that he is beyond or above this conflict. Yet the very definition of unemployment or poverty as a problem changes perceptions and hence the sociologist is nevertheless involved. The nature of this involvement becomes more clear when we look at the kind of activities social scientists are engaged in.

Studying the Beast
Seeley (1963) for example separates out two activities of social scientists:

1 the definition of problems for study;
2 and the analysis and detection of the causes of the problem.

The definition of a problem for study is of importance since problems are the particular phenomena we are concerned with. For example, the definition and re-definition of poverty as an area of scientific study has had a significant impact on its general perception, and indeed government policies designed to deal with it. Thus, the 'discovery' of poverty in the late nineteenth century by Booth, Rowntree and others, it has been argued, increased fears of socialism, and ultimately stimulated the 1911 Social Insurance Act – as Rimlinger (1971) put it 'To the extent that those who might become poor were forced to protect themselves from want, society as a whole, but particularly the rich, was protected from the poor. In this sense, social insurance has become an important form of protection for the rich' (p. 338).

In the 1950s, on the other hand, the general optimism of peacetime and the construction of the Welfare State in Britain made the results of the survey by Rowntree in 1951 (of poverty in York) particularly influential. He appeared to show that poverty had been reduced to the low level of 1½ per cent of the population. Poverty it seemed could be more or less disbanded as a problem. Yet only 14 years later poverty was re-discovered, again by academics, and re-entered the political and scientific arena as a serious issue for consideration (Abel-Smith and Townsend, 1965). Thus, social scientists have been crucial to the definition of poverty as a social problem.

Secondly, and most crucially for our purposes, the social scientist concerns himself with explanations – what are social problems and where do they come from? What causes them? Of course in some senses, everything is connected to everything else, so how do we choose the cause? Seeley argues that a cause is, in effect, that which will secure a desired change in the most convenient, economic or efficient way possible. Hence, we choose to exterminate mosquitos as the cause of malaria, since to do without human blood (another 'cause' of malaria) would obviously be a drastic and inconvenient solution.

Seeley suggests that it is in the field of social problems analysis that this choice of 'convenience' causes is most noticeable:

As I have said elsewhere, the cause of delinquency, 'other things being equal', is any one or more of the following: poor street lighting, alleys, immigration, paternal infidelity, differential association, neurotic acting out, broken homes, the American income distribution, lack of alternate meaningful activities, advertising and display, failure to nail down prized objects, the slum, the ecological organisation of the American city, materialism, its opposite; preoccupation with one's worth as a person, the law itself, the absurdity of society or the human condition; the want of religion, the nuclear family, the political system which needs crime which needs as a training ground prisons and reformatories; schools that engage few or no loyalties, the perversity of the individual delinquent, or his parents, or theirs; psychological ignorance, the unconscious wishes of those who deplore the activity or condemn the actors. 'Choose your pick', as they say. There can hardly be a question that all are involved, and an infinity – literally – of other candidates for causal ascription besides. And each of these 'causal factors' is also connected for the purposes of science with an infinity of other causes. The selection for reporting and hence attention of any one cause – say the ghettoization of Negroes in the Black Belt, leading to rent extortion, leading to overcrowding, leading to heightened necessities for certain types of experiences and escapes – is as clear an act of judgement (in the legal sense) as if when a bridge collapsed a judge were to select a particular passenger over it, as the cause of its downfall from the combined excessive weight of all of them on it at the time.

The selection of any one of these for study is a political act, an expression of a political position – a power-redistributing value-function that the social scientist knowingly or unknowingly holds. Let me leave this here for now as the cause-tax or etiology-fine theorem.

(Seeley, 1963, pp. 60–1)

Thus, the choice of which cause to study involves value bias and the involvement of the social scientist. But this is not a haphazard affair. There are definite pressures most clearly exercised by those agencies funding research to concentrate study on certain particular areas. For example, Sir Keith Joseph, just before the Conservatives lost office in 1974, announced a massive research effort amounting to hundreds of thousands of pounds, to study not merely poverty and other associated social deprivations, but a particular cause (the main one in his view) – the transmission of deprivation from one generation to another. In other words he funded the study of the way the poor hand on deprivation to their children (Rutter and Madge, 1976).

This, we may think, merely will add to our general knowledge about poverty. But it is not as simple as this. Seeley illustrates by looking again at delinquency:

Let me suppose a sociologist or psychologist interested in the rehabilitation of the imprisoned delinquent. He might be asked and he might assent to the study of any of the following, roughly ordered problems. How, after we have thoroughly strapped a defiant child, can we mitigate his feelings, so that he is not led by the feelings into a vicious cycle of further defiance and increased punishment. Or, how can we find a substitute punishment for strapping that would have the same effect – the breaking of resistance – without the too patent sadomasochistic risks. Or, how can administration be smooth and overwhelming without resort to patent punishment, defined as such? (I think this is the commonest type of problem our clients bring us). Or, given morally meaningless confinement how can we minimize coercion? Or, given the need for order and the absurd rules of the society, what alternatives can we find for confinement (e.g. free marijuana)? Or, what alternatives are there to the absurd rules, given the present sociopolitical structure? Or, what alternatives are there to that structure, given the need for national stability in the face of the cold war? Or, what alternatives to cold war, given no radical reconstruction in the minds and hearts of men?

(Seeley, 1963, p. 61)

He further asserts that success earlier in this list reduces the likelihood that a subsequent item will be examined. For Keith Joseph, the successful demonstration that the poor cause poverty in their children would avoid the more painful examination of whether it is the wealthy and the structure of inequality in society which causes poverty. Thus, the way we choose to examine a social problem is affected by complex assumptions, which Seeley maintains are typically in favour of leaving the status quo undisturbed.

As we shall argue in greater detail later in this chapter, this kind of bias in intellectual work can be best analysed through the concept of ideology.

A Reformulation

We have suggested that our case studies support the definition of social problems as the reconstitution of social grievances into soluble form as they are legitimated within the state, represented in the media, and ideologically recast in terms of individual and natural misfortunes. Yet there is overwhelming evidence of the failure to solve social problems in this form, combined with a surprising tolerance of such failure. Since academic social scientists are a crucial medium in this process we examined their contribution to the definitional outcome, particularly their biases introduced as a result of attempts to remain value-neutral.

If this bias in social science which lends support to the reconstitution of social grievances as social problems was merely an error or oversight remediable through a better analysis, then it would have been corrected a long time ago. However it seems there is a more stable process at work which constantly reproduces this approach to social problems. We can begin to consider the nature of this process by returning to the suggestion of Mannheim that ideological bias creeps into the analysis because of the self-interest of authors which shapes the way they look at the world. George and Wilding (1972b) have suggested that in modern society in fact only some people are able to sustain their own definition of the world by persuading others to agree with them in three ways:

i)   The definitions of those in dominant positions tend to become part of the major institutional order – the civil service, the law and the courts, the education system and so on. Thus the perceptions of a particular group are changed into *national* symbols or images. Thus 'scroungers' are despised not only by the rich, but the respectable working class also.
ii)   Appeals are made to the necessities of the economic system. For example inequality is seen as necessary as a stimulus to economic achievement, a view to which we are all asked to subscribe, yet which also justifies poverty.
iii)   Third there is a more direct control of the creation and circulation of cultural images. The mass media thus tend to convey ideological perceptions again justifying the status quo. For example recent research on the presentation of industrial news on television demonstrates a systematic bias against the interests of workers, and in favour of industrialists who are identified with national interests (Glasgow University Media Group, 1976).

Their third point has been stressed particularly by Habermas (1972) who suggests there is a tendency in modern society towards a conception of political and social issues in 'technical – problem' terms rather than as real conflicts. He argues that along with the increasing spread of ideas of rationality and problem solving into previously political areas, there grows a new legitimation of the status quo. In other words existing social and political arrangements are increasingly justified as rational, while any conflicts or difficulties which arise become technical problems theoretically amenable to logical analysis and therefore solution.

Social issues are one area in which this rational problem policy view has grown. Hence the recourse to a 'social problems' view of many areas of social life. But Habermas argues that to the extent that such apparent rationality actually conceals real differences of interest, for example between rich and poor, then that rationality becomes increasingly ideological in nature as it spreads. In other words the very attempt to foist certain particular interests on others in the guise of rationality, introduces ideological bias. As Ryan puts it:

All of this happens so smoothly it seems downright rational. First, identify the problem. Second, study those affected by it and discover in what ways they are *different* from the rest of us as a consequence of deprivation and injustice. Third, define the differences as the cause of the social problem itself. Finally, of course, assign a government bureaucrat to invent a humanitarian action programme to correct the differences ...

(Ryan, 1977, p. 66)

This account of bias in our understanding of social problems has two principal components: a view of ideology as class dominance, and an argument that in contemporary society problems which individuals and groups experience are transformed in cultural terms, particularly by the media, into issues that are properly resolved in a technical manner in the political sphere. However this argument has been criticised for over emphasising the passivity of the public as recipient of ideas and images circulated by the dominant class via the mass media. Both Parsonian sociology which emphasised socialisation via the internalisation of values, and structuralist Marxism which emphasises the human subject as the bearer of class forces, reduce human actors to empty shells. As Giddens (1979, p. 52) tersely observes; 'Parson's actors are cultural dopes, but Althusser's agents are structural dopes of even more stunning mediocrity.'

Abercrombie, Hill and Turner (1980) for example suggest, on the basis of an extensive historical review, that ordinary citizens have never been heavily influenced by dominant class ideas, even in the modern age with its greatly expanded production of media technology. Rather, they suggest that dominant ideologies are only important in sustaining cohesiveness *within* the dominant class's value system. This argument echoes Mann's (1970) earlier observation that the social cohesiveness of liberal democracies is an illusion at the level of social values. Only those with power need consistent values, he suggests, since everyone else can hold a variety of values so long as they pragmatically accept their role requirements.

If we abandon an explanation which rests on something akin to a conspiracy theory of class, we must think further about why the general public and academics alike have such a faith in the solution of their grievances as social problems in the political sphere. The obvious step to take is to suggest that people really do think that the state can help them, and indeed on occasions it does. However there are complications, since their experience of state help may include the giving up of some independence, or the receipt of unwelcome opprobrium (London Edinburgh Weekend Return Group, 1979). While it may be argued that this is merely the inevitable (natural?) consequence of bureaucratic organisation, we can explore this apparent contradiction in state activity (i.e. both help and control) by reflecting further on the nature of the state in modern society, and the way we think about it.

In modern society there is a formal split, particularly noticeable since the advent of Thatcherism, between an anarchic undemocratic private world of market and family and a formally democratic political sphere, supposedly guardian of the common good/interest. However economic and social crises increasingly compel the state to intervene even while it formally refuses to do so. This is because the very existence of the state is dependent on buoyant economic production and stable family reproduction to provide jobs, taxes and loans, and new workers. Thus economic and social conflicts are transferred to the political sphere, which however is contrained in its responses by the need to maintain the economy and the family. Thus while the world of the state is formally rational and neutral it becomes tainted by partisanship and ideology as conflicts appear within it.

Clearly the nature of these conflicts (including social problems) is crucial. If we merely mean disagreements between a myriad of different interests, we are suggesting no more than that the state continues its traditional role of a neutral umpire and rule-keeper. However if we suggest that these conflicts and social problems are the more fundamental ones between classes and genders, then it is more difficult to sustain a view of the state as a neutral. Rather it will be forced into taking sides – of one class against another, and one gender against another, since the conflicts it is asked to resolve affect its own conditions of existence.

Popular and academic appeal to the state to solve social problems is thus both a realistic request, based on common interests, yet one which rests upon an ideology of the formal separation of the state from the private sphere. Since in reality this formal separation is in continual danger of breaking down, social policies as responses to social problems become bound up with issues of class and gender conflict since they attempt at the same time to solve social problems and to sustain existing class and gender inequalities.

This formulation of the state as operating in a contradictory manner, rather than as a simple agent of class conspiracy, requires a more detailed elaboration, which we will consider in the next section. While there are a number of approaches to understanding the state, which we outlined in Chapter 1 (rationalist, élitist, corporatist, pluralist, and Marxist), we shall use one which we have found most useful with respect to elaborating social problems in terms of a theory of ideology – the Marxist approach. We shall consider a modified Marxist approach, developed from corporatism, in the final section of this chapter.

The State
There are several distinct approaches to understanding the state from a Marxist viewpoint. However they are not equally useful for understanding social problems and social policy. The first takes an 'instrumental' view of the state, by suggesting that it operates as an instrument in the hands of the ruling class. For example Miliband (1973, 1977) argues that because senior state personnel are frequently drawn from the ruling class, and capitalist enterprises are very effective pressure groups, the state acts on behalf of a class, conscious of its own interests. While we would agree with this analysis of early capitalist societies, it seems to us that it is simplistic when applied to Britain in the late twentieth century. Our evidence from the case studies is that the state may be operating on behalf of a ruling class in some areas, such as the macro-economic planning which affects inflation and unemployment. But in other areas it may also be responding to genuinely popular anxieties, such as for the control of mad people and juvenile criminals, or to the pressures of professionals and reformers, or to the real problems of specific groups such as blacks and women. These interventions cannot be interpreted simply as ruling class concerns, although the form in which such interventions are couched, and hence the frequent failure of such policies may well be a result of certain actions being out of bounds – bounds drawn by ruling class interests.

A second approach challenges this notion of the state as reducible to the interpersonal relations of the various groups that constitute the state. By contrast Poulantzas analyses:

social classes and the state as objective structures, and their relations as an objective system of regular connections, a structure and a system whose agents, 'men', are in the words of Marx 'bearers of it – trager'.

(Poulantzas, 1972, p. 242)

In other words, the growth of state intervention and the nature of social policies are not to be seen as the deliberate result of conscious class or individual actions, but rather the result of the immanent logic of the total system. This crucially paves the way for a conception of the state as relatively autonomous of the economic level of capitalist society which merely constrains the state 'in the final instance'. While such autonomy can also be located in Miliband's work (as the result of political 'slack' in the system), Poulantzas attempts to theorise this far more rigorously as a necessary aspect of the division of capitalist society into different instances or levels – the economic, the ideological, and the political.

It seems to us that despite the difficult language in which this second approach is expressed, it has a major advantage over the first, in that it can accommodate the notion of working class organisation and political presence in the modern capitalist state. Poulantzas argues that the ruling party within the state must weld together an effective power bloc (as Margaret Thatcher has done recently) out of the existing class forces available. Clearly, the balance of such forces is the key to understanding state activity, and hence social policy. This approach helps us to understand the development of welfare legislation in many European countries around the turn of the century in response to the potential and actual organisation of the working class in those countries into political parties. In England, the last quarter of the nineteenth century witnessed the beginnings of an organised labour movement, industrially and politically. During this same period, one finds a growing recognition by individuals within the capitalist class and the state that social reform was not synonymous with the demise of capitalism.

However, there are problems nevertheless with this approach. First of all, it has nothing to say about the extent of and limits to the autonomy of the political level and how the constraints of the economic level 'in the final instance' actually operate. In other words, it takes class power and its effect on the political level as a given. For example we may imagine that the ultimatum delivered to the Labour Government by the International Monetary Fund in 1976 is a clear example of the economic 'last instance', determining the beginning of the current era of restraint on social policy expenditure. Perhaps also the subjection since 1979 of state activities to the requirements of 'beating' inflation is a similar economic 'last instance'. Yet it is clear that controlling inflation is a political option, not an immanent requirement of a natural economy. Nevertheless structuralism excises almost all political voluntarism, and hence seems to have nothing to say about how the state changes. Thus for example if we wish to understand the source of the British state's recent attacks on social policy from this perspective, we are reduced to acknowledging that the balance of class forces at the political level has changed, but we do not know how to discover whether this is a case of the economic 'final instance'.

A third approach can be seen as a direct corrective to the weaknesses of the second. If Poulantzas separates out the balance of class forces into the political level, this approach asks instead about what developments and requirements are coming up from the economic level to which the state must respond. In other words, what are the needs of capital(ism) which constrain the state to act in certain ways? From this perspective, any autonomy that the state may appear to have is quite limited. Developments and crises in the economy are heavily determining of state policy. From the social policy perspective, our understanding of recent cuts in public expenditure extending across two different governments is considerably enhanced with this approach which directs our attention not so much to the state directly, but to the state operating within severe economic limits.

One well known recent variant of this approach is adopted by Ian Gough (1975, 1979) in his study of the British Welfare State. In a sense his is not a pure example for he argues that the state is both inextricably linked to economic forces, yet specific policies are hammered out through conscious class and pressure group conflict in a separate political sphere. Nevertheless, the economic dynamic is dominant. Gough relies on O'Connor's separation of capital accumulation and political legitimation as the two major tasks facing the capitalist state (1973). These primary tasks give rise to expenditure on social policy to ensure that there is labour available for production at minimal direct cost to the employer, and to ameliorate the worst disruptions generated by industrialisation.

In general, the strength of views which give real space to the economic dynamic as an integral part of state activity, is that they can explain why and from where the constraints upon the political system arise – they raise the economic 'final instance' to the status of full cabinet member! We can thus understand developments in social policy as continuously contingent upon economic changes, and the political tensions these generate as they appear within the state. Or, to put it more crudely, economic policy dominates social policy, while the state in general has relatively little autonomy.

However, our viewpoint from social problems indicates that this approach is still inadequate in certain respects. Firstly, it is clear that social policy has never really been a vital and central issue in political class conflict in the way that Gough suggests – certainly not when compared to the struggle over wages, industrial relations, and so on. The British TUC has never concerned itself as much with the social wage, as the industrial wage. Other groups who have struggled over social policy, such as clients, have never entered the political arena in anything like the codified way that Gough suggests conflicts are settled. Moreover, public opinion polls suggest considerable ambivalence towards the Welfare State (Taylor-Gooby, 1982). Secondly, the assumption that state activities are necessary and functional for capital, underlying much of this work, is confounded by the considerable evidence in case studies such as ours which demonstrates the failure of many social policies to achieve their objectives. These difficulties have given rise to a further reformulation of state theory, which is most relevant to understanding social problems and social policy.

The previous positions have all more or less accepted the separation of the political and economic levels, while suggesting various degrees of relative autonomy between them. A fourth position takes a different line by returning to Marx's separation in his critique of classical political economy, of 'appearances' and 'essences'. In a nutshell, he suggested that in bourgeois society what is in fact a unitary totality of social relations of exploitation is experienced as divided between autonomous economic individuals in the market and state regulation of that market. This appearance could only be penetrated by him through a materialist analysis of class struggle. This theory of knowledge central to Marx's method in *Capital* suggests that the economy and the state, far from being distinct spheres within their own 'rules for action', only appear to be so (Gold, Lo and Wright, 1975; Cypher, 1980). In essence, they are part of a unified set of social relations characterised by both exploitation and the class struggle generated by this. Class struggle then is not, as Gough suggests, merely to be found at the political level, but at the economic level also. Social and other state policies are attempts to respond to struggle generated there, in apparently 'political terms'. However, in the process, these struggles are continually reproduced and take the form of conflict over the nature or form of state policies.

Esping-Anderson, Friedland, and Wright (1976) suggest that struggle ranges along three dimensions: whether reproductive of capitalist social relations; whether in commodity or non-commodity forms; and whether at the level of production or circulation. They suggest that working class struggle in both the economy and the state is towards changes that are unreproductive of capitalist social relations. However, if forced to concede policies the state normally pushes for those that are reproductive of capitalist social relations.

We can illustrate this from our case studies. While the political demands which have appeared from blacks, women and mental patients have stressed autonomous organisation and community control of facilities, social policy has usually been in the form of professionally controlled goods and services provided at a meagre level. Rather than by guaranteeing the right to work as an activity divorced from its labour market status, the state deals with unemployment by policies to reinforce the commodity status of labour (youth training, better job centres, and so on).

This line of argument has been linked by Holloway and Picciotto (1978) to the so-called 'state-derivation debate' amongst West German writers, who have argued that the state is the form in which class struggle appears in capitalist society. From this point of view then social policy becomes an aspect of class struggle which is permanently in existence at both political and economic levels, but appears in the guise of rational debates about social problems and social policy solutions to them.

An important aspect of this movement from class conflict to the political solution of social problems, is the way in which only certain kinds of policy solutions acquire legitimacy:

the state is not a structure, it is an organisation; or, better, it is a complex of social forms organised so that it inflects all relations and ideas about relations in such a way that capitalist production, and all it entails, becomes thought of and lived as natural.

(Corrigan, Ramsey and Sayer, 1980, p. 10)

Thus certain social forms such as individualism and competition become naturalised, as the only possibilities: 'Well, that's the way things are, isn't it?' Where state intervention is necessary, it develops to contain and regulate struggle, rewriting its own history in passing to naturalise what has developed as inevitable (e.g. the 'progressive meeting of needs'). Further it aggressively marginalises through repression, or 'help', any alternatives such as working class autonomous welfare activity, international solidarity, and so on (Jones and Novak, 1980). This view helps us to understand why the state may often take an initiative in social policy which is not clearly demanded by labour, and furthermore why that initiative may or may not turn out to be successfully implemented (or functional for capital). In other words the state is formed by individuals and groups for the most part unaware of the nature of the struggles they are involved in, believing themselves rather to be struggling with natural forces such as 'inflation' or 'needs'.

Urry (1981) has extended this discussion to suggest that we must understand state forms not merely within the context of class struggles generated out of the sphere of production, but also in the context of other struggles (such as the women's movement). He draws heavily on Laclau's distinction between class struggle and classes-in-struggle, developed in the context of an analysis of fascism and ideology, in which petit bourgeois struggles are central to understanding developments, which are not simply reducible to a basic capital-labour antagonism. Laclau (1979) suggests that rarely is class struggle found in its pure form, necessitating the 'abandonment of the Platonic cave of class reductionism' (p. 12). Rather, such classes as peasant, petite bourgeoisie, etc., may be in struggle within a social formation, but not constituted directly by the mode of production:

> Through this kind of antagonism, the dominated sectors would not identify themselves as a class but as 'the other', 'the counterposed' to the dominant power bloc, as the *underdog* . . . this second contradiction is expressed through the interpellation of the agents as the *people*. The first contradiction is the sphere of class struggle: the second, that of popular-democratic struggle.
>
> (Laclau, 1979, p. 107)

Urry suggests that classes-in-struggle must be taken as an important element of what he defines as civil society, centred on the areas of social reproduction and the distribution of goods and services. While these are heavily structured by developments in the capitalist mode of production, they are also relatively autonomous, as a result of classes-in-struggle. Such autonomy is not, as is frequently argued, thus a 'requirement' of capital, or purely a result of the power of labour, but is generated by these struggles *and others*. This is the only way we can account for different forms of the capitalist state, (corporatist, authoritarian, etc.). This approach helps us to understand changes in social policy more clearly since social policy is also centred on Urry's civil society – the areas of distribution and reproduction. Indeed, Urry's account of the two main periods of capitalist development make social policy developments quite clear. He suggests that these phases are initially when the area of distribution is dominant in civil society and subsequently when the area of reproduction is dominant, reminding us that the timing and form of these changes is in no way pre-determined – they depend on the outcome of struggle. Urry suggests that the motive for change to the latter phase is to be found both in capital's desire to sustain demand (consumption) and self-reproduction (at a time when centralisation and concentration make this difficult), and in labour's desire to sustain wages and the level of consumption. Thus, for example, the British Welfare State is not simply a working class victory, but a change in social relations in civil society, in which various groups (capital, labour, professionals, insurance companies etc.) struggled to maximise their interests. The ideological significance of the celebrated appearance of the Welfare State as a working class victory, is belied by the continued existence of oppression contained within its forms, and not least the simple point that its functional equivalents (social and private insurance) have produced very similar levels of consumption and reproduction in other countries.

In this section then we see an emphasis on the unity of the system of social relations under capitalism, which only appears ideologically as separable into the state and the economy. In reality, both are reflections of class struggle (and classes-in-struggle). Changes in social policy are not merely 'influenced' by classes, they are class struggle, just as accumulation is. State policies are not, therefore, always clearly and consciously formulated or implemented, since struggles surround both processes. The recent successful creation of a dominant power bloc by Thatcher is not the 'defeat' of labour by capital, or 'required' by the economy, but in Jessop's (1977) terms a re-alignment during crises of classes-in-struggle, such as women voters or the SDP.

Class rule is thus not about the direct exercise of power, but the struggle to reproduce existing (unequal) social relations (Therborn, 1978).

We conclude from this all too brief examination of the state in relation to social problems, that we are dealing with the issue of ideology. Not only are there ideological tendencies in the way social problems are viewed, but the whole state apparatus by which they are processed can be theorised as ideology – as a way of perceiving issues which are essentially founded in economic and political conflict in the wider society. In the next section we therefore return to a discussion of ideology.

Ideology

In Chapter 1 we argued that only certain social problems attain a sufficiently legitimate status to be recognised in government policy. This seemed to entail two processes. First, the problem was construed in technical and administrative terms, rather than political terms. Second, we followed Mannheim (1960) to suggest that powerful social groups, particularly classes, had an interest in perceiving social problems in a way which did not threaten the status quo. These two processes of concealment or disguise, and the accommodation to class interests takes us to the heart of ideology. Mannheim's work was essentially historical and descriptive. In this section we shall be more analytical in our approach to ideology both with respect to social problems, and with respect to the nature of the state as an aspect of ideology.

In a comprehensive discussion of ideology Larrain (1979) suggests that there are four typical considerations employed in discussing and using the concept. First there is the question of ideology as a negative or positive concept. In its negative and critical form it emphasises the falsity or distortion of ideas; in its positive and neutral form it emphasises the common perceptions of a class through which the interests of that class are defended and promoted. Second, there is the question of ideology as a subjective or objective phenomenon. The subjective approach emphasises the ways in which individuals, groups or classes cannot grasp reality clearly; the objective approach suggests that deception is an essential part of reality itself, a part of the social structure whereby reality deceives the subject rather than vice versa. Third, there is the question of whether ideology applies to part or all of our thoughts. That is, are only some aspects of the total culture ideological, or is the ideological to be equated with all of that level of society which is social consciousness? Fourth, there is the problem of the relation between ideology and science. On the one hand science is non-ideological and can dispel ideology; on the other hand science is also a human product and thus itself may have ideological effects, for example in securing class interests.

Larrain suggests that ideology is used in different ways according to which of these aspects are stressed. Some authors, such as Althusser (1969) link them together to suggest that for example the objective, negative and all encompassing (of all social consciousness) nature of ideology is preferable. Larrain himself in a more recent book (1983) makes extensive use of the first aspect to suggest that amongst Marxist writers, ideology has clearly moved from a negative and critical concept formulated by Marx, to a positive and neutral concept in which it merely refers to the different viewpoints of different classes. We shall explore this positive approach later when we consider the work of Gramsci.

From the Camera Obscura to Fetishism

The most vigorous and original discussion of ideology is to be found in Marx's writings. In Larrain's terms Marx stressed a concept of ideology which was negative, objective and the antithesis of science, but which only applied to part of the total cultural world. His work was developed in two distinct phases, in relation to Feuerbach's materialism initially and later through his analysis of the commodity in volume one of *Capital.*

Marx fully supported Feuerbach's criticism of German idealism which had argued that human society was merely a reflection of the historical progress of independent ideas. Such a suggestion was mercilessly exposed in Feuerbach's study of Christianity. In the *Essence of Christianity,* Feuerbach reversed the relation between ideas and reality suggested by Hegel. He showed how the ideas and concepts of people are derived from reality, and thus do not create that reality, which exists outside of our minds and is merely perceived by us. Feuerbach argues this with reference to the Christian religion, which he places firmly on a secular base, for it springs up in response to various physical and psychological frustrations.

This argument of Feuerbach's became completely materialist in Marx's writing. He showed how this 'religious principle' or 'natural fetishism of human activity' pervaded all aspects of social reality. The state and wealth were also seen as things objectified and given powers beyond man's control:

The fact is, therefore, that definite individuals who are productively active in a definite way enter into these definite social and political relations . . . The social structure and the state are continually evolving out of the life-process of definite individuals; however, of these individuals, not as they may appear in their own or other people's imagination, but as they *actually* are . . . Consciousness can never be anything else than conscious being, and the being of men is their actual life process. If in all ideology men and their relations appear as in a *camera obscura*, this phenomenon arises just as much from their historical life process as the inversion of objects on the retina does from their physical life-process.

In direct contrast to German philosophy which descends from heaven to earth, here it is a matter of ascending from earth to heaven. That is to say, not of setting out from what men say, imagine, conceive, nor from men as narrated, thought of, imagined, conceived, in order to arrive at men in the flesh; but setting out from real, active men, and on the basis of their real life-process demonstrating the development of the ideological reflexes and echoes of this life-process . . . It is not consciousness that determines life, but life that determines consciousness.

(Marx and Engels, 1976, pp. 30–1)

Thus Marx focusses explicitly on the way people's lives, their social practices, give rise to consciousness – to the way that they understand their lives. However this is ideological to the extent that their lives contain contradictions; for example the fact of class dominance in a formally free and democratic society cannot be resolved through conventional social practice. That is, formal parliamentary democracy cannot be translated into real economic democracy within conventional social practice. Ideological consciousness serves to mask such a contradiction Marx suggests by enabling people to imagine that they are free to resolve conflicts as equal citizens in the political system. However this of course helps to deflect criticisms away from class dominance, and is therefore clearly to the advantage of the dominant class.

However, Marx at this stage (the 1840s) had no more precise an analysis of the key elements of people's 'life process'. His mature thoughts on Feuerbach's problem of the 'natural fetishism of human activity' appear much later in volume one of *Capital* where he sets out to analyse the key elements of the life process of modern society, i.e. capitalist production, by starting with its central element, the commodity. In a remarkable continuity of analysis he examines not the fetishism of religion or the state, as before, but the fetishism of commodities:

A commodity appears at first sight an extremely obvious trivial thing. But analysis bring out that it is a very strange thing . . . the enigmatic character of the product of labour . . . arises from . . . the measure of the expenditure of human labour-power [as] the value of the products of labour, . . . and the relationships between the producers [as] a social relation between the product of labour.

(Marx, 1976, pp. 163–4)

Thus Marx suggests that commodities are special in that the effort to produce them is measured in terms of their market values, not the real effort; and that the producers of commodities do not relate together directly but through the medium of apparently independent things – commodities:

The commodity-form, and the value-relation of the product of labour within which it appears, have absolutely no connection with the physical nature of the commodity ... the definite social relation between men themselves assumes here, for them, the fantastic form of a relation between things.

(ibid., p. 165)

Harking back to Feuerbach's concerns, he therefore suggests that:

to find an analogy we must take flight into the misty realm of religion. There the products of the human brain appear as autonomous figures endowed with a life of their own, which enter into relations with each other and with the human race. So it is in the world of commodities.

(ibid., p. 165)

Marx is suggesting that this dual effect of commodities (translating labour effort into a market value, and connecting producers indirectly through a market of apparently autonomous things) is a sophisticated and pervasive ideology. It enables exploitation since the price of labour (wages) is less than the real labour effort expended, leading to the expropriation of surplus labour; but it also enables us to experience a powerful sense of this relation as the natural outcome of a detached and independent market, under no-one's control. And this Geras (1972) has pointed out is not an illusion or trick, but a real and inescapable element of capitalist society.

While Marx starts his analysis at the heart of capitalist 'life process', the commodity, his use of fetishism can be extended to other relationships in society. Of particular note is the way political conflicts between people become displaced in an exactly similar way, to assume the 'fantastic form' of a relationship within the conventions of the state. For example Cohen (1978) argues that in our capitalist society class antagonism appears to us in a falsely autonomous and separate political realm of parliamentary democracy, which takes on the form of political conflict as a natural, inevitable fact of life. Rather, Cohen suggests, such conflict is peculiar to class divided societies, and would not appear in classless societies.

Wells (1981) extends this idea further to suggest that the connection between commodity, state and other possible fetishisms is the fundamental ideology in capitalist society of dissolving the real relations of dependency and group identity amongst people into isolated abstract individuals who are endowed with natural (usually selfish) propensities which must be curbed by another isolated and abstract entity, society. Real relations thus appear to be combinations of separate things – individuals and societies. Wells points out that this explains the commonsense view of the necessity of an autonomous 'thing' – the state – as minimally the upholder of the rules of fair play between (selfish) individuals, and maximally the helping hand for those unable to survive in the game as it is seen to be played.

With respect to social problems the idea of fetishism helps us to understand how fundamental conflicts between classes and genders come to be expressed in the more limited sphere of the Welfare State. Here such conflicts are neutralised into technical issues which do not address the origin of those conflicts, but rather draw our attention away into a safer world of rational policy making. Indeed Ginsburg (1979) suggests that 'the capitalist welfare state is one of the clearest examples of the fetishised form of the State' (p. 37), since it embodies a particularly extreme inversion of reality into an opposite appearance: the Welfare State strives in reality to suppress or contain class conflict to the advantage of the dominant class or gender by presenting itself in appearance as precisely the opposite – the defender of the rights and needs of the working class.

In our case studies ideology has a particularly useful role in helping us to understand why state policies have taken the form that they have, and in particular in helping us to understand the frequent failure of such policies. Clearly if social problems are an ideological expression in appearance of an altogether different reality, then policies based on an understanding of the issues only at the level of appearance will fail. Thus if we accept uncritically that madness is indeed an illness, we cannot understand why medical treatment not only is ineffective but has sanctioned unpleasant lives for the mad in the past. However, if we suggest that the medicalisation of an illness is, in appearance, the fetishisation of interpersonal conflict, in reality, then the history of professional and state policies for the mad is unravelled.

A similar picture appears in the case of violence against women. The myths of rape suggest in appearance the inverse of the reality which has been revealed in recent studies. However, state policy in terms of legal, educational and welfare provision in connection with rape has been heavily influenced by the myths/ideology of rape: rapists are disturbed strangers, victims provoke, nice girls aren't victims, and so on. Ryan's (1971) famous summary of welfare ideology as 'victim-blaming' neatly captures an essential aspect of this process of reversing in appearance what the real issue is. Women, delinquents, blacks, madmen, and greedy workers are blamed for possessing some quality which appears to cause the problems of rape, crime, racism, madness and inflation/unemployment; whereas our case studies show that these groups of people suffer the consequence of social processes and structures as much as initiate problems.

The Dominant Ideology

While Marx's discussion of ideology is very helpful, its development in terms of fetishism can be criticised on two counts. First it is a rather reductionist account of consciousness. By this we mean that ideology is conceived of as an automatic element in antagonistic class society, which can be *reduced to* the basic principles of capitalist economic relations – it is an almost mechanical necessity of the society of which it is a part. In this respect although ideology is an essential part of class conflict, since it masks reality to the advantage of the dominant class, it is conceived of without reference to the conscious activities of the dominant class itself in creating and manipulating ideas. Moreover, since ideas are essentially determined, any criticism or discussion is pointless.

A second criticism of Marx is that his faith in what is reality and what is appearance requires considerable scientific arrogance. The possibility that, as Mannheim suggested, all thought is potentially ideologically biased, and hence in principle contestable, is brushed aside by Marx's self-assurance that he has quite definitely arrived at 'the truth'.

In relation to these criticisms, twentieth century developments of Marx's work have taken two distinct directions. One, characterised by Anderson (1976) as 'western Marxism', has been a restatement, despite these criticisms, of the objective scientific and reductionist elements of Marx's work. Disappointed by the failure of revolutionary politics in the west to overthrow capitalism, and the tragedy of Stalinism in the east, western Marxism has retreated, Anderson suggests, into the world of philosophical logic. For example Althusser's (1969) stress on an anti-humanist, pessimistic theory offers no escape from the distortions of ideology even if the transcendence of capitalist society occurred. While appearing to allow for a degree of autonomy in the individual's understanding of his or her life process, Althusser ultimately suggests that our subjectivity is determined by ideology ('ideology interpellates the subject' in a famous phrase).

The other direction, characterised by Anderson as an exception to his general observation, is one which attempts to meet the two criticisms by placing political struggle rather than economic logic at the centre of the analysis. From this point of view ideology cannot be reduced to a necessary element in a commodity producing society, but is rather contingent upon the balance of political forces. In other words, of the two defining criteria of ideology we introduced earlier, class interest becomes more prominent and primary over the criterion of concealment. In Larrain's terminology, ideology becomes a positive aspect of a class viewpoint, is subjective, and cannot be rigidly separated from science.

This approach is more akin to the earlier formulation Marx used in the *German Ideology*, where he suggested that consciousness arises out of social practice. The notion of fetishism was built upon the social practice of commodity production – for the worker the experience of the 'dull compulsion' to work in order to live. However Marx also stressed a different kind of practice, which also produces consciousness, but of a different kind from fetishism. Gouldner (1980) has elaborated the difference between these two social practices in a project which, like Anderson's, tries to trace the development of modern Marxism:

There is, then, a tension between Marx's dismissal of idealism and his call to change the world . . . This ambiguity is reproduced in his conception of 'praxis'. Marx had two tacitly different conceptions of praxis or, as I will usually call it here, of practice: Praxis$_1$ is the unreflective labour on which capitalism rests, the wage labour imposed by necessity which operates within its confining property institutions and its stunting divisions of labour. While this labour inflicts an alienation upon workers, it also constitutes the foundation of that society, reproducing the very limits crippling workers. Here workers are constrained to contribute to the very system that alienates them. This conception of praxis is congenial to Scientific Marxism. In the second, more heroic concept of practice – Praxis$_2$, more congenial to Critical Marxism – emphasis is on a practice that is more freely chosen, most especially on political struggle. If Praxis$_1$ is the constrained labour that reproduces the status quo, Praxis$_2$ is the free labour contributing toward emancipation from it. In undertaking the first form of labour or practice, persons submit to necessity; in the second, however, they undertake a deliberate and Promethean struggle against it.

(Gouldner, 1980, pp. 33–4)

From this perspective, then, ideology also arises out of the struggle to resolve class and gender antagonisms. It becomes not the counterpoint, in disguise, of truth, but the world view of groups in struggle. Anderson identifies this exception to the general run of western Marxism in the work of Gramsci. Gramsci developed the idea that in modern capitalist societies ideology does not merely emerge automatically, but rather depends on whether the dominant class can organise a system of beliefs to which the general public freely submits. Observing the failure of the Russian revolution to spread to Western Europe, Gramsci argued that the dominant classes in the West were able to exercise hegemony over other classes by using ideology as a kind of social cement. However, there is a danger here of adopting a conspiracy theory of class dominance, which we criticised earlier in discussing George and

Wilding's (1972b) explanation of bias in social policy analysis. That view we suggested requires an overly passive model of the public as 'cultural dopes'. But Gramsci overcomes this problem by acknowledging that ideology is not just about an organised system of ideas for understanding social issues; just as important is the place of common-sense and folklore which comprise significant portions of the public's consciousness: 'it is not possible to separate what is known as "scientific" philosophy from the common and popular philosophy which is only a fragmentary collection of ideas and opinions' (Gramsci, 1971). Class dominance, or hegemony as Gramsci calls it, is thus also the subtle organisation of commonsense to naturalise ideas and possibilities which are in the interests of the dominant class. As Hall et al. (1978a) comment 'conspiracy theses play no part whatsoever in his work'.

Since, as Gouldner argues, we can distinguish two kinds of practice, we can distinguish two kinds of commonsense and two kinds of ideology. One is the commonsense or ideology arising from the dominant or fetishised view of capitalist social relations. The second, however, is an oppositional commonsense which grows out of struggle against such fetishised consciousness. The successful dominant class manages to either discount or incorporate the latter into the former in the style of Thatcher's now famous phrase, 'There is no alternative', which classically expresses Gramsci's point.

As we suggested earlier, therefore, we may doubt whether 'welfare-statism' is a working class victory, since it is the perfect expression of a dominant ideology in which a particular form of collective organisation of services comes to appear commonsensical, natural, practical and in comparison to which any alternative seems rather absurd – indeed the working assumption of traditional social administration. In our case studies we have therefore attempted to highlight the duality of commonsense in our subheadings of conventional and unconventional wisdom. Thus we have tried to separate and contrast two common senses about the nature of social problems and the appropriate collective response in pursuit of their solution. On the one hand the problems of crime, race, violence, unemployment and so on are natural misfortunes from which the Welfare State should protect its individual citizens. On the other hand these problems are seen to be perpetuated, but in a contained form, by the denial of their underlying origins and by the emasculation of alternative solutions. And this latter viewpoint or ideology only develops as a product in consciousness of oppositional practice by such groups as feminists.

We may explore Gramsci's twin aspects of ideology – formal philosophies and commonsense – and their uncertain outcome in the surrounding political struggle by considering more recent work on the analysis of popular culture on the one hand and the analysis of intellectual practice on the other. Both of these are relevant to social problems as they appear at both popular and intellectual levels.

Dominated Commonsense: The Media, and Professional Language

Popular culture has been the focus of work at the Birmingham Centre for Contemporary Cultural Studies since the 1960s. The director Stuart Hall (1980a) acknowledged that Gramsci's concept of hegemony 'played a seminal role in Cultural Studies' and 'has been one of the Centre's organising ideas'. Distancing himself from a purely relativist position associated with work of the Frankfurt School on cultural power, Hall's materialism nevertheless has encompassed an influential stream of work on contemporary British social life. While much of this has involved ethnographic observation to record popular culture in action, the most celebrated example being Paul Willis's (1977) study of the transition from school to work, the Centre's work on the media is most relevant to social problems. As we argued in Chapter 1 the media are an important mechanism for the popularisation and legitimation of social problems, and for the orchestration of public opinion in favour of any particular remedial action. The most sustained analysis by the Centre in this area was a monumental study of mugging (Hall, et al., 1978b) its appearance in the media, and its perception in relation to popular and official ideologies about policing. Some of these points have already been touched on in Chapter 5.

In introducing the book the authors observe that:

if we could abolish the word [mugging], that would have been our principal – perhaps our only – 'practical proposal'. It has done incalculable harm – raising the wrong things into sensational focus, hiding and mystifying the deeper causes.

However they acknowledge that 'you cannot resolve a contradiction by abolishing the label'. In other words the label, the ideology, is real and pervades popular, media, official and academic thought, and consequently it is necessary (as we have also argued):

to counter the view that the way books about 'social problems' are written is that investigators simply walk into the streets, their heads utterly void of any preconceptions about crime or society, look the 'empirical facts' in the face, and write about whatever 'problem' happens to sneak up behind them and hit them over the head with its presence. This is not a book like that. We doubt whether books of that order of innocence can be written about society – though there are plenty enough currently masquerading in that guise. (ibid. p. vii)

The Centre's analysis of the media is different from the model we presented in Chapter 1, where the media were seen as either educating, reflecting or manipulating public opinion about social problems. In a seminal paper Hall (1980b) recasts this typically mechanical model of communications by focusing upon the way that a raw historical event cannot be simply transmitted in its totality as a piece of information via the media to the audience. Thus mugging as a news item is much more than information about someone being attacked on a street. The term mugging assumed its modern form in America in the 1940s, and arrived in full blossom so to speak in Britain in the early 1970s:

> The label had no unsensational origins in Britain. It was a complex, social theme from its inception. It arrived in Britain already established in its most sensational and sensationalised form. It is hardly surprising, given this pre-history, that it triggered off at once its own sensational spiral. What is more the American representation in the British press may have helped to shape the nature of the unofficial reaction to 'mugging'; for if American 'mugging' arrived entramelled in the whole American panic about race, crime riot and lawlessness, it was also fully entramelled in the anti-crime, anti-black, anti-riot, anti-liberal, 'law-and-order' backlash. Thus, via the American transplant, Britain adopted, not only 'mugging', but the fear and panic about 'mugging' and the backlash reaction into which those fears and anxieties issued.

> (Hall, et al., 1978b, p. 28)

These powerful meanings associated with natural/historical events are particular representations of the significance of those events, ie., ideology. Hall's recasting of the media tries to include this ideological aspect since it is an important factor in the success or failure of dominant groups to achieve hegemony over popular understanding of 'problems' like mugging. Thus the simple model of 'transmitting-receiving' becomes 'encoding-decoding', because events are encoded into media transmissions in such a way that they invite the audience to decode them using

> dominant or preferred meanings. New, problematic or troubling events, which breach our expectancies and run counter to our 'common-sense constructs', to our 'taken-for-granted' knowledge of social structures, must be assigned to their discursive domains before they can be said to 'make sense'. The most common way of 'mapping' them is to assign the new to some domain or other of the existing 'maps of problematic social reality'.

> (Hall, 1980b, p. 134)

A good example can be found in the study by Brunsdon and Morley of the television programme Nationwide (1978). In the course of a detailed content analysis of the programme they found that social problems were consistently set in the context of individualised misfortunes which afflicted specific individuals as if the cause was a bolt from the blue. State or voluntary help was portrayed as benign and reassuringly supportive, while any connection with socially structured disadvantage was severed. Not surpisingly disabled people portrayed as accident of birth or environment were favoured subjects

However, remembering Gramsci's sensitivity to the p hegemonic pressures can be struggled against, it is r conclusion that the encoded messages will in fact be dec dominant code. Hall suggests that decoding may also occur with negotiated code in which, while dominant meanings are accepted in general (e.g. we should not pay ourselves more than the country can afford), their specific application contains adapted and even oppositional elements (e.g. in my industry we must strike to regain pay parity). Ultimately this decoding may move into a completely oppositional code whereby the invitation to use the dominant code is systematically rejected, so that for example 'national interest' is always reinterpreted as 'class interest'; and class or gender struggle in ideology is fully joined.

Such mechanisms surrounding the development of ideological forms in the struggle for and against hegemonic closure by one class or group over another can be developed beyond the media to include other areas of discourse such as the conversations between professionals and clients found throughout the Welfare State. Here we are beginning to move away from the orchestration of the commonsense level of ideology, to Gramsci's other level, of formal philosophies. He placed great significance on the role of 'intellectuals' in the development and circulation of ideologies. In particular he argued that 'organic' intellectuals were those who significantly organised ideologies which expressed the interests of particular classes and genders. While of course journalists can be organic intellectuals with respect to ideologies at the level of public opinion or commonsense, we are here thinking more in terms of doctors, teachers, lawyers, social workers, academics and so on.

Probably the most influential notion which studies of the representation of ideas by these organic intellectuals have recently drawn upon is Bernstein's (1971) distinction between elaborated and restricted linguistic codes. He demonstrates that working class language leaves many meanings implicit, relying on shared or mutual knowledge between people to fill in gaps. Middle class language on the other hand makes meanings more explicit, and elaborates the contents of communication thus freeing it from context. The difference is similar to the different language usage by intimates as compared to strangers. Many writers (including Bernstein himself) have been quick to realise the political implications of this observation, since restricted codes are available to all classes but elaborated codes are only available to the middle class: elaborated codes may make explicit the meanings (ideologies) in the interest of dominant groups in a way working class interests are not elaborated. Since public debate takes place in elaborated code, working class meanings tend to be excluded.

While Bernstein's work has been criticised for its elevation of the difference between language use into a hierarchy of preferred language use (Rosen, 1972), he nevertheless opened up a debate about class and language, which has developed to include gender and language (Spender, 1980), and race and language (Reeves, 1983). All of this work shares a concern about the way political interests are constituted in, and to a certain extent actually determined by language. Familiarised as the 'Sapir-Whorf' hypothesis in which world views of pre-industrial societies were understood as embedded in their languages, this notion has been given a critical usage with regard to differential language use by groups in conflict within a society since

A major function of sociolinguistic mechanisms is to play a part in the control of members of subordinate groups by members of dominant groups. This control is effected both by regulation and by constitution: by explicit manipulation and by the creation of an apparently 'natural world' in which inequitable relations and processes are presented as given and inevitable. Power differential provides the underlying semantic for the systems of ideas encoded in language structure.

(Fowler, et al., 1979, p. 2)

This is particularly the case where working class clients interact with organic intellectuals operating within a dominant elaborated code. Thus for example studies of doctors (Strong, 1979) and social workers (Baldock and Prior, 1981) as well as teachers (by Bernstein himself) illustrate clearly the use of language which directly or indirectly structures assumptions about appropriate conduct expected from patients, clients, pupils. In other words there is a restriction of legitimate meanings to the status quo which Marcuse (1964) classically expressed in terms of 'one-dimensionality'.

Mueller has developed a parallel argument in terms of 'repressive communication'. Starting from a position remarkably similar to (and which predates) Hall's model of encoding/decoding (Mueller, 1970), he argues that in addition to those effects in the media (which are discussed above) that he calls 'constrained communication', we should also distinguish 'arrested communication' (using a Bernstein-type restricted code model) and 'directed communication' typical in countries with limited press freedom (Mueller, 1973). However the common characteristic of all repressive communication is that

the language permits neither the articulation of subjectively experienced needs, nor realisation of maximum individuation or autonomy . . . On the class level the language used results in an incapacity to locate oneself in history and society.

(Mueller, 1970, p. 105)

Hence, returning to Gouldner's distiction, praxis$_2$ is severely inhibited.

This is a point stressed particularly by Pateman (1980), since he is concerned along with Gramsci about the possibility of counter-hegemonic developments. He also distinguishes heavily directed communication ('linguistic and cognitive exclusion'), media-constrained communication ('linguistic repression and cognitive mystification'), and arrested or restricted code communication ('linguistic alienation'), and details the way in which ideology is produced. However his analysis points towards the possibility of change in a way Mueller's does not. Perhaps the best example in recent years has been the challenge of feminism to 'man-made language' (Spender, 1980). For example Pateman shows how everyday language which he calls 'idle discourse' strenuously avoids any disagreement between people. The paradigmatically non-controversial topic is of course the weather, but if one of the participants begins to utter contentious remarks about race or gender perhaps, then the other makes strenuous efforts to neutralise the remarks by agreeing, ignoring them or changing the subject. There is a strong cultural expectation, in other words, for such conversations to be uncritical and non-political: 'Idle Discourse is the language of the powerless who accept their position' (p. 77). While Pateman does not elaborate his argument with respect to feminism, it is clear that consciousness-raising about gendered language is precisely an attempt to repoliticise language and challenge male hegemony, as our case study of violence against women makes clear.

The mechanisms identified in this section which are involved in transmitting a dominant ideology, and through which the dominant ideology is resisted – the media and language – may not necessarily be effective. There is some dispute about the extent to which popular resistance is successful. For example as we mentioned earlier in the chapter Mann (1970) and Abercrombie, et al., (1980) argue on the grounds of survey and historical analysis respectively that dominant values are more important to the creation of dominant class coherence than working class consent, the latter being achieved by the more pragmatic 'dull compulsion' of workers to sell their labour power on the market. Another argument is that some sections of the population have a real interest in current economic arrangements (for example owner occupiers) who will therefore freely support existing governments at elections (Dunleavy, 1979). But to build a model of public opinion about social policy in terms of the rational calculus of economic man, supposedly revealing his preferences in the economic or political market on the basis of considered choice, requires the suspension precisely of a theory of ideology about the way individuals perceive their interests using categories and information available to them via the media and language.

Dominated Intellectual Sense: Social Administration, Science or Ideology?

The ultimate intellectual production of language is of course not by professional workers but by those upon whom their knowledge base rests: academics, such as the authors of this book. If, as we have argued, ideology is the key to understanding *why* economic and political conflicts become processed into social problems for the state to solve, and if it is also the key to understanding *which* issues become social problems, then to the extent that academics shape those processes, which they do, we must consider academic work also as ideological.

Academic work has been extensively examined within the sociology of science. By returning to Larrain's four questions with respect to ideology, we can examine the sociological study of science as an attempt to locate academic work in social context and thereby to reveal its ideological content. In Larrain's terms, the sociology of science has traditionally developed a 1 negative, and 2 subjective critique of science in which, 3 part of the whole is regarded as biased and to that extent is to be, 4 radically separated as ideology from true science. More recent work has interestingly shifted in parallel with Gramscian Marxism towards a 1 positive (i.e. group interest), but still, 2 subjective, and 3 wholistic view of, 4 scientific activity which is socially constructed in the same way as any cultural activity including ideology.

Traditionally the sociology of science concentrated on the way in which social factors external to the scientific process helped or hindered scientists' progress towards discovering scientific truths, for example the bias we noted in the earlier section on studying social problems. The scientific knowledge thereby acquired was not itself questioned, so much as the scientists' own understanding of their work. Whereas scientists stressed the scientific community's commitment to openness, disinterest, rationality and so forth, sociologists found that quite strict mechanisms of social control shaped the development of scientific work in periods of 'normal' science, punctuated by periodic revolutionary shifts in dominant views as older paradigms broke down under the weight of accumulated anomalies in scientific results (Kuhn, 1970).

A good example is currently furnished by social administration itself which operated until the mid-1970s from within a dominant paradigm committed to the accumulation of facts in pursuit of the perfection of the Welfare State. Since that time the conditions of existence of the Welfare State have shifted dramatically as economic growth faltered and unemployment and inflation took off. As we have argued in the case study of these issues, public expenditure – the life-blood of the Welfare State – became the focus of various attempts to recast the Welfare State in the pursuit of new solutions. Consequently the dominant paradigm within social administration also began to disintegrate for it rested on the assumption of the essential viability of the Welfare State. In terms of Kuhn's analysis, social administration in the last 10 years has suffered a veritable overload of anomalous research findings which throw great doubt on the relevance of the previous approach to welfare studies. Again, as Kuhn suggests, previously marginalised paradigms begin to vie with each other as the potential new dominant paradigm, depending on the success with which each can explain the accumulated anomalies. No longer was it possible to accept the Welfare State as the naive solution of social problems. It now appeared to be the cause of many social problems, or at least irrelevant to their solution, from the point of view of the new currents within social administration – feminism, Marxism, and the 'new right' (Taylor-Gooby, 1985).

However the sociology of science has also accumulated anomalies within its own model. Mulkay (1972a, 1972b) suggests that periods of 'normal science', during which scientific facts are rapidly and efficiently accumulated, interspersed by revolutionary change, are actually unusual and mostly confined to special periods in the history of the pure or basic natural sciences. Moreover, he observes that social control in such a model is over-emphasised. Indeed one of the mechanisms of control – the exchange of scientific status and rewards for knowledge – actually continually generates scientific innovation rather than scientific routine. He argues that science consists more often of frequently changing unstable networks through which academics pass in pursuit of rewards in the process of which cross-fertilisation of ideas is the main generator of new knowledge. Thus, while control within dominant paradigms may be sought, in fact the use of rewards to control academic work only stimulates mobility and hence the production of new ideas. Indeed ironically it is often non-conformity which leads to innovation, while the conformity of aspiring academics in pursuit of rewards leads to stagnation in ideas (Davis, 1971).

We can again see the operation of this model in the analysis of social policy and social problems, as academics move into the field and bring with them ideas from other disciplines. While social administration has always drawn heavily on sociological ideas in the past, there has more recently been a marked growth of new models drawn from philosophy, political science, economics, history and so on. And as Mulkay suggests, the application of these models to traditional questions within social administration, is beginning to transform those questions themselves and hence the very nature of the subject.

However such a transformation raises the question of the status of the knowledge which is being generated in social administration. The sociology of science models outlined to this point have not questioned the status of knowledge itself; they have confined themselves, as we observed earlier, to a particular combination of Larrain's terms which stress social processes as, albeit necessary, hindrances upon science's pursuit of truth – that truth being determined by the nature of the empirical world itself. But the implication of teasing out ever more closely the way social relations generate knowledge is to lead to the question of whether it is in fact possible to discern knowledge which can in any valid way be disentangled from its social generation. Current developments within the field suggest a negative answer, implying that knowledge itself and not merely its production must be socially contingent.

Mulkay (1979) draws on recent work in the philosophy of science to argue that four essentials in the standard epistemology of natural science can no longer be sustained. First the principle that the material world is invariant and stable, he argues, lies in the eye of the beholder: 'The principle of uniformity is not an aspect of the natural world, but rather an aspect of scientists' methods for constructing their accounts of that world'. (p. 29).

Thus second, empirical statements are 'theory-laden', so that the radical separation of facts and theories in natural science cannot be sustained; and third, scientific observation must be fundamentally dependent on language, since it is an active process involving categorisation, inference and interpretation 'guided by and expressed in terms of a complex repertoire of symbolic formulations' (ibid., p. 49). Finally, Mulkay demonstrates that knowledge claims are not assessed by means of invariant, universal criteria. Qualities of simplicity, accuracy, scope, fruitfulness, elegance, falsifiability, factualness vary in meaning and are open to influence by authority, amongst other things. He concludes therefore that: 'there is nothing in the physical world which uniquely determines the conclusions of the scientific community.' (ibid., p. 61).

Clearly the consequence of this line of argument is that of a radical social constructionism, in which reality is located entirely within the consciousness of the scientific community. In Larrain's terms, again, we have moved to a positive concept of ideology in which consciousness merely varies from one group to another, such that it is a characteristic of all thought rather than partial sectors of it, and that there is no distinction between science (or truth) and ideology. However this is not necessarily a naive or simple relativism in which all thought is of equal status, since the basic defining criteria of ideology which we introduced right at the beginning of this whole section were that ideological thought disguises or mystifies reality in the interests of a group or class. This is a much stronger conception than the notion merely that all thought is socially constructed, as Berger and Luckmann (1967) have famously argued. In other words the scientific community, including that of social administration, not only is responsible for constructing truths which it actually perceives as objective and detached, but it does so in a manner designed to disguise this very process.

Typically this disguise is achieved by perceiving and presenting the construction of ideas or scientific findings as the *discovery* of them on the presumption that they already existed in the external world. Just to make the point more forcefully we can illustrate this process in the hard world of natural science, on the argument that if we can demonstrate the process there, then we can more readily accept it in the softer world of social science. We are looking therefore for an illustration of

how certain achievements in science are constituted as discoveries – and not how they occurred to an individual. This model focuses on how persons confer the status of 'discovery' on social events and how they determine and sanction the appropriateness of this category both for their own achievement and for those of others.

(Brannigan, 1981, p. 11)

A useful case study for our purposes is provided by Latour and Woolgar (1979) about the 'discovery' of a substance called TRF (H) [thyrotropin releasing factor (hormone)], which regulates the way substances are released by the pituitary gland. Their study was concerned to elucidate the way that the existence of TRF(H) became stabilised as an accepted fact:

our argument is not just that facts are socially constructed. We also wish to show that the process of construction involves the use of certain devices whereby all traces of production are made extremely difficult to detect.

This process they argue is centred around the splitting and inversion of statements within the laboratory context, those statements being concerned with the issue of whether a particular substance such as TRF(H) really exists – ie., whether it has been 'discovered', in conventional terminology:

From their initial inception members of the laboratory are unable to determine whether statements [about the real existence of a substance] are true or false, objective or subjective, highly likely or quite probable . . . once the statement begins to stabilise, however, an important change takes place. The statement becomes a split entity. On the one hand, it is a set of words which represent a statement about an object. On the other hand, it corresponds to an object in itself which takes on a life of its own. It is as if the original statement has projected a virtual image of itself which exists outside the statement . . . Before long, more and more reality is attributed to the object and less and less to the statement about the object. Consequently an inversion takes place: the object becomes the reason why the statement was formulated in the first place. At the onset of stabilisation, the object was the virtual image of the statement; subsequently the statement becomes the mirror image of the reality 'out there' . . . small wonder that the statements appear to match external reality so exactly: they are the same thing. (pp. 176–77)

Latour and Woolgar are at pains to distance this argument from the totally relativist position in which facts melt into perceptions. They are merely suggesting that 'out-there-ness is the consequence of scientific work rather than its cause' (p. 182), reserving, with Marx whom they quote approvingly, the point that 'an objective truth is not a theoretical but a practical question' (p. 179). However it is the extraordinary nature of inversion at the point at which reality is stabilised which fascinates them:

The result of the construction of a fact is that it appears unconstructed by anyone; the result of rhetorical persuasion in the agnostic field is that participants are convinced that they have not been convinced... as to circumstances, they simply vanish from accounts... Although it is unclear whether this kind of inversion is peculiar to science, it is so important that we have devoted much of our argument to specifying and describing the very moment at which inversion occurs (p. 240).

Needless to say, we can substitute 'social problems', or a particular social problem, for TRF(H) and draw the appropriate conclusion: social administration can be construed as an ideological activity in which certain elements of social reality are invisibly constructed: needs, rights, policies, problems, and so on.

However we have still to identify the second criterion for the establishment of an ideology – the interests served by it. Clearly even if the social production of knowledge is a contingent affair, this may be a random noise interfering with the main signal; and for the total relativist there is no main signal. But in ideology such interference is systematic – it serves the interest of a class or group. Whether or not the interference distorts totally or partially the production of true knowledge, it shapes the production of knowledge which is of use to different classes.

Unlike the establishment of the distorting effect of social processes on knowledge production, the identification of interests in relation to knowledge production has been difficult. Habermas (1971) suggests that there are different kinds of useful knowledge depending on the interests concerned. He suggests three general kinds of interest. First there is a technical interest in controlling objects in the environment. Second there is a practical interest in the development of inter-subjective understanding. Third there is an emancipatory interest in securing freedom from control and from distorted communication. These three interests are derived from Habermas's definition of the basic types of human action as work, language and domination. However these universal interests must be subdivided according to the way each of these kinds of action develop within certain groups such as social classes or genders. Thus owners of capital, or men, may have an interest in controlling objects, developing understanding, or securing freedom in a way which ignores or systematically denies such possibilities for other groups.

Nevertheless the demonstration of such interests in practice remains difficult. In an extended review of this problem Barnes (1977) is driven to the conclusion that there is not yet a satisfactory way of establishing the influence of interests, particularly concealed interests, on thought and belief. However, echoing Habermas he suggests that 'knowledge grows under the impulse of two great interests, an overt interest in prediction, manipulation and control, and a covert interest in rationalisation and persuasion' (p. 38). Of course we could always ask people what their interests are, but the subjective experience of wants may be open to artificial stimulation or temporary misperception. Alternatively we could presume that an individual would make choices on the basis of real interests given the perfect opportunity – the kind of 'original position' used by philosopher's to establish what constraint-free ideals might be (Rawls, 1972; Habermas, 1970).

With respect to the study of social policy and social problems, the identification of interests which may motivate social administration as an intellectual activity and hence encourage ideological distortion has been hotly contested. For example welfare knowledge has been claimed to advance the interests of, amongst others, common human needs, the functioning of an advanced industrial society, professional service providers, men, ruling class political dominance and economic production, working class needs, and so on. And knowledge production, empirical or normative, based on these different interests has indeed varied widely in its content.

The question remains as to identifying which knowledge is valid. The total relativist, as the total determinist, forecloses the possibility of criticism: the former on the grounds that all knowledge is valid; the latter on the grounds that knowledge is determined (as in the process of fetishism) by material life and is hence immutable. How, then, can we know which approach to understanding social policy and social problems to choose? Our case studies suggested, we argued earlier, that social administration had encouraged an understanding of social problems which produced repeated failure in terms of social policy. This seems to preclude a pragmatic solution to the question in terms of choosing the analysis which works, since not working does not seem to invalidate a particular analysis. However, in terms of ideology, social administration may in fact be working well, since it successfully constructs knowledge in a manner which disguises the nature of that construction, and which serves dominant class and gender interests. Thus we can in fact choose between knowledges if we are clear about the interests they purport to serve.

For example, in parallel to Habermas and Barnes's distinction between knowledge-constituting interests in prediction and control on the one hand, and understanding and meaning on the other, Abercrombie

(1980) suggests that relativism is conventionally resolved by an appeal either to the 'Doctrine of Proletarian Truth' (the working class understanding of modern social life is unbiased), or the 'Doctrine of Autonomous Science' (science actually works, whatever the source of its ideas, in terms of successfully controlling the natural world.) Brannigan (1981) more formally argues for the separation of methodological relativism (all thought is socially constructed) and ontological relativism (all thought is equally valid), and rejects the latter but not the former. We can therefore consider the possibility of varying social administration studies along two dimensions. One is the traditional question of whether it can actually identify mechanisms of social intervention which 'work' – the very stuff of evaluation studies which have grown enormously in technical complexity since the 1960s. The other is the political question of whose side it is on – which class, gender, race, age-group, etc. actually benefits. A combination of these two ways of identifying knowledge validity is evident throughout all of our case studies.

Unfortunately much effort is expended in social science generally, and social administration in particular at the moment, in moving unproductively from one dimension to the other: each is posited as a critique of the other. Those who seek technical knowledge in the knowledge – constitutive interest of prediction and control regard those who seek political knowledge in the knowledge – constitutive interest of meaning and emancipation as of doubtful validity, and vice versa. As Mills (1970) observed tersely the choice seems to be between knowledge which is true but trivial, and knowledge which is important but speculative.

The nature of this mutual critique appears to be the operation of a double irony: that the truths available to scientifically valid work tend to be small ones, and that large truths are difficult to pin down scientifically. Thus, for example, we observed in Chapter 6 the juxtaposition of the sophisticated Treasury model for predicting the British economy in the short term, and the theoretical divisions in economics over the long term, fundamental nature of the economy.

Nevertheless the use of such ironic reinterpretations of the work of others remains popular – we have after all set out in this book to construct an ironic analysis of traditional social problems. The trick is to be able to show that other explanations are undermined by the revelation of their concealed interests, while ducking the return fire:

The ironicist struggles for balance on a particularly greasy pole. If he moves too far in one direction, he could slide disastrously towards total relativism, at which point his colleagues might say he had fallen from the pole altogether. But rhetorically he needs at least occasionally to stretch out an arm in that direction. His solution at these times is to increase the grip of his other arm, anchoring himself more firmly than ever in the reflective [empiricist] end of the pole.

(Woolgar, 1983, pp. 255–6)

The art of course is to change arms without being caught out, but there is a constant danger of slipping!

Resolving Social Problems: From Crisis to Corporatism

In this chapter we have answered three questions set at the beginning – why social problems, why state solutions, and why continued support for such solutions which frequently fail – in terms of the concept of ideology. We have suggested that this explanation holds good not only for the general public's apprehension of problems and their solution, but also for the academic world of social administration. Just as we have suggested that a social problem seems to be a contestable concept, open to competing definitions, then solutions to such problems must similarly vary since the way the problem is defined (what is wrong) indicates the solution (what is right). Thus, for example, if as Ryan (1977) suggested victims are blamed, then logically victims should be changed. Ideology then is as relevant to the way solutions are conceived as it is to the way problems are conceived.

In recent times the ideological currents surrounding debates about social problem solution have greatly increased. Both popular and academic support for the Welfare State has faltered. Recent election results seem to indicate a marked popular disaffection, while as we indicated earlier social administration academics are suffering a severe bout of paradigmatic uncertainty (Mishra, 1984). Clearly these changes, too, can be addressed through ideology since they are changes in consciousness about the Welfare State's ability to solve social problems. This point is particularly reinforced by the observation that despite the size of the current government's majority, the Welfare State is *not* being dismantled wholesale, and opinion polls suggest that popular disaffection is actually reserved for minor parts of the Welfare State (Taylor-Gooby, 1982).

The range of alternatives being debated to the traditional social problem solving activities of the Welfare State have by now been well reheased in print (George and Wilding, 1976; Mishra, 1984). Logically there are two ways to achieve better solutions: alter the mechanisms with which to change the social conditions, or redefine the problem. Many approaches do both. For example the present government is in principle committed to a reduction in 'inefficient' state welfare activity, and an increase in private and 'community' care. However, it is also concerned to change the acceptable range of legitimate social problems. Thus unemployment is inevitable, inequality is essential, yet crime is intolerable.

From the point of view of ideology, it is the link between mechanisms for problem solution and definitions of the problem which is crucial. On the one hand the perceived mechanisms available determine what can be solved; but on the other hand what should be solved determines the mechanisms required. The former link can be explored through a range of positive theories of what the state is, such as we listed in Chapter 1 (rationalist, élitist, pluralist, corporatist and Marxist). The latter link however is related to the range of normative political platforms in struggle over welfare policies (new right, Marxist and so on). Clearly these two ranges of views overlap at certain points, to embrace both positive and normative elements. Indeed positive theories of the state are used by both left and right in the attempt to gain support for their normative commitment to particular welfare policies. It is at this point that academic work becomes enmeshed in practical politics in a direct way.

One of the most subtle of these interactions between state theories and political goals has been the suggestion that the modern state is approaching crisis point (defined theoretically) and must therefore be changed, but in a direction which happens to suit the normative position of the analyst. This is a well known ploy in more mundane walks of life such as medical practice or even the car and house repair industries: declare an emergency, preferably on rather technical grounds, and then offer the sucker a solution which you want him to have and which he is now (ideally) hysterically grateful for. Every fairground operator and market hawker knows how to play this trick. Yet in the world of politics it is still played successfully, in order to combat or advance the kind of grievance – claims at the heart of Spector and Kitsuse's (1977) model of social problems. For example the 'father' of modern state crisis theory, James O'Connor (1973), drew heavily for his model on the fiscal crisis of American cities, exemplified by the spectacular collapse in 1974/75 of confidence in bonds regularly floated by New York City to pay its monthly salary liabilities. In O'Connor's terms this is a classic example of the contradiction between the economic liabilities of the modern state in providing an infrastructure for capital accumulation, and the limits of its political legitimacy in sustaining those liabilities (in this case both raising taxes, and borrowing commercial money to meet taxation short falls).

However the history of this event (see especially Shutt, 1982; Marcuse, 1981) reveals a rather different story. There is no doubt that objectively New York City has *no* trouble in repaying its bonds regularly, as it and other cities had done in the past. However there is considerable evidence of the dissatisfaction that Wall Street Bankers working in Manhattan had with the increasingly liberal welfare policies of New York City politicians. New York has traditionally been one of the highest per capita welfare spenders, particularly under the myriad of permissive programmes set up during the extraordinary burst of welfare policy making in the 1960s. Rather than the manifestation of a theoretical crisis, the New York fiscal crisis was engineered by a small group of bankers who held the city to ransom. In return for money they forced the city government to hand over all of its economic affairs to the Municipal Assistance Corporation (later called the Emergency Financial Control Board) made up of the said bankers. Democratic controls were thus suspended, and thousands of jobs were cut to save money.

Thus this crisis was not the logical outcome of a contradiction of late capitalism. Rather it was the successful use of a label (which incidentally had been increasingly taken up by the media in the months leading up to 1974) as a device for initiating desired changes. It has been used similarly with respect to restructuring American social security provisions (Freeman and Adams, 1982) and closer to home in the exchange rate 'crisis' which allowed the IMF to impose public expenditure cuts on the 1976 Labour Government.

Clearly the use of this label, if it works, can be a successful lever in politics. However, to cry wolf too often obviously undermines its effectiveness. For example, extensive discussions of 'crises of crisis management' by Offe (1976) and 'legitimation crises' by Habermas (1976) have sparked off a derivative literature in social administration (George and Wilding, 1984; Taylor-Gooby, 1985; Mishra, 1984), which tends to take the notion of crisis seriously if critically. Yet the overwhelming impression of the British Welfare State in the 1980s is of relative continuity. Certainly it has handled unemployment in terms of the cost of social security quite effectively, and public expenditure cuts and privatisation are still relatively mild, taken overall. The crisis, if anywhere, is in terms of our perceptions of the Welfare State. But if as we have suggested this might be a manufactured impression in the pursuit of a particular hegemonic project, the left may be contributing negatively by reinforcing the possibility of 'new right' policy changes. Certainly claiming a crisis is a high risk strategy if it also opens up the possibility of policy alternatives in the interests of other groups.

For example, if we pursue this 'confidence trick' model of politics a little further we can suggest that the manufacture of crisis is not the complete story. Even more important is the subsequent requirement to 'cool the mark out' (Goffman, 1952). If by the mark in this case we mean not the victim of a confidence trick, but the range of legitimate political opinion, then not the creation of crisis but its legitimate resolution on terms favourable to a particular set of political interests is the key pay-off from 'crisis management' (in Offe's terms). And this bears all the hallmarks of our earlier definition of ideology – mystification in the interests of particular groups.

We are not here arguing any particular strategy, such as 'not rocking the boat', rather we are merely sceptical of the validity of arguments positing a theoretical state crisis which are then used to underpin normative political goals. Yet if crisis has been overplayed, and the Welfare State survives, our earlier analysis of social problems and their solutions as shaped within ideology remains: social problems generally fail to be solved by the state, yet they cannot be perceived and tackled in any other way. We can merely ask, where next?

If it seems unlikely that left or right will actually be able to realise the substantial changes they would wish, then some continuance of current arrangements is most likely to be the case for the rest of this century. Those current arrangements, despite social administration's commitment in the past to a collectivist ideal, have always been a mixture of state, voluntary, commercial and private (ie. family and neighbourhood) solutions to the social problems of the day. Indeed there has been a resurgence of normative rationalisation for this mixed system under the banner of the 'mixed economy of welfare' (Beresford and Croft, 1984).

While it must be apparent that we are critical of this system, we are driven to the conclusion that it will continue. How will it be described in the twenty-first century? A possible model under recent discussion in the social administration literature (Offe, 1982; Cawson, 1982; Mishra, 1984) (again derivative of a debate within sociology in the 1970s (Winkler, 1977; Panitch, 1980)), is the notion of corporatism. While this, like the 'mixed economy of welfare', has been used as a normative ideal upon which to base future welfare policies (especially by Mishra, 1984, Chapters 4 and 6), we are here merely concerned with explanation rather than prescription.

If as we have argued, conflicts are transformed into social problems and channelled into the Welfare State by ideology, then the Welfare State clearly rests on the particular apprehension by major groups in society of the best way of achieving their interests. Quite simply this apprehension is of working within the system rather than changing it. To this extent struggle and protest have become institutionalised or incorporated. This was the burden of Dahrendorf's (1959) seminal analysis of class conflict in recent times, and the notion of the 'embourgeoisement' of the working class (Goldthorpe et al., 1969). While this picture was taken to (now ridiculed) extremes in Bell's (1961) thesis of the end of ideology, the presumed re-emergence of open conflict in the 1970s has itself been much exaggerated, not least in the terms of 'crisis' which we have criticised.

The continued management of conflict is explained in the corporatist model as a combination of the functional representation of economic interests such as trade unions and business groups directly in the political system (i.e. bypassing the formal representative mechanisms), and linked to this the state planning and direction of national economic factors such as wages, prices and investment. Although some writers, especially Winkler (1977), have extended this model to mean a new mode of production ('beyond' capitalism and socialism), its recent use is a more modest kind of 'monopoly pluralism' in which key interests are organised to influence state actions (Schmitter and Lehmbruch, 1979).

Unfortunately corporatism has frequently been regarded as distasteful by the left because it has been considered solely on the grounds of its normative implications. For example Mishra's (1984) clear normative endorsement of it has provoked a sharp condemnation in a recent review (Deacon, 1984). Yet socialists have been very reluctant to ask not whether the 'current crisis' is at long last the beginning of the end of capitalism, but rather the necessary, but painful, question of what the grounds are for the continued existence of capitalism.

Offe (1982) has asked this question, and found himself face to face with corporatism. A more technical and sophisticated exercise has been undertaken by Aglietta (1979) in his review of the development of American capitalism from the point of view of Marxist economics. He suggests that each era of capitalist development ('regime of accumulation') has to arrange sufficient demand (via a 'consumption norm') to sustain profitable production. He sees the Keynesian era of demand management and Welfare State organised consumption as a particularly successful 'regime of accumulation'. But his analysis is most relevant here for outlining what the next era will look like, if capitalism is to survive. The answer includes not surprisingly the expanded commodification of services, with an associated change in the consumption norm to ensure the availability of markets; but most significantly his answer also includes solidly corporatist control over incomes policies and investment decisions.

This model has been elaborated in a hybrid with the Marxist view, and applied to social policy by Cawson (1982). He points out that corporate groups do not merely press their demands on the state (as in the pluralist model), but that they also act as agents of policy implementation. Cawson's model does not merely focus within the 'black box' of policy implementation however, but attempts to incorporate the kind of ideological and class influences we have discussed earlier in Marxist theories of the state:

What marxist theories of the state lack is a vigorous theory of corporatism which would seek to specify the limits of class analysis and pose the problem of state power as something to be explained rather than as something that can be reduced to the power of social classes.

(Cawson, 1982, p. 52)

His model is therefore a necessarily multi-layered one.

Most previous writing on corporatism has stressed the incorporation of economic producer interests within the overall division of labour. Cawson suggests therefore that corporatism is most developed in social policy where welfare 'producers' are most powerfully organised, such as the professional groups in the National Health Service, and to a lesser extent in higher education, town planning and the personal social services. But he also suggests that as capital accumulation faltered in the late 1960s, those areas where welfare producers were not well organised were 'incorporated from above' by regionalising local services such as energy and water supply or by injecting managerial arrangements into social services, local government, and so on:

In short, the competitive-pluralist sector of politics diminished in importance as production-based state intervention, articulated through corporate modes of representation, came to greater prominence.

(ibid., p. 104)

The consequence of this is that liberal democratic theory grossly underestimates the effects of powerful corporate interests, which are regarded as improper:

This has produced the bizarre situation whereby everybody – except, apparently, the Prime Minister Mrs. Thatcher – accepts the reality of the power exercised by corporations and trade unions, but nobody can justify it.

(ibid., p. 109)

If Cawson's modified political economy is on the right path, then social problems will continue to be addressed towards the state with the ever greater conviction that it should be the purveyor of solutions. Calls for localism and democratisation (such as those made by Hadley and Hatch (1981)) will remain pious hopes, but for the same reasons the siren calls of the right will be confined similarly in practice to the margins of social policy.

Conclusion

In this book we have tried to move conventional wisdom about social problems. By outlining the weaknesses of the social problems literature in Chapter 1, and discussing a variety of specific social problems in subsequent chapters, we challenged the assumption that social policy is simply a way of solving such problems. The remarkable failure of social policies in this assumed task, yet their continued legitimacy, can only be understood by looking more closely at the way problems and policies are perceived, professionally, publicly and academically. To this end we have argued that an appreciation of ideological distortion in the perceptions of these three groups should be the central feature of an adequate explanation of social problems.

References

Aall-Jilek, L.M., 1965, 'Epilepsy in the Wapagor tribe in Tanganyike', *Acta. Psychiat. Scand.*, vol. 61, pp. 57–86.

Abel-Smith, B. and Townsend, P., 1965, *The Poor and the Poorest*, Bell & Hyman.

Abercrombie, N., 1980, *Class, Structure and Knowledge, Problems in the Sociology of Knowledge*, Basil Blackwell.

Abercrombie, N., Hill, S., and Turner, B.S., 1980, *The Dominant Ideology Thesis*, Allen and Unwin.

Aglietta, M., 1979, *A Theory of Capitalist Regulation: the U.S. Experience*, New Left Books.

Ahmed, P.I. and Plog, S.C. (eds), 1976, *State mental hospitals, what happens when they close*, Plenum Medical Book Co.

Allen, F., 1974, *The Crimes of Politics*, Harvard University Press.

Allen, F., 1981, *The decline of the rehabilitative ideal*, Yale University Press.

Althusser, L., 1969, *For Marx*, Penguin Books.

Althusser, L., 1971, *Lenin and Philosophy and Other Essays*, New Left Books.

Amir, M., 1971, *Patterns of Forcible Rape*, University of Chicago Press.

Anderson, O.W., 1968, *The Uneasy Equilibrium, Private and Public Financing of Health Services in the United States 1875–1965*, College and University Press.

Anderson, P., 1976, *Considerations on Western Marxism*, New Left Books.

Armstrong, D., 1983, *Political anatomy of the body, medical knowledge in Britain in the twentieth century*, Cambridge University Press.

Attlee, C.R., 1920, *The Social Worker*, Bell & Hyman.

Baker, J., 1979, 'Social Conscience and Social Policy', *Journal of Social Policy*, vol. 8, no. 2, pp. 177–206.

Baldock, J. and Prior, D., 1981, 'Social Workers Talking to Clients: a study of verbal behaviour', *British Journal of Social Work*, pp. 19–38.

Barker, M., 1981, *The New Racism*, Junction Books.

Barnes, B., 1977, *Interests and the Growth of Knowledge*, Routledge and Kegan Paul.

Barrett, L., 1977, *The Rastafarians, Dreadlocks of Jamaica*, Heinemann.

Bart, P., 1981, 'A study of women who both were raped and avoided rape', *Journal of Social Issues*, vol. 37, no. 4, pp. 123–37.

Baruch, B. and Treacher, A., 1978, *Psychiatry observed*, Routledge and Kegan Paul.

Becker, H.S., 1963, *Outsiders*, Free Press.

Bell, D., 1961, *The end of ideology*, Collier Books.

Ben-Tovim, G. and Gabriel, J., 1982, 'The politics of race in Britain 1962–79', in Husband, C. (ed.), *Continuity and Change*, Hutchinson.

Beresford, P. and Croft, S., 1984, 'Welfare Pluralism: the new face of Fabianism', *Critical Social Policy*, vol. 3, no. 3, pp. 19–39.

Berger, P.L. and Luckmann, T., 1967, *The Social Construction of Reality*, Allen Lane.

Bernstein, B., 1971, *Class, Codes and Control*, vol. 1, Routledge and Kegan Paul.

Bilton, K., 1968, 'Children in trouble', *Child Care News*, no. 75, pp. 9–10.

Binney, V., Harkell, G. and Nixon, J., 1981, *Leaving Violent Men: A Study of Refuges and Housing for Battered Women*, Women's Aid Federation.

Black Report, 1980, in Townsend, P. and Davidson, N., 1982, *Inequalities in Health, The Black Report*, Penguin.

Blackstone, W., 1765, *Commentaries on the Laws of England*, Clarendon Press.

Block, F., 1979, 'The ruling class do not rule', in Quinney, R. (ed.), *Capitalist Society*, Dorsey Press.

Booth, C., 1887, 'Condition and occupations of the people of the Tower Hamlets 1886–7', paper given to the Royal Statistical Society.

Booth, W., 1890, *In Darkest England and the Way Out*, International Headquarters of the Salvation Army.

Borkowski, M., Murch, M. and Walker, V., 1983, *Marital Violence: Community Response*, Tavistock Press.

Bott, E., 1976, 'Hospital and Society', *British Journal of Medical Psychology*, vol. 49, pp. 97–140.

Bottoms, A.E., 1974, 'On the decriminalisation of the English juvenile courts', in Hood, R. (ed.) *Crime, Criminology and Public Policy*, Heinemann.

Bourne, H., 1953, 'The insulin myth', *Lancet*, vol. 2, pp. 964–8.

Bourne, J. and Sivanandan, A., 1980, 'Cheerleaders and Ombudsmen, the Sociology of race relations in Britain', in *Race and Class*, vol. XXI, no. 4, pp. 330–52.

Box, S., 1971, *Deviance, Reality and Society*, Rinehart and Winston.

Box, S., 1981, 'Preface' in Schrag, P. and Divoky, D., *The Myth of the Hyperactive Child and Other Means of Child Control*, Penguin Books.

Bradshaw, J., Cooke, K. and Godfrey, C., 1983, 'The impact of unemployment on the living standards of families', *Journal of Social Policy*, vol. 12, part 4, pp. 433–52.

Brake, M., 1980, *The Sociology of Youth Culture and Subcultures*, Routledge and Kegan Paul.

Brannigan, A., 1981, *The Social Basis of Scientific Discoveries*, Cambridge University Press.

Breines, W. and Gordon, L., 1983, 'The new scholarship on family violence', *Signs*, vol. 8, no. 3, pp. 490–531.

Brittan, S., 1981, *How to End the 'Monetarist' Controversy: a journalist's reflections on output, jobs, prices and money*, (Hobart Paper No. 90), Institute of Economic Affairs.

Brittan, S. and Lilley, P., 1977, *The Delusion of Incomes Policy*, Temple Smith.

Brown, G. W. and Harris, T., 1978, *Social Origins of Depression: a study of psychiatric disorder in women*, Tavistock Publications.

Brownmiller, S., 1975, *Against Our Will*, Penguin Books.

Brunsdon, C. and Morley, D., 1978, *Everyday Television: 'Nationwide'*, British Film Institute.

Bulmer, M., (ed.), 1980, *Social Research and Royal Commissions*, Allen and Unwin.

Bulmer, M., 1983, 'An Anglo-American Comparison', *American Behavioural Scientist*, vol. 26, no. 5.

Burns, T., 1977, 'The organisation of Public Opinion', in J. Curran, M. Gurevitch, J. Woollacott (eds), *Mass Communication and Society*, Edward Arnold.

Butler, D. and Kavanagh, D., 1980, *The British General Election of 1979*, Macmillan.

Calnan, M., 1982, 'A review of government policies aimed at primary prevention', in Alderson, M. (ed.), *The Prevention of Cancer*, Edward Arnold.

Carlebach, J., 1970, *Caring for children in trouble*, Routledge and Kegan Paul.

Carpenter, M., 1968, *Reformatory schools*, Woburn.

Carlyle, T., 'Past and Present', Book one, chapter one, in Shelston, A. (ed.), 1971, *Thomas Carlyle: Selected Writings*, Penguin Books.

Cashmore, E., 1979, *Rastaman*, Allen and Unwin.

Cashmore, E. and Troyna, B., 1983, *Introduction to Race Relations*, Routledge and Kegan Paul.

Castel, R., 1976, *L'ordre psychiatrique: l'age d'or de l'alienisme*, Editions de Minuit.

Castles, S. and Kosack, G., 1973, *Immigrant workers and the class structure in Western Europe*, Oxford University Press.

Cavenagh, W. E., 1966, 'What kind of court or committee', *British Journal of Criminology*, vol. 6, no. 2, April, pp. 123–38.

Cawson, A., 1982, *Corporatism and Welfare, Social Policy and State Intervention in Britain*, Heinemann Educational Books.

CDP, 1977, *Gilding the Ghetto, The State and the Poverty Experiments*, CDP Inter-Project Editorial Team.

Chester, R. and Streather, J., 1972, 'Cruelty in English Divorce: some empirical findings', *Journal of Marriage and the Family*, vol. 34, no. 4.

Children in trouble, Cmnd. 3601, 1968, HMSO.

Clare, A., 1976, *Psychiatry in Dissent*, Tavistock Publications.

Clark, L. and Lewis, D., 1977, *Rape: the price of coercive sexuality*, Toronto Women's Press.

Clarke, M., 1975, 'Social Problem Ideologies', *British Journal of Sociology*, vol. 26, no. 4.

Clifton, J., 1984, 'Refuges and self help', in N. Johnson (ed.), *Marital Violence*, Sociological Review Monograph.

Cloward, R. and Ohlin, L., 1960, *Delinquency and Opportunity*, Free Press.

Coard, B., 1971, *How the West Indian Child is Made Educationally Subnormal in British Schools*, New Beacon Books.

Cobbe, F.P., 1878, 'Wife Torture in England', *Contemporary Review*, vol. 32, pp. 55–8.

Cochrane, A.L., 1972, *Effectiveness and Efficiency*, Nuffield Provincial Hospitals Trust.

Cohen, A.K., 1955, *Delinquent Boys: The Culture of the Gang*, Free Press.

Cohen, G.A., 1978, *Karl Marx's Theory of History, A Defence*, Oxford University Press.

Cohen, S., 1972, *Folk Devils and Moral Panics*, Paladin.

College of General Practitioners, 1960, 'A survey of the Epilepsies in General Practice', *British Medical Journal*, vol. 2, pp. 416–22.

Connell, N. and Wilson, C., 1974, *Rape: the first sourcebook for women*, New American Library.

Conrad, P., 1976, 'The discovery of hyperkenesis – notes on the medicalisation of deviant behaviour', *Social Problems*, vol. 23, pp. 12–21.

Conrad, P., 1981, 'On the medicalisation of deviance and social control', in D. Ingleby (ed.), *Critical Psychiatry*, Penguin Books.

Conrad, P. and Schneider, J., 1980, *Deviance and Medicalisation, from Badness to Sickness*, C.V. Mosby.

Conservative Party, 1979, *Conservative Manifesto 1979*, Conservative Central Office.

Cooper, D., 1970, *Psychiatry and Anti-Psychiatry*, Paladin.

Cooper, J., 1970, 'The children and young persons act 1969', *Child Care News*, no. 96, pp. 2–5.

Cooper, J., 1983, *The Creation of the British Personal Social Services 1962–1974*, Heinemann.

Corrigan, P. and Leonard, P., 1978, *Social Work Practice Under Capitalism*, Macmillan.

Corrigan, P., Ramsey, H. and Sayer, D., 1980, 'The state as a relation of production', in Corrigan, P. (ed.), *Capitalism, State Formation and Marxist Theory*, Quartet Books.

Crewe, I., 1983, 'How Labour was Trounced All Round', *Guardian*, 14 June, p. 20.

Crocetti, G.M., Spiro, H.R. and Siassi, I., 1974, *Contemporary Attitudes Toward Mental Illness*, University of Pittsburgh Press.

Croft, J., 1978, *Research in criminal justice*, Home Office Research Study no. 44, HMSO.

Croft, J., 1980, *Research and criminal policy*, Home Office Research Study no. 59, HMSO.

Croft, J., 1981, *Managing criminological research*, Home Office Research Study no. 69, HMSO.

Croft, J., 1982, *Concerning crime*, Home Office Research Study no. 75, HMSO.

Cross, M., 1982, 'The manufacture of marginality' in Cashmore, E. and Troyna, B. (eds), *Black Youth in Crisis*, Allen and Unwin.

Cypher, J.M., 1980, 'Relative state autonomy and national economic planning', *Journal of Economic Issues*, vol. 14, no. 2, pp. 335–8.

Dahrendorf, R., 1959, *Class and Class Conflict in an Industrial Society*, Routledge and Kegan Paul.

Davis, M.S., 1971, 'That's interesting! Towards a phenomenology of sociology and a sociology of phenomenology', *Philosophy of the Social Sciences*, 1, pp. 309–344.

Deacon, B., 1984, Review of Mishra, R., *The Welfare State in Crisis*, Harvester Press, in *Critical Social Policy*, vol. 10, Summer, pp. 151–2.

Dear, M.J. and Taylor, S.M., 1982, *Not On Our Street, Community Attitudes to Mental Health Care*, Pion.

de Boer, C., 1983, 'The polls: attitudes towards unemployment', *Public Opinion Quarterly*, vol. 47, pp. 435–42.

Delamont, S. and Ellis, R., 1979, *Statutory and Voluntary Responses to Domestic Violence in Wales*, S.R.U. Working Paper No. 6, Department of Sociology, University College, Cardiff.

Denney, D., 1983, 'Some dominant perspectives in the literature relating to multi racial social work', *British Journal of Social Work*, vol. 13 pp. 149 74.

Disney, R., 1979, 'Recurrent spells and the concentration of unemployment in Great Britain', *Economic Journal*, March, pp. 109–19.

Dobash, R. Emerson and Dobash, Russell, 1980, *Violence Against Wives: A Case Against the Patriarchy*, Open Books.

Drakeford, M., 1982, 'Probation: custody in the Community?', *Critical Social Policy*, vol. 1, no. 3.

Durkheim, E., 1964, *The Division of Labour in Society*, Free Press.

Dunleavy, P., 1979, 'The urban bases of political alignment', *British Journal of Political Science*, 9, 2.

Economist, The, 16 June, 1984.

Ely, P.J., Swift, A.K. and Sutherland, A., 1985, *Control Without Custody*, Scottish Academic Press.

Esping-Anderson, G., Friedland, R., and Wright, E.O., 1976, 'Modes of class struggle and the capitalist state', *Kapitalistate*, vol. 4–5, pp. 186–220.

Evason, E., 1982, *Hidden Violence*, Farset Press.

Faragher, T., 1985, 'The police response to violence against women in the home', in Pahl, J. (ed.), *Private Violence and Public Policy*, Routledge and Kegan Paul.

Faulk, M., 1974, 'Men who assault their wives', *Medicine, Science and the Law*, vol. 7, no. 2.

Ferrard, M.L. and Hunnybun, N.K., 1962, *The Caseworker's Use of Relationships*, Tavistock.

Feuerbach, L., 1957, *The Essence of Christianity*, Harper and Row.

Finch, J. and Groves, D. (eds), 1983, *A Labour of Love: Women, Work and Caring*, Routledge and Kegan Paul.

Foot, P., 1965, *Immigration and race in British politics*, Penguin.

Ford, J., Morgan, D. and Whelan, M., 1982, *Special Education and Social Control*, Routledge and Kegan Paul.

Foucault, M., 1967, *Madness and Civilization*, Tavistock Publications.

Foucault, M., 1973, *The Birth of the Clinic*, Tavistock Publications.

Fowler, R., Hodge, B., Kress, G. and Trew, T., 1979, *Language and Control*, Routledge and Kegan Paul.

Frankenberg, R., Johnson, N., Dawson, B. and Faragher, T., 1980, *Battered Women's Project*, University of Keele, Report presented to the Department of Health and Social Security.

Freeman, G., and Adams, P., 1982, 'The politics of social security', in Stone, A. and Harpham, E.J. (eds), *The Political Economy of Public Policy*, Sage.

Freeman, M.D.A., 1979, *Violence in the Home*, Saxon House.

Freeman, M.D.A., 1980, 'Violence against women: does the legal system provide solutions or itself constitute the problem?', *British Journal of Law and Society*, vol. 7, pp. 215–41.

Friedson, E., 1970, *Profession of medicine: a study in the sociology of applied knowledge*, Dodd, Mead and Co.

Frieze, I.H., 1983, 'Investigating the causes and consequences of marital rape', *Signs*, vol. 8, no. 3, pp. 532–53.

Fuller, R.C. and Myers, R.R., 1941, 'The natural history of a social problem', *American Sociological Review*, vol. 6, pp. 320–29.

Gayford, J.J., 1975, 'Wife battering: a preliminary survey of 100 cases', *British Medical Journal*, vol. 1, pp. 194–7.

Gelles, R.J., 1974, *The Violent Home*, Sage Publications.

George, V. and Wilding, P., 1972a, *Motherless Families*, Routledge and Kegan Paul.

George, V. and Wilding, P., 1972b, 'Social Values, Social Class and Social Policy', *Social and Economic Administration*, vol. 6, no. 3.

George, V. and Wilding, P., 1976, *Ideology and Social Welfare*, Routledge and Kegan Paul.

George, V. and Wilding, P., 1984, *The Impact of Social Policy*, Routledge and Kegan Paul.

Geras, N., 1972, 'Marx and the Critique of Political Economy', in Blackburn, R. (ed.), *Ideology in Social Science, Readings in Critical Social Theory*, Fontana.

Giddens, A., 1979, *Central Problems in Social Theory, Action, Structure and Contradiction in Social Analysis*, Macmillan.

Ginsburg, N., 1979, *Class, Capital and Social Policy*, Macmillan.

Gladstone Committee, 1895, *Report from the departmental committee on prisons*, C 7702, HMSO.

Glasgow University Media Group, 1976, *Bad News*, Routledge and Kegan Paul.

Glyn, A. and Sutcliffe, B., 1972, *British Capitalism: workers and the profits squeeze*, Penguin Books.

Glynn, S. and Booth, A., 1983, 'Unemployment in Interwar Britain: the case for re-learning the lessons of the 1930s?', *The Economic History Review*, vol. XXXVI.

Goffman, E., 1952, 'Cooling the Mark Out: some aspects of adaptation to failure', *Psychiatry*, XV, pp. 445–463.

Goffman, E., 1961, *Asylums: essays on the social situation of mental patients and other inmates*, Pengiun Books.

Goffman, E., 1969, 'The insanity of place', *Psychiatry*, vol. 32, pp. 357–88.

Goffman, E., 1971, *Relations in Public*, Penguin Books.

Gold, D.A., Lo, C.Y.H. and Wright, E.O., 1975, 'Recent developments in Marxist theories of the capitalist state', *Monthly Review*, October, pp. 40–1.

Goldthorpe, J., Lockwood, D., Bechhofer, F. and Platt, J., 1969, *The Affluent Worker in the Class Structure,* Cambridge University Press.

Gostin, L., 1977, *A Human Condition,* MIND.

Gough, I., 1975, 'State expenditure in advanced capitalism', *New Left Review,* vol. 92, pp. 53–92.

Gough, I., 1979, *The Political Economy of the Welfare State,* Macmillan.

Gould, J. and Kolb, W., 1964, *A Dictionary of the Social Sciences,* Tavistock Publications.

Gouldner, A.W., 1963, 'Anti-minotaur: the Myth of a Value-Free Sociology', in Stein, M. and Vidich, A. (eds), *Sociology on Trial.* Prentice-Hall.

Gouldner, A.W., 1980, *The Two Marxisms, Contradictions and Anomalies in the Development of Theory,* Macmillan.

Gramsci, A., 1971, *Selections from the Prison Notebooks,* Lawrence and Wishart.

Green, A., 1975, *Social Problems: arena of conflict,* McGraw-Hill.

Groth, A.N., 1979, *Men Who Rape,* Plennon Press.

Guardian, 11 August 1981.

Habermas, J., 1970, 'Toward a theory of communicative competence', in Dreitzel, H.P. (ed.), *Recent Sociology No. 2, Patterns of Communicative Behaviour,* Macmillan.

Habermas, J., 1971, 'Technology and Science as "ideology" ', in *Toward a Rational Society, Student Protest, Science and Politics,* Heinemann, pp. 81–122.

Habermas, J., 1972, *Knowledge and Human Interests,* Heinemann.

Habermas, J., 1976, *Legitimation Crisis,* Heinemann.

Hadley, R. and Hatch, S., 1981, *Social Welfare and the Failure of the State, Centralised Social Services and Participatory Alternatives,* Allen and Unwin.

Haines, H.H., 1979, 'Cognitive Claims-making, Enclosure, and the Depoliticization of Social Problems', *Sociological Quarterly,* vol. 20.

Hall, P., Land, H., Parker, R. and Webb, A., 1975, *Change, Choice and Conflict in Social Policy,* Heinemann.

Hall, S., 1980a, 'Cultural Studies and the Centre: some problematics and problems', in Hall, S., Hobson, D., Lowe, A., and Willis, P. (eds), *Culture, Media, Language,* Hutchinson, pp. 15–47.

Hall, S., 1980b, 'Encoding/Decoding', ibid, pp. 128–38.

Hall, S., Lumley, B. and McLennan, G., 1978a, 'Politics and Ideology: Gramsci', in Centre for Contemporary Cultural Studies, *On Ideology,* Hutchinson, pp. 45–76.

Hall, S., Critcher, C., Jefferson, T., Clarke, J. and Roberts, B., 1978b, *Policing the Crisis, Mugging, the State, and Law and Order,* Macmillan.

Hall Williams, J.E., 1977, 'The contribution of the judiciary to penal policy-making' in Walker, N. and Giller, H. (eds), *Penal policy-making in England*, papers presented to the Cropwood Round-Table Conference, December 1976. University of Cambridge Institute of Criminology.

Halmos, P., 1965, *The Faith of the Counsellors*, Constable.

Hanmer, J. and Leonard, D., 1984, 'Negotiating the problem: the DHSS and research on violence in marriage', in Bell, C. and Roberts, H. (eds), *Social Researching: Politics, Problems, Practice*, Routledge and Kegan Paul.

Hanmer, J. and Saunders, S., 1984, *Well-Founded Fear: a Community Study of Violence against Women*, Hutchinson.

Harrington, M., 1963, *The Other America: Poverty in the US*, Macmillan.

Harrison, A., 1984, 'Economic policy and expectations', in Jowell, R. and Airey, C. (eds), *British Social Attitudes: the 1984 Report*, Gower.

Hay, A., Soothill, K. and Walby, S., 1980, 'Seducing the public by rape reports', *New Society*, 31 July, pp. 214–5.

Hayek, F.A., 1962, *The Road to Serfdom*, Routledge and Kegan Paul.

Heald, D., 1983, *Public Expenditure: its defence and reform*, Martin Robertson.

Heidenheimer, A.J., Heclo, H. and Adams, C.T., 1983, *Comparative Public Policy: The Politics of Social Choice in Europe and America*, 2nd edn., Macmillan.

Hilbourne, J., 1973, 'On Disabling the Normal: The Implications of Physical Disability for Other People', *British Journal of Social Work*, vol. 3, pp. 497–504.

Hill, M., 1983, 'Government responses to unemployment', in Loney, M. et al. (ed.), *Social Policy and Social Welfare*, Open University Press, pp. 241–54.

Hiro, D., 1971, *Black British White British*, Penguin.

Hirsch, F., 1977, *The Social Limits to Growth*, Routledge and Kegan Paul.

Hirschi, T., 1969, *The Causes of Delinquency*, University of California Press.

H.M. Treasury, 1984, *The Next Ten Years: Public Expenditure and Taxation into the 1990s*, Cmnd. 9189, HMSO.

Hoghughi, M., 1983, *The Delinquent – Directions For Social Control*, Burnett Books.

Holloway, J. and Picciotto, S. (eds), 1978, *State and Capital, A Marxist Debate*, Edward Arnold.

Holman, R., 1978, *Poverty*, Martin Robertson.

Homer, M., Leonard, A. and Taylor, P., 1984, *Private Violence: Public Shame*, Cleveland Refuge and Aid for Women and Children.

Hood, R., 1965, *Borstal Re-assessed*, Heinemann.

Hook, S., 1962, *From Hegel to Marx*, University of Michigan Press.

Horton, J., 1966, 'Order and conflict theories of social problems as competing ideologies', *American Journal of Sociology*, vol. 71, no. 6.

Hough, M. and Mayhew, P., 1983, *The British crime survey: first report*, Home Office Research Study no. 76, HMSO.

Howell, R.C., J.P., 1967, *The Treatment of Young Offenders in Sweden*, Justice of the Peace Ltd.

Hudson, B., 1984, 'Predicting the unpredictable', *Community Care*, 2nd February.

Hunt, A., 1966, 'Enforcement in probation casework', *British Journal of Criminology*, vol. 4, no. 3.

Husband, C., 1982, *Race in Britain*, Hutchinson.

Ingleby, D., 1982, 'The social construction of mental illness', in Wright, P. and Treacher, A. (eds), *The problem of medical knowledge, examining the social construction of medicine*, Edinburgh University Press.

Ingleby, D., 1983, 'Mental health and social order', in Cohen, S. and Scull, A. (eds), *Social Control and the State*, Martin Robertson.

Ingleby Report, 1960, *Report of the committee on children and young persons*, Cmnd 1191, HMSO.

Illich, I., 1975, *Medical Nemesis: the expropriation of health*, Calder and Boyars.

Jackson, S., 1978, 'The Social Context of Rape', *Women's Studies*, vol. 1, no. 1.

James, E., 1970, *America Against Poverty*, Routledge and Kegan Paul.

Jarvis, F.V., 1966, 'The probation service – the effect of the white paper', *British Journal of Criminology*, vol. 6, no. 2, pp. 152–9.

Jefferys, M., 1975, 'Foreword', in Cox, C. and Mead, A. (eds), *A sociology of medical practice*, Collier-Macmillan.

Jenkins, R., 1982, *Managers recruitment procedures and black workers*, Working papers on ethnic relations, no. 18, Birmingham research unit on ethnic relations.

Jenkins, R. and Troyna, B., 1983, 'Educational myths, labour market and realities', in Troyna, B. and Smith, D. (eds), *Racism, School and the Labour Market*, National Youth Bureau.

Jessop, B., 1977, 'Recent theories of the capitalist state', *Cambridge Journal of Economics*, vol. 1, pp. 361–4.

Jessop, B., 1980, 'The transformation of the state in post-war Britain', in Scase, R. (ed.), *The State in Western Europe*, Croom Helm.

Jessop, B., 1982, *The Capitalist State*, Martin Robertson.

Johnson, A.G., 1980, 'On the prevalence of rape in the United States', *Signs*, vol. 6, no. 1, pp. 136–46.

Johnson, T., 1972, *Professions and Power*, Macmillan.

Jones, C. and Novak, T., 1980, 'The State and Social Policy', in Corrigan, P. (ed.), *Capitalism, State Formation and Marxist Theory*, Quartet books.

Jones, K., 1972, *A History of the Mental Health Services*, Routledge and Kegan Paul.

Jones, K. and Tillotson, A., 1965, *The adult population of epileptic colonies*, London, British Epilepsy Association.

Jordan, B., 1971, 'Probation in the sixties', *Journal of Social and Economic Administration*, vol. 5, no. 2, pp. 125–38.

Kahan, B.J., 1966, 'The child, the family and the young offender: revolutionary or evolutionary?', *British Journal of Criminology*, vol. 6, no. 2, pp. 159–69.

Katznelson, I., 1973, *Black Men White Cities*, Oxford University Press.

Keating, P. (ed.), 1976, *Into Unknown England 1866–1913*, Fontana.

Kendell, R.E., 1981, 'The present status of electro convulsive therapy', *British Journal of Psychiatry*, vol. 139, pp. 265–83.

Kennedy, M.C., 1982, 'The economy as a whole', in Prest, A.R. and Coppock, D.J. (eds), *The U.K. Economy*, Weidenfeld and Nicholson.

Kittrie, N.N., 1971, *The Right to Be Different: deviance and enforced therapy*, Johns Hopkins Press.

Klass, A., 1975, *There's Gold in Them Thar Pills: an inquiry into the medical-industrial complex*, Penguin Books.

Koestler, A., 1959, *The Sleepwalkers*, Hutchinson.

Kowalczewski, P.S., 1982, 'Race and Education – racism diversity and inequality implications for multi racial education', *Oxford Review of Education*, vol. 18, no. 2, pp. 145–60.

Kuhn, T.S., 1970, *The Structure of Scientific Revolutions*, 2nd Edition, University of Chicago Press.

Labour Party, 1983, *The New Hope for Britain: Labour's Manifesto 1983*, London.

Laclau, E., 1979, *Politics and Ideology in Marxist Theory*, Verso.

Laing, R.D., 1965, *The Divided Self: an existential study in sanity and madness*, Penguin Books.

Larrain, J., 1979, *The Concept of Ideology*, Hutchinson.

Larrain, J., 1983, *Marxism and Ideology*, Macmillan.

Latour, B. and Woolgar, S., 1979, *Laboratory Life, the Social Construction of Scientific Facts*, Sage.

Lea, J., 1980, 'The contradictions of the sixties race relations legislation' in National Deviancy Conference, *Permissiveness and control*, Macmillan.

Lee, P. and Raban, C., 1983, 'Welfare and Ideology', in Loney, M.,

Boswell, D. and Clarke, J. (eds) *Social Policy and Social Welfare,* Open University Press.

Lemert, E., 1967, *Human Deviance, Social Problems and Social Control,* Prentice Hall.

Lennox, W.G., 1960, *Epilepsy and Related Disorders,* Churchill.

Leonard, P. and McLeod, E., 1980, *Marital Violence: Social Construction and Social Service Response,* University of Warwick, Department of Applied Social Studies.

Lester, A. and Bindman, G., 1972, *Race and Law,* Penguin Books.

Little, A., 1978, 'Schools and race', in *5 views of multi racial Britain,* Commission for Racial Equality.

Littlewood, R. and Lipsedge, M., 1982, *Aliens and Alienists: Ethnic Minorities and Psychiatry,* Penguin Books.

Livingstone, P., 1978, *The leisure needs of Asian boys aged 8–14,* Scout Association.

London Edinburgh Weekend Return Group, 1979, *In and Against the State, Discussion Notes for Socialists,* Conference of Socialist Economists.

London, Jack, 1903, *The People of the Abyss,* 1962 edition, Arco Publications.

London Rape Crisis Centre, 1978, *Second Report,* Rape Counselling and Research Project.

London Rape Crisis Centre, 1982, *Third Report,* Rape Counselling and Research Project.

London Rape Crisis Centre, 1984, *Sexual Violence: the Reality for Women,* The Women's Press.

Loney, M., 1983, *Community Against Government, the British CDP, 1968–78,* Heinemann.

Longford Report, 1964, *Crime – a challenge to us all,* Labour Party.

Lowson, D., 1975, 'The ethos of probation' in Mays, J.B. (ed.), *The Social Treatment of Young Offenders,* Longman.

McCabe, S. and Treitel, P., 1983, *Juvenile justice in the United Kingdom: comparisons and suggestions for change,* London, New Approaches to Juvenile Crime.

McClintock, E.H., 1963, *Causes of Violence,* St. Martin's.

McKeown, T., 1979, *The Role of Medicine, Dream, Mirage or Nemesis,* Basil Blackwell.

Manis, J.G., 1976, *Analysing Social Problems,* Praeger.

Mann, M., 1970, 'The social cohesion of liberal democracy', *American Sociological Review,* vol. 35, no. 1.

Mannheim, K., 1960, *Ideology and Utopia,* Routledge and Kegan Paul.

Marcuse, H., 1964, *One Dimensional Man,* Routledge and Kegan Paul.

Marcuse, P., 1981, 'The targeted crisis: on the ideology of the urban fiscal crisis and its uses', *International Journal of Urban and Regional Research,* vol. 5, p. 330.

Marris, P. and Rein, M., 1974, *Dilemmas of Social Reform,* Penguin Books.

Marsden, D., 1978, 'Sociological perspectives on family violence', in *Violence and the Family,* Martin, J. (ed.), Wiley.

Marx, K., 1976, *Capital,* vol. 1, Penguin Books.

Marx, K. and Engels, F., 1976, *The German Ideology,* ch. 1, Progress Publishers

Marx, K., 1964, *Theories of Surplus Value,* Part I, Lawrence and Wishart.

Mauss, A.L., 1975, *Social Problems as Social Movements,* J.B. Lippincott.

May, M., 1978, 'Violence in the Family: an Historical Perspective', in Martin, J. (ed.), *Violence and the Family,* Wiley.

Mays, J.B. (ed.), 1975, *The Social Treatment of Young Offenders,* Longman.

Mepham, J. and Ruben, David-Hiller (eds), 1979, *Issues in Marxist Philosophy, vol. II: Materialism,* Harvester.

Merton, R., 1957, *Social Theory and Social Structure,* Free Press.

Merton, R.K. and Nisbet, R., 1971, *Contemporary Social Problems,* 3rd ed., Harcourt Brace Jovanovich.

Middlemass, K., 1979, *Politics in Industrial Society, The Experience of the British System since 1911,* Deutsch.

Migdall, S.D., 1980, 'Domestic violence – has the act beaten it?', *Family Law,* vol. 9, no. 5, p. 136.

Miliband, R., 1973, *The State in Capitalist Society,* Quartet Books.

Miliband, R., 1977, *Marxism and Politics,* Oxford University Press.

Mill, J.S., 1869, *The Subjection of Women,* Oxford University Press.

Millham S., Bullock, R. and Hosie, K., 1978, *Locking Up Children,* Saxon House.

Mills, C. Wright, 1956, *The Power Elite,* Oxford University Press.

Mills, C. Wright, 1963, 'The Professional Ideology of Social Pathologists', in *Power, Politics and People,* Ballantine.

Mills, C. Wright, 1970, *The Sociological Imagination,* Penguin Books.

Minford, P. & Peel, D., 1981, 'Is the Government's economic strategy on course?', *Lloyd's Bank Review,* No. 140, April, pp. 1–19.

Mishra, R., 1984, *The Welfare State in Crisis: Social Thought and Social Change,* Wheatsheaf Books.

Monger, M., 1964, *Casework in Probation,* Butterworth.

Montagu, E., Q.C., 1965, speech at NAPO/ACCO Middlesex Branches Conference on the White Paper.

Moore, R., 1975, *Racism and Black Resistance,* Pluto Press.

Morell, D.H., 1969, 'Social work and the community' in *Social work and the community,* London, Association of Child Care Officers.

Morgan, D., 1975, 'Explaining mental illness', *Archives Europeennes de Sociologie*, vol. 16, pp. 262–280.

Morgan, M., Calnan, M. and Manning, N., 1985, *Sociological Approaches to Health and Illness*, Croom Helm.

Moriarty, M.J., 1977, 'The policy-making process – how it is seen from the Home Office', in Walker, N. and Giller, H. (eds), *Penal policy-making in England*, Papers presented to the Cropwood Round-Table Conference, December 1976, University of Cambridge Institute of Criminology.

Mueller, C., 1970, 'Notes on the repression of communicative behaviour', in Dreitzel, H.P. (ed.), *Recent Sociology No. 2, Patterns of Communicative Behaviour*, Macmillan.

Mueller, C., 1973, *The Politics of Communication, A study in the Political Sociology of Language, Socialisation, and Legitimation*, Oxford University Press.

Mulkay, M., 1972a, 'Cultural Growth in Science', in Barnes, B. (ed.), *Sociology of Science*, Penguin Books.

Mulkay, M., 1972b, *The Social Process of Innovation, a Study in the Sociology of Science*, Macmillan.

Mulkay, M., 1979, *Science and the Sociology of Knowledge*, Allen and Unwin.

Mullard, C., 1982, 'The state's response to racism: towards a relational explanation', in Ohri, A., Manning, B. and Curno, P. (eds), *Community Work and Racism*, Routledge and Kegan Paul.

National Opinion Polls (N.O.P.), 1975, *Political Bulletin*, February, p. 12.

National Opinion Polls (N.O.P.), 1976, 'Unemployment', *Political, Social and Economic Review*, No. 8, October, pp. 9–14.

National Opinion Polls (N.O.P.), 1980, *Political, Social and Economic Review*, No. 27, October, p. 4.

National Opinion Polls (N.O.P.), 1982, 'Unemployment', *Political, Social and Economic Review*, No. 38, September, pp. 4–6.

Navarro, V., 1976, *Medicine Under Capitalism*, Croom Helm.

O'Connor, J., 1973, *The Fiscal Crisis of the State*, St. Martin's Press.

Offe, C., 1975, 'The theory of the capitalist state and the problem of policy formation', and 'Introduction to Part III – legitimacy versus efficiency', in Lindberg, L.N., Alford, R., Crouch, C. and Offe, C. (eds), *Stress and Contradiction in Modern Capitalism*, Lexington Books.

Offe, C., 1976, ' "Crises of crisis management": elements of a political crisis theory', *International Journal of Politics*, vol. 6, no. 3, pp. 29–67.

Offe, C., 1982, 'Some contradictions of the modern welfare state', *Critical Social Policy*, vol. 2, no. 2, pp. 7–16.

Ohri, A., Manning, B., and Curno, P., (eds), 1982, *Community Work and Racism*, Routledge and Kegan Paul.

Oliver, M., 1979, 'Epilepsy, Self and Society: A Study of Three Groups of Adolescent Epileptics', (unpublished PhD Thesis, University of Kent).

Packman, J., 1975, *The child's generation: Child care policy from Curtis to Houghton*, Basil Blackwell.

Pahl, J., 1978, *A Refuge for Battered Women*, HMSO.

Pahl, J., 1979a, 'Refuges for battered women: social provision or social movement', *Journal of Voluntary Action Research*, vol. 8, no. 1–2, pp. 25–35.

Pahl, J., 1979b, 'The general practitioner and the problems of battered women', *Journal of Medical Ethics*, vol. 5, no. 3, pp. 117–23.

Pahl, J., 1980, 'Patterns of money management within marriage', *Journal of Social Policy*, vol. 9, no. 3, pp. 313–35. Reprinted in Rosenfeld, J. (ed.), *Relationships: the Marriage and Family Reader*, Scott Foresman and Company.

Pahl, J., 1981, *A Bridge over Troubled Waters: a Longitudinal Study of Women who went to a Refuge*. Report presented to the Department of Health and Social Security.

Pahl, J., 1982a, 'Men who assault their wives: what can health visitors do to help?', *Health Visitor*, vol. 55, pp. 528–30.

Pahl, J., 1982b, 'Police response to battered women', *Journal of Social Welfare Law*, November, pp. 337–43.

Pahl, J., 1983, 'The allocation of money and the structuring of inequality within marriage', *Sociological Review*, May, pp. 237–62.

Pahl, J., 1985, *Private Violence and Public Policy*, Routledge and Kegan Paul.

Panitch, L., 1980, 'Recent theorisations of corporatism: Reflections on a Growth Industry', *British Journal Sociology*, vol. 31, no. 2.

Parker, H. and Giller, H., 1981, 'More and less the same: British delinquency research since the sixties', *British Journal of Criminology*, vol. 21, no. 3.

Parker, S., 1985, 'The legal background', in Pahl, J. (ed.), *Private Violence and Public Policy*, Routledge and Kegan Paul.

Parry, N. and Parry, J., 1976, *The Rise of the Medical Profession: a Study of Collective Social Mobility*, Croom Helm.

Parsloe, P., 1978, *Juvenile Justice in Britain and the United States: the balance of needs and rights*, Routledge and Kegan Paul.

Parsons, T., 1964, 'Definitions of health and illness in the light of

American values and social structure', in his *Social Structure and Personality*, Free Press.

Parton, N., 1981, 'Child Abuse, Social Anxiety and Welfare', *British Journal of Social Work*, vol. 11.

Pateman, T., 1980, *Language, Truth and Politics*, 2nd ed., Jean Stroud.

Pearson, G., 1983, *Hooligan – a history of respectable fears*, Macmillan.

Phillips, B., 1979, *Patterns of Juvenile Crime*, Peel Press.

Piachaud, D., 1978, 'Inflation and income distribution' in Hirsch, F. and Goldthorpe, J.H. (eds), *The Political Economy of Inflation*, Martin Robertson.

Pinchbeck, I. and Hewitt, M., 1969, *Children in English society, vol. 1, from Tudor times to the eighteenth century*, Routledge and Kegan Paul.

Pippard, J. and Ellam, L., 1981, 'Electro convulsive treatment in Great Britain', *British Journal of Psychiatry*, vol. 139, pp. 563–568.

Pitts, J., 1979, 'Doing your bird on the H.P. The changing shape of intermediate treatment', *Howard Journal*, vol. 18, no. 1, pp. 17–28.

Pizzey, E., 1974, *Scream Quietly or the Neighbours will Hear*, Penguin.

Poulantzas, N., 1972, 'The problem of the capitalist state', in Blackburn, R. (ed.), *Ideology in Social Science*, Fontana.

Pryce, K., 1979, *Endless Pressure*, Penguin Books.

Rabkin, J.G., 1975, 'The role of attitudes toward mental illness', in Guttentag, M. and Struening, E.L. (eds), *Handbook of Evaluation Research*, Sage.

Radical Science Journal, 1981, no. 11.

Radical Statistics Group, 1980, *Britains Black Population*, Heinemann.

Rampton Report – *Committee of inquiry into the education of children from ethnic minority groups; the West Indian children in our schools*, Interim report Cmnd 8273, HMSO.

Rawls, J., 1972, *A Theory of Justice*, Oxford University Press.

Reeves, F., 1983, *British racial discourse, a study of British political discourse about race and race-related matters*, Cambridge University Press.

Reeves, F. and Chevannes, M., 1981, 'The underachievement of Rampton', *Multi Racial Education*, vol. 10, no. 1.

Rex, J. and Tomlinson, S., 1979, *Colonial immigrants in a British city*, Routledge and Kegan Paul.

Richardson, J.J. and Moon, J., 1984, 'The politics of unemployment in Britain', *Political Quarterly*, vol. 55, pp. 29–37.

Rimlinger, G.V., 1971, *Welfare Policy and Industrialisation in Europe, America and Russia*, Wiley.

Roberts, K., et al., 1983, 'Young black and out of work', in Troyna, B. and Smith, D. (eds), *Racism, school and the labour market,* National Youth Bureau.

Roper, B., 1982, 'Rival Ideologies' in Elcock, H. (ed.), *What Sort of Society? Economic and Social Policy in Modern Britain,* Martin Robertson.

Rose, G., 1961, *The Struggle for Penal Reform,* Stevens and Sons.

Rose, R., 1984, *Do Parties Make a Difference?* Macmillan.

Rosen, H., 1972, *Language and Class: A Critical Look at the Theories of Basil Bernstein,* Falling Wall Press.

Ross, J., 1983, *Thatcher and Friends: the Anatomy of the Tory Party,* Pluto Press.

Rotenberg, M., 1978, *Damnation and Deviance: the Protestant Ethic and the Spirit of Failure,* Free Press.

Rothman, D.J., 1971, *The Discovery of the Asylum: Social Order and Disorder in the New Republic,* Little, Brown and Co.

Rothman, D.J., 1980, *Conscience and Convenience: The Asylum and its Alternatives in Progressive America,* Little, Brown and Co.

Rothman, D.J., 1983, 'Social control: the uses and abuses of the concept in the history of incarceration', in Cohen, S. and Scull, A.T. (eds), *Social Control and the State,* Martin Robertson.

Rowntree, S., 1902, *Poverty: a Study of Town Life,* Macmillan.

Royal Commission on the National Health Service, 1979, Cmnd 7615, HMSO.

Rubington, E. and Weinberg, M.S., 1977, *The Study of Social Problems,* 2nd edition, Oxford University Press.

Rusche, G. and Kirckheimer, O., 1939, *Punishment and Social Structure,* Columbia University Press.

Russell, D. and Howell, N., 1983, 'The prevalence of rape in the United States revisited', *Signs,* vol. 8, no. 4, pp. 688–95.

Rutter, M. and Giller, H., 1983, *Juvenile Delinquency – Trends and Perspectives,* Penguin Books.

Rutter, M. and Madge, N., 1976, *Cycles of Disadvantage,* Heinemann.

Ryan, W., 1971, *Blaming the Victim,* Pantheon Books.

Ryan, W., 1977, 'Blaming the victim: ideology serves the establishment' in Wickman, P. (ed.), *Readings in Social Problems: Contemporary Perspectives,* Harper and Row.

Sayers, J., 1984, 'Sexual contradictions: on Freud, psychoanalysis and feminism', University of Kent (unpublished paper).

Scarman, L. Rt. Hon. Ld., 1981, *The Brixton disorders 10–12 April 1981,* Cmnd 8427, HMSO.

Scheff, T.J., 1966, *Being mentally ill: a sociological theory,* Aldine.

Scheff, T.J., 1975, *Labelling Madness*, Prentice-Hall.

Schlegel, A., 1972, *Male Dominance and Female Autonomy*, Hraf Press.

Schmitter, P.C. and Lehmbruch, G. (eds), 1979, *Trends Towards Corporatist Intermediation*, Sage.

Schur, E.M., 1980, *The politics of deviance, stigma contests and the uses of power*, Prentice-Hall.

Schwab, J.J. and Schwab, M.E., 1978, *Sociocultural Roots of Mental Illness*, Plenum Press.

Schwendinger, J. and Schwendinger, H., 1983, *Rape and Inequality*, Sage Publications.

Scott, P., 1966, 'The child, the family, and the young offender', *British Journal of Criminology*, vol. 6, no. 2, pp. 105–112.

Scott, R.A., 1970, 'The construction of conceptions of stigma by professional experts', in Douglas, J.D. (ed.), *Deviance and Respectability, the social construction of moral meanings*, Basic Books.

Scull, A.T., 1977, *Decarceration, community treatment and the deviant – a radical view*, Prentice-Hall.

Scull, A.T., 1979, *Museums of Madness, the social organisation of insanity in 19th century England*, Allen Lane.

Scull, A.T. (ed.), 1981, *Madhouses, mad-doctors, and madness, the social history of psychiatry in the Victorian era*, Athlone Press.

Sedgwick, P., 1982, *Psycho Politics*, Pluto Press.

Seebohm Report, 1968, *Report of the committee on local authority and allied personal social services*, Cmnd 3703, HMSO.

Seeley, J.R., 1963, 'Social Science? Some probative problems', in Stein, M. and Vidich, A. (eds), *Sociology on Trial*, Prentice-Hall.

Select Committee Report, 1975, *Violence in marriage*, HCP 1974–5, 553 II.

Sheriff, P.A., 1983, 'State Theory, Social Science, and Governmental Commissions', *American Behavioural Scientist*, vol. 26, no. 5.

Sherman, A., 1979, 'Britain's urge to self destruction', *The Daily Telegraph*, 9 September 1979.

Shutt, J., 1982, 'Rescuing New York City, 1975–1978', in Forrest, R., Henderson, J. and Willians, P. (eds), *Urban Political Economy and Social Theory*, Gower.

Sieber, S.D., 1981, *Fatal Remedies, the ironies of social intervention*, Plenum Press.

Sivanandan, A., 1976, *Race, class and the state, the black experience in Britain*, Race and Class pamphlet 1, Institute of Race Relations.

Sivanandan, A., 1982, 'From resistance to rebellion: asian and afro caribbean struggles in Britain', *Race and Class*, vol. 23, nos. 2/3, pp. 111–52.

Smart, C., 1969, 'Colin Smart on parliament', *Child Care News*, no. 89, pp. 15–18.

Smith, D., 1981, *Unemployment and racial minorities in London*, Policy Studies Institute.

Smith, D., 1977, *Racial disadvantage in Britain*, Penguin Books.

Snowdon, B. and Osborne, M., 1982, 'Inflation and Unemployment' in Elcock, H. (ed.), *What Sort of Society? Economic and Social Policy in Modern Britain*, Martin Robertson.

Solomos, J., Findlay, B., Jones, S. and Gilroy, P., 1982, 'The organic crisis of British capitalism and race: the experience of the seventies', in CCCS, *The Empire Strikes Back*, Hutchinson.

Spector, M. and Kitsuse, J.I., 1977, *Constructing Social Problems*, Cummings.

Spender, D., 1980, *Man Made Language*, Routledge and Kegan Paul.

Stapleton, R.C., 1981, 'Why recession benefits Britain', *Journal of Economic Affairs*, vol. 2, no. 1, pp. 7–11.

Stark, E., Flitcraft, A. and Frazier, W., 1979, 'Medicine and patriarchal violence', *International Journal of Health Services*, vol. 9, no. 3.

Starnes, C.E., 1976, 'Contemporary and historical aspects of officially defined poverty in the United States', in Zimmerman, D.H., Weider, D.L. and Zimmerman, S. (eds), *Understanding Social Problems*, Praeger, pp. 36–68.

Straus, M., 1978, 'Wife beating: how common and why' in Eekelar, J. and Katz, S. (eds), *Family Violence*, Butterworths.

Straus, M., Gelles, R.J. and Sternmetz, S.K., 1980, *Behind Closed Doors: Violence in the American Family*, Anchor Books.

Strong, P.M., 1979, *The Ceremonial Order of the Clinic*, Routledge and Kegan Paul.

Szasz, T., 1966, 'Wither Psychiatry', *Social Research*, Vol. 33.

Szasz, T., 1971, *The Manufacture of Madness, a comparative study of the Inquisition and the Mental Health Movement*, Routledge and Kegan Paul.

Szasz, T., 1972, *The Myth of Mental Illness, Foundations of a Theory of Personal Conduct*, Paladin.

Szasz, T., 1974, *Ideology and Insanity*, Penguin Books.

Tarling, R., 1983, 'Unemployment and crime', *Research Bulletin*, no. 15, pp. 28–33, Home Office.

Taylor, D.C., 1979, 'Some Psychiatric aspects of Epilepsy' in Harrington, R.N. (ed.), *Current Problems in Neuropsychiatry. Schizophrenia, Epilepsy and the Temporal Lobe*, Headley Bros.

Taylor, F., 1974, *Race School and Community*, National Foundation for Educational Research.

Taylor, I., 1978, 'Juvenile justice system', unit 22, *Social work, community work, and society*, course DE 206, Open University.

Taylor, I., 1981, *Law and Order – Arguments for Socialism*, Macmillan.

Taylor, I., Walton, P. and Young, J., 1973, *The New Criminology – For a Single Theory of Deviance,* Routledge and Kegan Paul.

Taylor, L. and Cohen, S., 1976, *Escape Attempts. The Theory and Practice of Resistance to Everyday Life,* Penguin Books.

Taylor-Gooby, P., 1982, '2 Cheers for the Welfare State: public opinion and private welfare', *Journal Public Policy,* vol. 2, pp. 319–46.

Taylor-Gooby, P., 1985, *Public Opinion, Ideology and State Welfare,* Routledge and Kegan Paul.

The child, the family and the young offender, Cmnd. 2742, 1965, HMSO.

Therborn, G., 1978, *What Does The Ruling Class Do When It Rules?,* New Left Books.

Thomas, J.E., 1972, *The English Prison Officer Since 1850,* Routledge and Kegan Paul.

Thorpe, D.H., Smith, D., Green, C.J. and Paley, J.H., 1980, *Out of care: The community support of juvenile offenders,* Allen and Unwin.

Tierney, J. (ed.), 1982, *Race, Migration and Schooling,* Holt.

The Times, 1969, obituary of D.H. Morrell, 13.10.69, p.10, col.g, and tributes 20.12.69, p.10, col.h, and 24.12.69, p.8, col.g.

Toland, S., 1980, 'Changes in living standards since the 1950s', *Social Trends No.10,* HMSO, pp. 13–38.

Tomlinson, S., 1980, 'The educational performance of ethnic minority children', *New Community,* vol. 8, no. 3, pp. 213–34.

Tomlinson, S., 1982, *A Sociology of Special Education,* Routledge and Kegan Paul.

Toner, B., 1977, *The Facts of Rape,* Arrow.

Townsend, P., 1976, *Sociology and Social Policy,* Penguin Books.

Treacher, A. and Baruch, G., 1981, 'Towards a Critical History of the Psychiatric Profession', in Ingleby, D., *Critical Psychiatry, the Politics of Mental Health,* Penguin Books.

Trombley, S., 1981, *'All that Summer She was Mad', Virginia Woolf and Her Doctors,* Junction Books.

Troyna, B. and Smith, D. (eds), 1983, *Racism, School and the Labour Market,* National Youth Bureau.

Tuke, S., 1813, *Description of the Retreat,* York: W. Alexander.

Tutt, N., 1981, 'A decade of policy', *British Journal of Criminology,* vol. 21, no. 3, pp. 246–56.

Tutt, N., 1982, 'An overview of intervention with young offenders. The political and legal contexts', in Feldman, P. (ed.), *Developments in the study of criminal behaviour, vol. 1, The prevention and control of offending,* John Wiley and Sons.

Upton, M., 1980, 'Reviving Rowntree: poverty lines and the levels of Social Security benefits for the unemployed', *Social Policy and Administration,* vol. 14, pp. 36–46.

Urry, J., 1981, *The Anatomy of Capitalist Societies, the Economy, Civil Society and the State,* Macmillan.

Van Den Bergh, P., 1978, *Race and Racism,* John Wiley.

Walker, E., 1979, *The Battered Woman,* Harper and Row.

Walker, H., and Beaumont, B., 1981, *Probation Work: Critical Theory and Socialist Practice,* Basil Blackwell.

Walker, M.J. and Brodsky, S.L., 1976, *Sexual Assault,* Lexington Books.

Walker, N., 1974, 'Lost causes in criminology', in Hood, R. (ed.), *Crime, Criminology and Public Policy. Essays in honour of Sir Leon Radzinowicz,* Heinemann.

Walker, N. and Giller, H. (eds), 1977, *Penal policy-making in England.* Papers presented to the Cropwood Round-Table Conference, December 1976, Cambridge, University of Cambridge Institute of Criminology.

Walker, N. and Marsh, C., 1984, 'Do sentences affect public disapproval?' *British Journal of Criminology,* vol. 24, no. 1, pp. 27–48.

Walmsley, R. and White, K., 1979, *Sexual Offences, Consent and Sentencing,* Home Office Research Unit Report, HMSO.

Warnock Report, 1978, *Special Educational Needs,* Cmnd 7212, HMSO.

Wasoff, F., 1982, 'Legal protection from wife beating: the processing of domestic assaults by Scottish prosecutors and criminal courts', *International Journal of Sociology of Law,* vol. 10, pp. 187–204.

Watson, J.A.F., 1970, *The Juvenile Court – 1970 Onwards,* Shaw.

Weber, M., 1949, *The Methodology of the Social Sciences,* Free Press.

Weir, A., 1977, 'Battered women: some perspectives and problems' in Mayo, M. (ed.), *Women in the Community,* Routledge and Kegan Paul.

Wells, D., 1981, *Marxism and the Modern State, An Analysis of Fetishism in Capitalist Society,* Harvester Press.

West, J., 1969, book review, *Howard Journal,* vol. 18, no. 3, pp. 178–180.

Wiedemeyer, N., 1976, 'The polls: do people worry about the future?', *Public Opinion Quarterly,* vol. 40, pp. 382–391.

Williams, B., 1982, 'Probation – the coercive tilt', *Bulletin on Social Policy,* vol. 11.

Willis, P., 1977, *Learning to Labour: How Working Class Kids get Working Class Jobs,* Saxon House.

Wilson, E., 1983, *What Is To Be Done About Violence Against Women?* Penguin Books.

Winkler, J.T., 1977, 'The Corporate Economy: Theory and Administration', in Scase, R. (ed.), *Industrial Society: Class, Cleavage and Control,* Allen and Unwin, pp. 43–56.

Women's Aid Federation, 1980, *Annual Report 1979–80,* obtainable from WAF(E), 374 Grays Inn Road, London, W1.

Women's Aid Federation Research Group, 1981, 'Violence to Women in the Home: a Research Strategy', paper presented to the DHSS seminar on Violence in the Family at the University of Kent.

Woolgar, S., 1983, 'Irony in the Social Study of Science', in Knorr-Cetina, K.D. and Mulkay, M. (eds), *Science Observed,* Sage.

Wootton, B., 1959, *Social science and social pathology,* Allen and Unwin.

World Health Organisation, 1948, *Constitution.*

Young, J., 1975, 'Working-Class Criminology', in Taylor, I., Walton, P. and Young, J. (eds), *Critical Criminology,* Routledge and Kegan Paul.

Zola, I., 1972, 'Medicine as an institution of Social Control', *Sociological Review,* vol. 20, pp. 487–504.

Index